HMS *Arethusa* in the Grand Harbour, Valletta, Malta. 1843.
by Joseph Schranz
Copyright Sotheby's (from a private collection)

To Kevin and Kate,
With best wishes from the author,
Tim Price.

A HUNDRED YEARS BEHIND THE TIMES

The History of Bisley in Surrey

Tim Price

Published by

An Imprint of Melrose Press Limited
St Thomas Place, Ely
Cambridgeshire
CB7 4GG, UK
www.melrosebooks.co.uk

FIRST EDITION

Cover designed by Catherine McIntyre

ISBN 978-1-908645-17-3

Printed and bound in Great Britain by:
TJ International Ltd, Padstow, Cornwall

CONTENTS

LIST OF ILLUSTRATIONS

INTRODUCTION

Though most of us are aware of the ever-increasing rate of change in our busy lives, we often forget, or may never have known, about many important things that have affected us to some extent in times past. For example, how often has one bemoaned the lack of information on the back of a photograph, or the failure of a deceased relative to tell us more about our family history. Some changes occur suddenly, while others are so gradual that they are barely perceptible at first. Their effect can be quite profound, even life-changing, yet conversely there are times when they hardly impinge upon our routine, if at all. We may even question whether the benefits really outweigh the disadvantages. Nevertheless, whatever the circumstances, the inexorable progress of modern life can often be viewed with greater clarity by having knowledge of the past, and it is largely this aspect of our social history that has led me to share the events in the following chapters that have shaped the village of Bisley, the place in which I have lived virtually all my life.

I have to confess that the urge to make notes of such things stems from my early boyhood in post-war years, when I became fascinated with the natural environment and observed how variable was the appearance from year to year of the flowers and insects which were to become an absorbing interest in later life.

Torn between reluctance to display my limited literary skills, of which I am acutely aware, and a growing desire to pass on information about this corner of Surrey which, small as it is, has had a long and interesting history, I eventually decided to take the latter course of action and produce this book. Faced with the growing realisation that I might depart this world without firstly having passed on material collected over many years, and seeing a dwindling number of people whose memory is longer than mine, I resolved two years ago that I should not wait a minute longer to start writing a history of the village. Even so, some long-standing friends who would have been potential contributors died before I had a chance to hear their experiences, while others who did provide very useful material have not lived to see it published.

Many things that happened centuries ago in Bisley may cause a little surprise, yet some of the changes which have occurred within living memory might be even more astonishing, especially to the younger generation whose experience is limited to today's standards. Who, for instance, would think that the A322, the busiest non-trunk road in Surrey, so we are told, was a rough unmade track called Port Lane until the 1920s, when it was first dressed with a tarred macadam surface?

We cannot begin to imagine what Bisley will be like in 2100, any more than the Reverend Joseph Cater could foresee the invention of aeroplanes and plastics, or the discovery of antibiotics, or the impact that cars would have in today's world when, in the year 1892, he wrote 'Bisley Bits', the first history of this village.

Forty years have elapsed since Britain abandoned the LSD coinage system of pounds, shillings and pence, and introduced decimalisation of the pound sterling. Nowadays few people can readily convert from one to another and for them terms such as 'ten bob', 'half a crown', 'florin', 'tanner' and 'thrupenny bit' have little or no meaning. As there are so many references in this book to the superseded coinage, one of the appendices contains a conversion table from what is now commonly called 'old money' into decimal currency.

July 2012 TRSP

ACKNOWLEDGEMENTS

I wish to thank everyone who has helped and encouraged me with this project, which was an immensely interesting and absorbing task throughout, though far more time-consuming than I could possibly have imagined at the outset. I must start by thanking Gill Burn and Jen Martin who generously permitted me to copy photographs from the Burn and Martin Collection, and to the Surrey History Centre staff for allowing access to this material and also to records compiled by and copyright of Surrey County Council Heritage Conservation Team. I am indebted to the British Library for permission to use the John Hassell illustrations of St John the Baptist Church, and to Sotheby's for their copy of the Joseph Schranz painting of HMS *Arethusa* in a private collection, the whereabouts of which took over a year of painstaking investigation in England and Malta to trace. I am grateful for the use of other photographs to John Baker, Felicity Cavey, Peter Fidczuk, the Lens of Sutton Collection, Jim Henbest, the National Rifle Association and Joan Roberts.

Many friends have assisted with most useful original information, reminiscences and clarification of abstruse details, including Felicity Cavey, Nick Cavey, Joan Cheeseman, Ralph Cheeseman, Beryl Daborn, Robin

Daborn, John Fertig, Peter Fuller, Cyril Goff, Keith Martin, Phyllis Martin, Marilyn Meller, Tom Meller, Lorna Tongue, Melvyn Tongue and Richard Wilson. There are also many individuals whom I should have wished to thank but who sadly are no longer alive to see the inclusion of information which they so kindly contributed. My sincere thanks go to Dr Marco Grilli for guidance on the papal registers of the Vatican Secret Archives and to Peter Beesley of the Guildford Diocesan Registry for information on ecclesiastical appointments. Ted Molyneux, the Curator and Archivist of the National Rifle Association Museum, has been most helpful in correcting my mistakes and directing me to various sources in connection with information about the NRA. Chris Bunch has been exceptionally generous with his time and expert guidance on the railways of Bisley Camp. Sharon Cross, the former Curator of Surrey Heath Museum, deserves special thanks for reading my draft and providing sound advice and encouragement on the production of the book.

Lastly, but by no means least, I owe an incalculable amount to my wife, Jo, who has helped me in so many ways and, without complaint, has put up with unwelcomed piles of paperwork around our house and has sustained me with countless cups of tea while I have been shut away in the seclusion of my study for hours and hours, evening upon evening.

Chapter 1

WHAT'S IN A NAME?

Before spelling became standardised around the 1800s, small rural villages frequently had many variations on the way their names were spelt, largely because those who put pen to paper often had to write down these unfamiliar place names relying entirely on the spoken word uttered by locals, most of whom, if not all, could neither read nor write. The older the village the more varied and quaint the names often became. Bisley in Surrey was no exception to this general rule, having had at least twenty different ways of spelling this simple name at various times in its long history, which dates back over a thousand years.

Busseleghe was one of forty or so places named in the royal charter of AD 933[(1)] when King Athelstan confirmed the lands belonging 'to the familia of Chertsey Minster'. Though it is tempting to suggest that 'confirmation' in this context implies lands that were already possessed, one should not presume this to be the case, and it would be prudent to discount the possibility of a settlement at Bisley before this date unless firm evidence comes to light. This tiny hamlet was next recorded just three decades later in

AD 967[2] when the property and privileges of Chertsey Abbey were confirmed by King Edgar stating: '*…v mansae apud Chabeham cum Busseleghe…*' which translates as '5 hides[3] at Chobham with Bisley'. Interestingly, we shall see that these two adjacent villages are to be linked in various ways from time to time in later history.

There is a much earlier charter of AD 672 x 674[4] in which Frithwald (*Frithuwold*), the subregulus of Surrey, with the consent of Wulfhere, king of Mercia, gave a large estate to Erkenwald Abbot of *Coroteseye* (Chertsey), part of this estate being *Chebeham* (Chobham). Although Bisley was not mentioned, other parts of the village were clearly named in the bounds appended to this Latin document. However, the bounds were written in Old English and it is now generally agreed that they were not contemporary and there seems to be no evidence that they even belonged to it. Some of the bounds appear to have been updated[5] to include later alterations to the landholding. One should also remember that 'seventh-century kingdoms grew and shrank from one year to the next'[6], a situation that may have continued for hundreds of years, and it was not unknown for documents to be attached together, even changed and forged, in order to lay claim to land. However, it is generally accepted that the information contained in this copy does support the authenticity of the charter, as the way in which the Latin text is written, and also the inclusion of some unusual place names in Old English form, are unlikely to have been the work of a medieval forger. The original part was probably made at an early date, possibly very close to the ascribed date, and the details are now widely regarded as being trustworthy.

The bounds attached to this charter are divided into three areas, and those for *Chabbeham* (Chobham) list several places that are recognisable as being local to Bisley:- '*… Andlange hagan to fhyþeke mere… forþ rigte ofer þane feld to Cuscetes hagen. Sua bi þan hagen to Cumore. Of Cumore to þe stondinde stone.*' This translates as '… along the enclosure to Fhytheke Mere (believed to refer to Stafford Lake by its location) … fork right over the field to Cuscetes (Cowshot) enclosure. So by the enclosure to Cumore (Cow Moor). Of Cumore (Cow Moor) to the standing stone.' It is remarkable that so many of the boundary points, including some of these local ones, can still be identified some thirteen centuries later.

Until comparatively recently there were actually three standing stones within four miles of each other, which unfortunately led to some confusion in the late 1800s and early 1900s, as exemplified in the following extract from a book[(7)] by Henry Curtis[(8)] which unknowingly refers to all three:-

> There is a tradition that Bisley Manor once extended to the Standing Stone, that ancient boundary mark mentioned in an old Saxon Charter as the extreme South-West limit of the demesne of Chertsey Abbey. This portion… in Cowshot may have then been within its bounds. Standing Stone Hill is marked on the Map of the Manor and Parish of Pirbright, 1805-7. Speaking of it by its old name, 'The Stondyng Stone', the Rev. Mr.

> Owston[9] says it was undermined by a man excavating for boulders, sometime early in this [the XIXth] Century, and this caused its fall. I had this from Russell, formerly stone-getter, who for many years lived in the old farmhouse, now converted into the Vicarage. Miss Cawthorn says that Richard Saunders, when a young man, remembered taking shelter under the Standing Stone – a huge piece of ironstone, on the north side of the Railway line. He stated that the navvies, when making the South-Western Railway, threw it down for a joke. There is another, and, I understand, a larger stone on the north side of the Basingstoke Canal, near the gun, mounted on one of the hills near the stone, prior to the Great War, but no longer in existence, for the testing of gunpowder by the Chilworth Powder Mill Company.

Dr Curtis firstly refers to the stone marking the south-westerly limit of the abbey's territory, which was the Mainstone (mighty stone) situated on Mainstone Hill on the western side of Cow Moor which accords with the clockwise order of names listed on the ancient bounds. The boundary point shown on modern maps separating the three discrete communities of Blackdown, Pirbright and West End, may not have moved at all over the centuries but, even if it has, it is still no more than 230 yards (210 metres) from the original spot.

The second stone, marked as 'Standing Stone Hill' on the 1807 Map of Pirbright, is clearly marked over two miles away (4 km) from Mainstone Hill, and is on the opposite side of the canal not far from Tunnel Hill on Pirbright Common.

The third standing stone 'on the north side of the Basingstoke Canal' was the closest of the three to the canal, situated on Cowshot Hill near the mortar used in the 1800s for proving tests for the various formulations of Chilworth black powder.

The sporadic occurrence of such boulders on local heaths was not uncommon in former times, but the largest example still to be found is perched on top of the highest point in North West Surrey – High Curley at Lightwater.

The Chertsey bounds were beaten again in AD 1446, but once more the record appears to be written at a later date and may or may not be an exact copy of the original. It states[10] *'and fro thennes to potterneweye. And fro potternewey to Cowschotherne and fro thennes to Cowmor' and fro thens to the stondyngestone.'* This is generally consistent with the details of the former event. The accounts of both perambulations clearly list a sufficient number of points of identification, recognisable to this day, to define the southern and western extremities of the monastical landholding and they corroborate other evidence that Bisley was owned by Chertsey Abbey.

Large construction team building Wilcot House

The current spelling of Bisley was first recorded in 1587, although other variations continued to appear from time to time for another two hundred years or so. A list of all the known spellings is shown in **Appendix A**, though more could await discovery. Nowadays, we tend to pronounce the name of the village with a 'z' rather than an 's', but who is to say that either way is any more correct than, say, one of the medieval variations? We presume that the current one is right solely on the basis that it is generally accepted, but if we were able to consult our ancient forebears they might insist that we have corrupted their correct version!

There are numerous examples of topographical features within our village where the former names appear to have been altered slightly as a result of mis-spelling, simplification or just mis-pronunciation. These include Stafford Lake (Stavek Lake, 1561), Reidon Hill (Riding Hill, 1603), High Hoglees (le Hogleaze, 1609), Stickledown (Stykeeldon, 1369) and Colony Bog (Colyngle Mor, 1369 and Coldingley Bog, 1688). Other local names have been deliberately changed. The inhabitants of Chattering Row, no doubt perceiving disparagement by association, chose to rename their lane 'Chatton Row' in 1783. Similar stories come from Windlesham, where Dog Kennel Lane dropped the suffix 'Dog', and from the town of Guildford where Spital Street was renamed Upper High Street. Short distinctive names often remain unchanged, whereas those that are cumbersome or difficult to pronounce tend not to last long. Perish the thought that Arethusa Way may one day become 'Harry Shoes Way'! Who now, one wonders, realises that there should be an apostrophe between the 'n' and the 's' in Queens Road or, for that matter, is aware that it was once Queen Lane, named after Queen Anne in 1711. Place names are sometimes conveniently altered to avoid confusion. There were once two Water Lanes in Bisley and so one was changed to Watery Lane. (Perhaps now is the time to consider differentiating more clearly between postal addresses on the common to the west of Bisley Recreation Ground, stated as being Bisley Green, and those to the east, known as The Green.) The pleasant little unspoilt Public Bridleway, called Kiln Lane since the early 1600s, which runs from beside The Fox Inn to Bisley Church, has all too frequently been wrongly associated with lime works, of which none has ever existed in this area for the very reason that there are no outcrops of lime or chalk anywhere near here. In fact the very opposite condition exists throughout much of Bisley as it lies on the highly acidic Bagshot Series of Sands on which heathland vegetation thrives. Kiln Lane and Kiln Close, named in parish records in 1666, actually refer to the brick and tile works that flourished there for just over a hundred years and closed in the early 1700s. Warbury Lane dates from 1577 and Bullhousen Farm from 1607 (Bulrowsen Wood) but, despite much searching, the origins of these names cannot be traced. Grindstone Handle Corner is so named as it rather aptly describes the shape of the parish boundary around part of the southern end, though the name itself is comparatively modern. Several points on the boundary were identified by trees, of which Polled Oak Slade (Powld Oak, 1605, and Poldok, 1609) is a good example.

Few of the dwellings encountered today still retain names that convey some long-standing connection with their locality, though Newbridge Cottage, Ford Farm and Pound Cottage are among those that do. Names are sometimes associated with people, examples of which include Miles Green (John Myles, 1483), Clews Farm (William and Mary Clew moved there after marrying in 1764) and Cobbetts Farm (Robert Cobbett, 1583). Dwellings are sometimes renamed by their occupants for a variety of reasons. A house on the main road was called Pashcralda in 1968 by combining the first two letters of the Christian names of the whole family who lived there: Patricia, Sharon, Craig, Alan and Darren! The reason why Raspberry Grove was changed to Strawberry Farm has been forgotten over the passage of four generations, but it is said that the opportunity to do so was taken when all dwellings had to be named when the postal service was expanded in mid-Victorian times. One suspects that the naming of Strawberry Fields, a 1970s development towards the north end of the village, had more to do with a popular song of the time than the cultivation of soft fruit, although Mr William Graham, the former owner at Montrose, did sometimes grow a few strawberries in the field behind his house.

Clews Farm by John Baker

Scarcely a hundred years ago almost every field, close, plat, pasture, meadow, orchard and paddock could readily be identified by name, often a very distinctive and appropriate one that was quickly recognisable by those deriving their living from working the land. Unfortunately, the importance of field names has diminished to the extent that they are now all but forgotten. Maybe a few of the older generation will still recognise Willows Five Corner, Dead Hills, Three Corner Field, Pightle, Long Slip, The Hoppit, Hither Loam Field, Snowdrop Meadows and Hashed Five Acres, and possibly others too.

The name Dead Hills is interesting and may be attributable to the fact that the land was unproductive because it was worn out and deficient in body and nutrients – 'hungry', they would have said. On the other hand it may have a more sinister origin. The name certainly pre-dates the plague of the mid-1600s and may well refer to the place used as the communal burial ground for victims of the Black Death, which spread throughout the land three hundred years earlier. The Black Death pandemic reached Dorset in 1348 and within a year had spread as far as Yorkshire. Over a thousand villages were severely depopulated or wiped out altogether, and between a third and a half of the entire population of England, which was about three to four million people, succumbed to the disease. It took nearly two hundred years for the country to recover and for numbers to reach the former level. Those who died in this plague were often interred together in trenches and covered with lime to prevent the spread of infection, as were victims of another dreadful pestilence – anthrax. The place known as Dead Hills in Bisley was far removed from habitable property and may have referred to the mounds of soil which were a visible reminder of the dreadful tragedy that had befallen the village.

Parcels of land in Bisley were generally quite small and this was reflected in many of their names: Pightle, a small piece of land[11] [Middle English *pichel, pightel*], is a relatively common name in Surrey; Hoppit [OE *hoppet*] is also a small enclosure; the author is proud to retain the ancient name of a long and narrow sliver of land called Long Slip [ME *slipe*]; and Hashed Five Acres, as the name suggests, was separated from a larger area, named The Great Coppice (of which there is now no trace), in order that it could be cleared and cultivated.

Part of Cowshot Common at the south-western end of the village lies outside the perimeter of Bisley Camp, but it is owned by the military authorities. The suffix '…shot(t)', when used as the second element of a place name, like Cowshot above, is derived from the Old English *scēat* which refers to a strip of land and is usually associated with a tree or an animal, as in Aldershot, Bagshot (badger?), Oxshott and Ewshot. Occasionally a form of *scēat* is used alone, the best local example being Sheet's Heath. John Field[12] states that it comprises 'a block of arable land, consisting of a number of selions[13] or lands, running in the same direction, and having at either end a headland on which the plough-team could turn'. Synonymous with furlong or flatt, names ending with '…shot(t)' are largely restricted to NW Surrey and just a little way beyond into the neighbouring county of Hampshire. Further afield, place names containing this element are almost unheard of and, interestingly but perhaps only coincidentally, they were all adjacent to heathland and, in most cases, still are. Maybe the component became corrupted by the local dialect and, in which case, one would expect its usage to be restricted in this way.

Even some old village families have not escaped the widespread problem of mis-spelt names. One branch of a local family remained Collier whilst another changed the spelling to Collyer. It seems that Elliott and Elliot, and possibly even Eliot, share a common ancestry. Undoubtedly, 'Gorge', 'Henery', 'Charls', 'Elianer', 'Eliazbath' and 'Charlote' would have preferred their respective entries in the first Bisley Census to have been spelt correctly but, even if they had spotted the mistake, it would have taken more than a little courage to challenge the literary proficiency of the official clerk compiling the list. In fact, all eighteen Henrys were spelt 'Henery', but, there again, every one of them probably called themselves 'Henery'.

---

(1) *Electronic Sawyer*

(2) Ibid

(3) A hide was an undefined and sometimes very variable area of land on which taxation was based.

(4) *Electronic Sawyer.*

(5) *Chertsey Cartulary.*

(6) *Early Medieval Surrey.*

(7) *Curates and Vicars of Pirbright, Surrey*

(8) Henry Curtis, BS & MD (London), FRCS, Consult. Surg. Metroplitan Hosp. London, lived at Furze Hill, Pirbright.

(9) Revd. Francis Owston, MA. Vicar of Pirbright from 1851 to 1888.

(10) *Chertsey Cartulary*.

(11) *English Field Names*.

(12) Ibid.

(13) **Selion:** A small strip of land often lying between the furrows of cultivated land and which was also capable of cultivation, yet so small that it would usually be rented by one of the poorer inhabitants.

Chapter 2

THE ESTABLISHMENT OF THE CHURCH

Bisley has been in existence for so long that it is now impossible to determine a precise date of establishment of either the early settlement or its place of worship. The farther back one delves into history, the more sparse local records become, especially when researching the early Middle Ages. It is now generally thought that the tiny hamlet which eventually was to become the village of Bisley developed as a result of the construction of a primitive chapel of ease close to a spring(1) with a dependable supply of potable water.

Could the location of Bisley Church have been chosen to satisfy both the material and spiritual needs of travellers? It is indeed situated very close to the spring and was within a day's journey on foot of the two most important monastic settlements in the area, the Benedictine Abbey of St Peter at Chertsey and the first Cistercian monastery in Britain – Waverley Abbey at Farnham. It was located more or less on the direct route between them and afforded the weary foot traveller shelter for the night, a place of prayer for the soul and refreshment for the body near at hand. There would have been a significant amount of interaction and intercommunication between the two ecclesiastical communities – even greater had the monks all belonged to the same religious order. Nevertheless, there certainly would have been an increasing number of people going to and fro as these establishments of religious, cultural, judicial and civil authority grew in size, prosperity and influence. Many itinerant traders and villagers would have relied heavily upon the sale of goods and services required by the abbeys as well as by the fast-growing communities beyond their precincts and in other towns.

Chertsey Abbey had been established(2) in AD 666 x 669 by Erkenwald (or Eorcenwald), its first Abbot. Originally it would have been no more than a simple wooden building(3) with around 50 monks, but during the next 800 years it was rebuilt twice and extended to such an extent that it grew into one of the grandest monastic structures in the kingdom, owning over 50,000 acres of land spread across several counties. Malden(4) states in his first book on Surrey that 'The local abbey of Chertsey towered, in the size of its fief, above any other monastery that held lands in the county.' It has been said that the Chertsey estate was once one of the largest in the England, comparable(5) with those at Reading, Glastonbury and Bury St Edmunds.

Bisley Church would undoubtedly have been a convenient stopping point for travellers making their way between the two abbeys, but this apparently feasible explanation for the establishment of St John the Baptist Church, then seemingly located, as it is now, some distance from the populated part of the village, is seriously flawed for the simple reason that Waverley Abbey was not founded until 1128, nearly two centuries after the first record of a church at Bisley.

Bisley Church by C T Cracklow

The original village settlement of Bisley may have comprised no more than a handful of primitive structures erected by peasants, who were scarcely able to scratch a living, trying to cultivate the poor quality arable land using primitive implements and techniques, and by keeping livestock on the tracts of impoverished heathland. They would have been heavily dependent upon their rich and venerable masters at the abbey to provide assistance in return for such limited services as they could render. Benedictine monks were known to have encouraged cultivation of the poorest soils and would have helped where necessary but, being not only pious but also very astute in matters of commerce, probably benefitted most from the reciprocal arrangement; an arrangement that did not always run smoothly. The monks would have ensured that there was a chapel at Bisley for the local inhabitants, but this still does not bring us much closer to ascertaining when the church might have been established.

One may surmise that there was a place of worship here in pagan times long before Christianity spread across the country, particularly as we know that such springs were accredited with supernatural powers of healing by the Celts and Saxons. They were also venerated by the Romans, who sanctified them in the name of one of their goddesses of springs and fountains. Early Christians were quick to see the benefit in adopting pagan buildings[(6)] and festivals and, if that is what they did in Bisley, then John the Baptist, to whom both the 'Holy Well' and the church are dedicated, would have been the obvious choice of patron saint. Paganism was not easily wiped out[(7)], especially in sparsely populated rural areas, and there would have been a long transitional period before it was more or less eradicated by the conversion of most of the population to Christianity. Paganism and Christianity may have existed in strange juxtaposition in many areas for a long while, although one may reasonably assume that Bisley was an early Christian outpost of Chertsey Abbey, possibly coming under its ownership from as early as the 7th century. A pagan origin does seem the most plausible explanation for the establishment of a simple place of worship at Bisley.

St John the Baptist Church (south side). 1961

The approximate location of the present-day Church of St John the Baptist in Bisley appears to have been identified in a very early document. A recently published book[(8)] based upon a doctoral thesis on early medieval Surrey, states 'The Pyrford charter-bounds of 956 pass around the irregular west end of modern Horsell parish. Unfortunately they cannot be plotted exactly, but at some point between *per leage* (Parley Farm) and *mint byrge* (Mimbridge) was an enclosure or meadow called *eceles hamme*. This must have lain near, perhaps almost adjoining, the medieval church of Bisley some fifty yards from the boundary. Bisley is an enclave on the edge of the great Chertsey Abbey estate; the nondescript little church need be no older than the 12th century, though it probably appears in Domesday Book as a chapel of Chobham. Although the area is not one of intensive Roman settlement, this seems a significant association between an *eccles* name and a standing church: It is conceivable that some cult had survived around the church site, or around the nearby holy well of St John the Baptist where parishioners were still being baptised within recorded memory.' The author, John Blair, explains that the place name element *eccles*, a derivation of late Latin *ecclesia*, probably implies contact between the early Germanic settlers and native churches with Latin-speaking priests or worshippers, and he cites Bisley as being a new and topographically significant example. Dr Blair also illustrates the location of *eceles hamme* by overlaying the information recorded in the bounds onto a simplified modern map of the village and surrounding area. He also qualifies his assertion that an alternative interpretation would be to place one of the landmarks, *mylen felda*, near modern Millbrook, which would space the boundary points less evenly and leave *eceles hamme* at the north-west corner of Horsell parish, further, but still not very far, from Bisley Church.

The Domesday Survey carried out in 1085-86 was a mammoth undertaking for its day and provides a vast quantity of important information about the country at that point in time. It does not specifically mention Bisley though it is generally believed that the entry for Chobham: '*Ibi æccla et alia capella*': 'There (is) a church and another chapel', refers to Bisley Church as being one of these two places of worship. Some authorities suggest[(9)] the church was at Bisley, and the chapel, dedicated to St Lawrence, was at Chobham. The chapel would have been whichever one had no resident priest, but without firm evidence we shall never know. It is not surprising that Bisley was not recognised as a separate village when the survey was compiled, for the widely scattered inhabitants, few as they were, would easily have been accepted as being part of the wider community of Chobham. After all, Chobham stretched far and wide even in comparatively recent times, with a West End extending to the Chobham Ridges along the Maultway, a North End (a substantial part of which was cut off by the railway in the mid-1800s and renamed Wentworth) and a Valley End (where the Church of St Saviour, built in 1837, became the place of worship for the somewhat isolated community already established there).

As previously mentioned, Bisley was reliant upon assistance from the monks at Chertsey who no doubt exacted due recompense in some form or another. Whether that *quid pro quo* was balanced too heavily in favour of the abbey or whether the village simply became confident enough to seek more independence is not entirely clear, but an event of great importance to Bisley occurred in the 13th century when one individual challenged the authority of the abbey in a most audacious way. This is how the Reverend Joseph Cater[(10)] describes it in the first book about the history of Bisley over a hundred years ago:-

'Shortly after John Sawbridge[11] became Bishop of Winchester in the year 1283, being the eleventh year of King Edward I, a sharp dispute arose between the Rector of Bisley and the Abbot of Chertsey, Bartholomew de Winchester. The cause of the quarrel appears to have been, strange to say, the burial of the dead. Several persons in the neighbourhood having died, their bodies were brought to Bisley to be interred, and the rector saw no reason for refusing them Christian burial in the ground around his church. The matter having reached the ears of the abbot, he complained to Thomas, the then rector, insisting that the burials properly belonged to the abbey, and that all fees accruing therefrom should be forfeited to the Abbot. The rector maintained his ground, but ultimately a kind of compromise was effected: the abbey conceding to the Rector of Bisley and his successors the right of interment of all inhabitants of the parish, together with all the payments by way of fee, the Rector on his part agreeing to render "to the abbey once every year three pounds of wax to sustain the lights of the Holy Cross". The ancient candle then in use was composed of strings surrounded by wax, and was regarded as quite a luxury. The poorer classes used splinters of wood

> fatted or dipped in pitch. The agreement was afterwards confirmed by the Bishop of Winchester, and the burial of all deceased inhabitants of Bisley has remained with the rector of the parish ever since.'

The abbey was involved in many disputes during the 13th and 14th centuries, the more serious ones sometimes ended in litigation or papal arbitration but minor ones were usually resolved by straightforward mediation 'in order to save extortion' upon the abbey's dwindling resources.

Of all the stories about the history of Bisley, Thomas's victory is one of the best known, and yet, like so many legends that have been repeated time and again, it may include some significant errors that have come to be accepted as truth. The question was raised recently as to whether this event actually occurred in 1283 or several decades earlier, and whether Thomas was just a humble farmer-cum-part-time-rector or a very influential figure in the Christian church. Doubt seems to have arisen in some minds because the account is so similar in many respects to part of the history of the adjacent village of Chobham. Comparing the two stories, there are indeed similarities but in other respects the details are markedly different.

There certainly seems to have been a priest called Thomas who refused to pay for the customary transportation of corpses from Bisley to Chertsey, who successfully petitioned for the 'right of sepulchre', and who had to supply beeswax to the abbey every year on the Feast of St Michael for making fine quality candles for the high altar. Up to this point these events closely match those for Chobham.

Turning now to Chobham's history, the following details are well-documented[(12)]:- Master Thomas of Chobham was born between 1158 and 1168 and died between 1233 and 1236. He was a learned scholar and theologian who studied at Paris and Oxford, he wrote influential works on moral theology, a handbook for preachers and a notable collection of Latin sermons that survive to this day. From this point onwards the details become less certain. Before holding the benefice of Chobham, Master Thomas was Sub-Dean of Salisbury and his eminent standing within Christian circles might well have ensured consideration by Pope Honorius the Third, to whom he was said to have pleaded for a churchyard at Chobham and the right to perform burials. This was supposedly done over the head of the Abbot of Chertsey who was adamant that the corpses must be brought forward and on which, of course, lucrative burial fees would be due. It is claimed that a papal brief granting permission was issued which Brother Adam (Abbot of Chertsey) and Peter de Roches (Bishop of Winchester) quickly endorsed. The abbot had been outmanoeuvred but not beaten. To save face, he demanded that Chobham must supply 6lbs (pounds) of beeswax and a fee of twenty shillings per year in return for this right.

Comparing the two stories, it seems highly unlikely that there were two priests, both called Thomas, both of whom were granted the right of burial by papal edict. Bisley's Thomas would never have been able to receive the attention of the Pope over the heads of the Abbot and the Bishop unless he had been equally as influential as his counterpart in Chobham and also well known by those close to the Pope. On the other hand, there could have been just one incumbent for both villages, Master Thomas of Chobham, who held the benefices of Chobham and Bisley either concurrently or at overlapping times, as indeed five other priests[(13)] were to do subsequently. If so, surely he would not have had to petition the Pope on a similar cause on two separate occasions. Even if he had, then the date from which burials could be performed in Bisley cannot be as late as 1283, as is generally claimed, but decades earlier, as the second appeal must have been determined during his lifetime. The most plausible explanation is that Bartholomew de Winchester (otherwise known as Bartholomew de Winton) conceded the right of burial, and the attendant fees, to the priest at Bisley in 1283, or thereabouts, following the precedent set at Chobham. By settling on similar terms, any repetition of the embarrassment suffered those 68 years earlier would have been avoided.

The reference to papal intervention seems to have been unfounded because painstaking research of the Vatican Secret Archives[(14)] has revealed no mention of these events, nor of the issue of any edict, during the papacies of Honorius III (1216–1227) or Martin IV (1281–1285), suggesting that the matter was settled not in the Vatican but at Chertsey or Winchester.

Reliance upon details passed by word of mouth across many generations because of the lack of substantive records, frequently results in unintended errors and sometimes deliberate embellishment and exaggeration, and so perhaps the name of the incumbent at Bisley was at some stage mistakenly confused with that of his more eminent fellow priest at Chobham – we may never know.

The possession of a graveyard in those days was a very significant mark of prestige. Some villages turned their churchyards into veritable stockades, not just to keep out wandering livestock but also to protect families from marauding gangs and robbers who roamed the countryside in those early troubled times.

The great abbey at Chertsey dedicated to St Peter, which had such a powerful influence upon the tiny hamlet of Bisley, was finally sacked in 1537 under Henry VIII when he ordered the dissolution of the monasteries, and today there is virtually no trace of this fine building. It was largely demolished to provide materials for the construction of Oatlands Palace near Weybridge and by the mid-1700s all the remaining stonework had been taken for re-use elsewhere.

---

(1) A spring, known as St John the Baptist Well.
(2) *Anglo-Saxons Charters.*
(3) *Chertsey Abbey.* Runnymede BC
(4) Malden. *Vict. Hist. Surrey.*
(5) *Chertsey Abbey.* Wheeler.
(6) *Surrey Heath in the Dark Ages .*
(7) Ibid.
(8) *Early Medieval Surrey.*
(9) Malden. *Vict. Hist. Surrey.* & Schueller. *Hist. Chobham.*
(10) *Bisley Bits.*

(11) John de Pontissara (otherwise John de Pontoise) c.1240-1304, Bishop of Winchester from 1282.

(12) *Cart. Sax.*

(13) Revds Richd Ode, Thos Ganton, Allen Walter, Geo Clarke-Gayton & Richd Cecil.

(14) Regista Honorii III & Les Registres de Martin IV.

Chapter 3

BISLEY BELLS

St John the Baptist Church at Bisley now has the oldest bell in Surrey, since an earlier 13th century one at the Church of St Peter & St Paul, Chalden, was stolen in 1970 and probably melted for its scrap value. Chalden's ancient bell was believed to have been cast in Italy and had been re-hung in the porch above the main door in 1902 in order to make room in the tower for a new peel of six bells. Bisley's oldest bell is unlikely to suffer the same fate as it is securely contained beneath the broach spire within a substantial framework, from which it cannot be removed without dismantling much of the second floor of the belfry.

The oldest Bisley bell, the middle one of three all cast in England, was made between 1307 and 1315. It is inscribed '+ FRATERNITAS FECIT ME IN HONORE BEATE MAREIE'[(1)] in ¾" (20mm) high, widely-spaced letters of a most unusual style. The 'fraternity' so described and who 'made me in honour of the Blessed (Virgin) Mary', would not have been from the monastic community at Chertsey Abbey that owned Bisley at that time, but a body of externs attached to the abbey. Great privilege and protection were bestowed upon holders of this title who, in return, were expected to render certain obligations and services from time to time.

However, those who cast the bell would have had absolutely no experience of such work, relying entirely upon the bell-founder's instructions and working under his close supervision. They would have carried out all the manual work: digging and lining the ground, constructing and firing the furnace, operating the bellows, and pouring the molten metal into the sand mould. The bell may have been cast in the field beside the church, where the other two bells were to be made four centuries later, but it could have been cast within or close to the precincts of the abbey and then hauled to Bisley.

Inscription on the middle bell.

The inscription is not cast into a band below the shoulder, where one would expect to see it, but on the angle of the shoulder itself, but it is the distinctive style of lettering that indicates that it was the work of Richard de Wymbish, according to Stahlschmidt[(2)] who was an eminent authority on local bells and a Master of the Worshipful Company of Founders.

There are only two examples of bells cast by Richard de Wymbish still in existence, the other being at Goring in Berkshire. Richard had a brother, Michael, who was also a bell-founder working in this area around the same time, but Stahlschmidt maintains that it is almost certainly the work of Richard, an assertion that is supported by a recent paper[(3)] on a number of bronze vessels designed for hand-washing at meals that were cast by him. The similarity of the letters of the Bisley inscription to those on one of the vessels is described thus: 'The style of the lettering and of the initial cross-fleury… is in fact very similar to those used by certain London bell-founders of the early 14th century. The most striking parallel noted is on a bell at Bisley, Surrey, but there is also a general similarity to the inscription on a bell at Goring cast by Richard Wymbish.' One may question whether any characteristic style of alphabet alone would have been sufficiently individualistic to identify the work of a single person, but in the absence of dissenting opinion it seems that the 'fraternity' bell at Bisley can reliably be attributed to Richard de Wymbish.

The belfry has two other bells: a tenor bell marked 'W E FECIT. 1710' that is reliably attributed as the work of William Eldridge (1634–1716), whose family established the Chertsey foundry in 1622; and a treble bell inscribed 'Thom^{s} Swaine made me 1781. James Stedman, Churchwarden.' Swain (as his name is spelled nowadays) was descended from William Eldridge and was from Longford, near

Colnbrook, in the former county of Middlesex. He lived from 1752 to1781. Both of these bells are believed[4] to have been founded in the field beside the church, where proof might be found if archaeological excavations were ever to be carried out.

The 1710 and 1781 bells were actually replacements for two earlier ones of which nothing is known other than their inclusion on an inventory carried out in 1553, demanded by Protestant reformers intent on removing all remaining relics and signs of the Catholic religion. The inventory[5] showed that the church had already been stripped of most of its valuables, many of which had been destroyed, although a few items may have been hidden, particularly if the secondary purpose of the exercise had become known which was that Edward VI's commissioners were confiscating valuable goods for the King. The list is very short but it clearly shows that there had been three bells:-

Bysley Pariche Churche

Imprimis	*j*	*Chalice of silver*
Item	*j*	*cope*
Item	*j*	*vestment of silke*
Item	*j*	*surplus*
Item	*iij*	*belles in the steeple*

All whiche is commyted to the custody of Thomas goring, John Hone, John Cobbett, John Rwtter, the vjth of October in the vjth yere of the reign of owre sovereign Lord.

In 1981, Whitechapel Bell Foundry were invited to inspect the bells and to quote for any recommended repairs. Their report was duly considered by the Parochial Church Council:-

The bells form a ring of three, as follows:-

	Diameter	Approx. Weight	Approx. Note	Date
Tenor bell	2′7″	6 cwt	B	1710
2nd bell	2′5½″	5 cwt	C#	Early 14th C.
Treble bell	2′3″	3¾cwt	D#	1781

All the bells appear to be sound but are only fair for tone and tune although some improvement could be effected by careful treatment under the tuning machine. The canons or supporting loops are intact and they still retain the cast-in clapper staples although a false one has been bolted through the crown of the second. They are all somewhat indented, especially the tenor and owing to the clapper being too long the indentation is fairly close to the lip and we would advise not using it until the matter has been corrected. It will be necessary, in the event of any restoration, for the clappers to strike on unworn surfaces; this will entail cutting out the cast-in clapper staples and drilling centre holes through the crowns so that new and independent ones can be fitted to enable the clappers to swing in an altered direction; the advantage of this is that the cast-in staples, being of iron, are usually the cause of old bells becoming cracked due to rust and consequent expansion and their removal does help to prevent this happening.

The installation generally appears to be just as it was installed back in the 18th century and it would seem that practically nothing has been done since. The fittings are in very poor condition. The headstocks are of elm with the old hoop type gudgeons running in plain gunmetal bearings, both of which are worn; the elm shews much evidence of infestation but we understand that all timbers have been treated. The wheels are poor and oversize. The clappers are of poor shape and proportion, very loose at the point of swing and all ironwork is heavily corroded. The supporting ironwork has the old coarse threads and the two smaller bells are loose on the headstocks. The pulleys, over which the bell ropes 'fall' are just crude reels.

The bell frame is of oak and probably 18th century construction but using older timbers. It is of post and brace construction and

> arranged for the three bells to swing side by side in the North/South direction. It takes its bearing on the belfry floor which is supported by beams below. Some of the timbers have been cut back in places to allow the bells to swing and there is evidence of infestation. We are of the opinion that the structure is serviceable to allow the bells to be just 'chimed on the swing' but not suitable for proper ringing where bells turn full circle. We consider, however, that the bells must be re-hung with all new fittings as we are of the opinion that they are past any reasonable form of repair. It would be quite in order to fit iron levers instead of wheels as this would effect quite a reasonable economy.
>
> We therefore enclose a detailed estimate of what we consider should be done but in view of the cost involved we also shew the relative costs of doing one, two or three bells.

The three quoted prices were £1,006-00, £1,708-00 and £2,466-00 respectively for one, two or all three bells to be refurbished concurrently. The report was duly considered and it was agreed that all three bells needed to be refurbished, although the price was more than could reasonably be afforded. In order to minimize the cost, three volunteers[6] undertook the work using materials supplied by the foundry. The tenor bell was rotated by a quarter-turn as this presented a striking area with much less wear on the sound ring. The same result was achieved by turning the other two half-a-turn each as they were more worn on one side than the other and, as the bells would be restricted to tolling in future, the clappers would no longer strike both sides. New headstocks[7] and straps were fitted, plummer blocks with self-aligning sealed bearings replaced the old gudgeons and their plain gunmetal bearings, metal levers were substituted for the dilapidated wooden wheels, and various other parts were renewed or replaced. The work was completed in 1982 and the total cost of materials was £581.67. Most of the obsolete 18th century fittings, including hand-made iron nuts and headstock straps, were placed in the intermediate room beneath the belfry, where they remain to this day. During the course of repair an unusual artefact was discovered beside the bell frames. It was a mid-to-late 19th century torpedo-shaped bottle, with a pointed end instead of a flat base, that contained a small amount of hardened brown wood glue. The bottle was very thick, pale green, about ten inches (250mm) long and heavily embossed with the words 'Genuine Superior Aerated Water. J. Schweppe & Co, 51 Berners Street, Oxford St, London'. Known as a Hamilton bottle or 'egg bottle', it was designed so that it could only be laid on its side so that the cork would be kept moist, preventing the escape of carbonated gas. The bottle had obviously been re-used for glue, perhaps for repairing some of the lighter wooden parts of the bell wheels in late Victorian or Edwardian times. All three bells are marked by fairly recent bird-staining because squirrels have damaged the cladding around the belfry, enabling pigeons to gain entry. These holes and other defects have been patched and droppings have been swept from the floor of the chamber. However, surface stains on the bells cannot be removed without vigorous cleaning, which would spoil the patina that has developed over the course of time.

---

(1) Note the spelling of 'MAREIE' which is often mis-spelt elsewhere.

(2) *Surrey Bells.*

(3) *Medieval 'Bronze' Tripod Ewers from Wales.*

(4) Personal communication with W A Hughes, Chairman & Managing Director, Whitechapel Bell Foundry.

(5) *Surrey Arch Coll.*

(6) Ken Atkins, Brian Jackson & Tim Price.

(7) The headstock was inverted on the middle bell to increase the pull required to chime it.

Chapter 4

RECTORS

Bisley has a long and impressive list of incumbents spanning over 700 years, but there are gaps where the register has been lost on three occasions. Sadly, there is now virtually no prospect of the missing registers ever being found. It seems quite likely that records for the period 1346 to 1366 are missing as a result of the turmoil that followed the Black Death, which swept across England killing between a third and a half of the population within two years of its arrival in 1348. The disease was possibly the most deadly pandemic in human history. It is thought to have returned with varying degrees of virulence during almost every generation and this could account for the loss of later records too. This, of course, is all pure supposition as there is no evidence to support it. However, it is recorded(1) that John de Benham, who was Abbot of Chertsey from 1346–61, died of the 'Great Pestilence'; a vicar of Chobham is thought to have been a victim and maybe the benefice of Bisley was at some time '*defectus per pestilentem*' – vacant as a result of the plague. One has only to study the records to see that half of Bisley's rectors appointed during the 14th and 15th centuries lasted in post no more than two calendar years, suggesting that some, at least, may have fallen victim to the Black Death. The years 1465 and 1466 show no less than four people were instituted as Rectors of Bisley, which is quite surprising, as parish priests were not usually offered retirement by the bishop, even when they became too frail to discharge their duties. To do so would have burdened the parish with the cost of supporting them in old age, and so many incumbents simply died in office. It was also unusual for priests to move from parish to parish as frequently as they do nowadays.

Rector, Vicar or Curate? The majority of early medieval priests were rectors (Latin *regnare* to rule) who were entitled to receive the whole tithe in addition to the produce resulting from their own labours. Each held his benefice for life, unless he disgraced himself. As the demand for churches increased, the bishops encouraged lay founders to present their churches to a monastery whose abbot or prior then nominally became rector but usually employed a deputy or *vicarius* to serve each parish. These vicars ultimately obtained an ordinance (whence 'ordination') granting them security of tenure, though they could claim only a small part of the tithe. By the end of the Middle Ages more than a quarter of English parishes were held by vicars. Correctly, the curate is the rector or vicar as he or, increasingly these days, she is entrusted with 'the cure of souls'. In general speech, however, the word is used to denote an ordained assistant who helps the incumbent in the performance of parochial duties, but they should properly be called assistant curates.

We know very little about early holders of the benefice of Bisley apart from Thomas, the first Rector, whose brilliant achievement in winning the right of burial is described in detail in Chapter Two and also in the Reverend Joseph Cater's book, 'Bisley Bits'. Cater provides us with a list of his predecessors, including the dates of their institution and their patron, but his list contains a few inaccuracies and omissions. These have been corrected where possible in **Appendix B**, which also includes subsequent appointments from 1895 to the present day. No doubt all the 'Clerks in Holy Orders' left their mark on Bisley in their own individualistic way, but just a few of them are selected here.

The Reverend Robert Grous (Rector from 1530 to 1560)
During his very long Rectorship, Robert Grous lived through a period of great turmoil for the church in Britain that began with the downfall and death of Cardinal Wolsey, followed by the King's divorce, the dissolution of the monasteries and the Reformation. It was Henry VIII who appointed Grous, and Cardinal Wolsey had conducted his Institution, and so Grous had to tread a very careful path. His adaptable views must surely have been every bit as flexible as those of 'the Vicar of Bray' in order to keep his position safe. Grous's legacy for Bisley was to compile the first Parish Register, starting with a baptism[(2)] in 1561. His early entries were later copied into what is now the earliest surviving register, headed:-

> *The Register booke of the parish church of bisley, in ye countie of surrey, newly written in the yeare of o~ Lord God, 1598, and in ye fortith yeare of the raigne of o~ most gracious Sovraigne Lady*

> *Elizabeth by the grace of God Queen of England, ffrannce and Ireland, Defender of the ~~ ancien-nte christian catholic ffaith so wherein is contayned all christenings, weddinge and burialls commanded by her Ma*[tie] *to be made for divers good causes and considerations.*

The Reverend John Hill (Rector from 1561 to 1588)

Under the direction of the Archbishop, who was concerned about the standard of his clergy, parishes were asked to send a report indicating: the order to which the incumbent belonged; whether he was married; what was his education; was he resident in the parish; was he willing to provide hospitality to visitors to the parish; where was he normally to be found; was he licensed to preach and did he hold any other benefices. The response from Bisley was that the Revd Hill was in full orders; unmarried; moderately learned; resident; hospitable; spent his time in the parish; was not licensed to preach and held the livings of Bisley and Windlesham in plurality.

Not only is it doubtful that anyone in the village would have felt sufficiently competent to assess his scholastic achievements, let alone bold enough to assert with such understatement that he was 'moderately learned', but it is questionable whether anyone else could even write. If he was the only person capable of completing the questionnaire, he might well have demonstrated such modesty, making light of his qualifications in the presence of his Churchwardens.

His background is mentioned in a letter(3) from a

Windlesham historian who said, '… as far as I can make out his career was as follows: Christ Church, Oxford, BA 1550; MA 1555; BMed 1560; BD 1561; Rector of Bisley 26, March 1561–1588; Canon of Westminster, 1561; Rector of Windlesham, 10th March 1516–1588 and Canon of Canterbury 1567. John Hill was what may be termed "a pluralist" (a not uncommon matter in those days), and he would have to find someone to help him to serve one or other of his cures. Hill died in 1588.'

The Reverend Richard Massey, MA (Rector from 1610 to 1658 or 1659)

Massey appears in Foster's *Alumni Oxon* as 'Richard Massy, of Cheshire, pleb Brasenose Coll matric. 14 Feb 1588/9, aged 13'. If this is the same person who held the Rectorship of Bisley, he would have been about 34 years of age when he was instituted as Rector, having previously completed eight years as Rector of Weybridge. More significantly, this would make him 82 years old in 1658 when he was fined for non-attendance at the Court Baron. Dr Curtis[4] claims that Massey is the person named in extracts[5] of that Court Baron held at Pirbright on 18th January 1858, at which 'Richard Massey, Clerk' heads the list of twenty tenants fined 'iiijd' (four old pence) 'for default of appearance att the Court Baron then and there holden'. Curtis further suggests that his non-appearance was not due to age or inadvertence but to a refusal to recognise the jurisdiction of the Lord of the Manor of Pirbright, who claimed ownership of part of the 'waste' of a small Manor called 'Cowshete' (the modern Cowshot) upon which rent was payable. This was disputed by the Rector of Bisley who attested that by tradition it had always been glebe land belonging to Bisley Rectory. It appears that a portion of land by the Standing Stone did lie within the bounds of Bisley and, if appendant to the Rectory of Bisley, would necessarily be tithe free. The matter was still unresolved almost two centuries later when a corpse was found on Cowshot Common. The people of Bisley denied any liability for disposal of the body, possibly because ownership of that part of the common was not disputed. The record shows that the burial fee was paid by Pirbright. However, Bisley was still claiming the alleged glebe land when beating the bounds in 1841. Curtis also quotes from Manning & Bray[(6)]:-

> There is a small Manor in the northern part of the parish of Pirbright, extending into Bisley, to the rectory of which it is annexed, called Cowshete, – the modern Cowshot – which holds of the manor of Pirbright, paying the yearly acknowledgement of a peppercorn. About the year 1615, George Austen, Esq, of Shalford, purchased of Edward Remnant, the 'Manor of Cowshott, in Pirbright', and conveyed it, with other lands by deed inrolled in Chancery, to certain persons [mentioned in the text] upon trust, for the uses of his Will. By his Will, da: 1 April, 1619, he gave it to his son Robert Austen, but by a Codicil, da: 8 Nov., 1620, he devised it to certain persons [mentioned in the text] upon trust, to

> employ the rents, &c., for the benefit of the then Parson of Bisley, and the Parsons and Incumbents for the time being, to whom it did some time belong, until it was found, in the time of the late Queen Elizabeth [ER1], to be a concealment[7], the Parson paying 3s. a year reserved to the Queen. It consisted of a small coppice, and some small quid-rents, amounting to £1 7s. 3d. This small and once independent Manor of Cowshot – the property of the National Rifle Association since the year 1889, when the training camp was removed from Wimbledon – is now, and has been for years, included under that of Pirbright.

Quoting the Reverend Frances Owston, Curtis adds, 'A small parcel of land in it is the Glebe[8] of Bisley Rectory and tithe-free', which was correct, though unbeknown to Curtis the glebe was compulsorily purchased by the War Department, together with other parcels of land scattered around the periphery of its main landholding, a year after Owston relinquished the incumbency at Pirbright.

The Reverend Dr Andrew Lamont, DD (Rector from 1660 to 1711)

The first parish register contained a note stating that Lamont conducted a service in accordance with the Book of Common Prayer[9] on 24th August 1662 and that he read the Thirty Nine Articles contained therein. Another note refers to the order for prohibition of clandestine marriages that was publicly read in church by Lamont on Sunday 6th March 1686.

Dr Lamont dutifully served for over half a century in Bisley, longer than anyone else before or since. He is best remembered for giving two substantial sums of money (50 pounds on one occasion and 100 pounds on another[10]) to be invested in land, from which the rents were to used for charitable purposes. Four cottages in Queen Lane (now Queens Road) with gardens and some additional land were bought after Lamont's death and rented to the poor. The last of these Charity Cottages was demolished in 1973 following sale by private treaty from which the proceeds were invested; the interest that accrues is paid annually to the needy.

Cater[11] recognised the esteem in which this great man was held: 'The inhabitants of Bisley will ever have cause to remember with gratitude the residence among them of Dr Andrew Lamont, not only on account of his benefaction of one hundred pounds which he left for the poor, but also in consequence of the manifest interest which he took in all parochial matters. It is as though at the time they would guard against any possibilities of his being forgotten that they have two separate entries of his interment.'

The Reverend Richard Cecil MA.

The Reverend Richard Cecil, MA (Rector from 1786 to 1810)

Cecil was a remarkable man who gave up a business career in his mid-twenties to study theology, enter the church and become a prolific religious writer and one of the most notable preachers of his day. On being presented with the livings of Bisley and, four years later, Chobham, he declared that both parishes were in a wretched state[(12)]

in which ignorance and immorality prevailed to a very awful degree. Few persons attended the church and many regarded Sunday only as a day of sport and amusement. Furthermore, he found that there was 'no house to either of the livings, except a ruin inhabited by a labourer, nor any that could be engaged for Mr. Cecil's residence'. He spent several years in temporary accommodation until 1807, when 'a convenient house with eleven acres of ground' was provided for him at Chobham at a modest rent, though he never took up permanent residence, only using it for several months each summer while taking services at the two villages. He spent most of his time in London where the fame of his evangelistic preaching brought him lectureships at many notable churches, including St John's Chapel in Bedford Row, with which he was most prominently associated.

After Cecil's death, his works were published by an old friend who wrote in the rambling introduction an exegesis of his character and his religious pronouncements. The book is entitled 'Cecil's Remains'[(13)] in which Cecil recalled his first impression of Bisley:-

> 'It is completely out of the world. The farmers in these parts are mostly occupiers of their own land. They crowded round me when I first came, and were eager to make bargains with me for the tythe. I told them I was ignorant of such matters, but that I would propose a measure which none of them could object to. The farmers of Bisley should nominate three

farmers of Chobham parish; and whatever those three Chobham farmers should appoint me to receive, that they should pay. This was putting myself into their power indeed, but the one grand point with me was to conciliate their minds, and pave the way for the Gospel in these parishes. And so far it answered my purpose. I had desired the three farmers to throw the weight, in dubious cases, into the farmers' scale.' Thus he quickly gained the deepest respect of the villagers and greatly increased the Sunday congregations. He said, 'I hardly think it likely that a man could have been received in a more friendly manner than I have been. About 500 people attend at Chobham, and 300 at Bisley. While I am grave and serious they will allow me to say or do anything. For instance; a few Sundays since it rained so prodigiously hard when I had finished my sermon at Bisley, that I saw it was impracticable for any body to leave the Church. I then told the people that as it was likely to continue for some time, we had better employ ourselves as well as we could, and so I would take up the subject again. I did so; and they listened to me readily for another half-hour, though I had preached to them three-quarters of an hour before I had concluded. All this they bear, and think it nothing strange.'

Some of 'Cecil's Remains' are very illuminating while others, conversely, are quite abstruse. A copy acquired by the author some years ago has the following annotation on the flyleaf written by a former owner:- 'Carl Chatham after listening to Cecil's preaching, on his way with a companion, confessed that he was greatly impressed, but said he could not understand him! Was there anyone that could?'

We should not judge him unfairly as he was undoubtedly a most talented communicator. In his younger days Cecil had also been an accomplished violinist, musician(14), poet and passionately fond of fine art; and yet these worldly pleasures were all but abandoned on his turning to Christ in his mid-twenties. He suffered from rheumatism from an early age and at 60 suffered a bad stroke and died two years later. A portrait of Cecil, presented after his death to the Parish of Bisley by a Chobham resident, is handed on to each succeeding Rector as a sort of mascot.

The Reverend F B Gourrier (Rector from 1857 to 1861)

Under the Inclosure Award of 6th August 1858 when Bisley's common fields were enclosed, Gourrier was allotted 6 acres 1 rood 33 perches (2.6 hectares) on which he was quickly provided with a glebe house erected by public subscription that raised £504 9s. 0d. 'Bisley Bits' lists the fifty or so individuals who contributed, starting with the name of Queen Victoria who gave £50. We are not told whether there had ever been a previous parsonage house.

The Reverend George J Wild (Rector from 1865 to 1872)

The Rectory was considerably enlarged in 1866 to meet the growing needs of the new Rector but, as no record seems to exist of the cost being borne by the diocese, it seems that Wild paid for the work out of his own pocket.

The Reverend Walter Eaton, MA (Rector from 1872 to 1881)

With explicit instructions from the Bishop who had 'urged on one the necessity for immediate restoration', Eaton wasted no time in setting up an appeal for £700 'to plainly but decently restore the church'. He sent off numerous letters of request and quickly raised £800, enough to start replacing the almost derelict chancel – falling down, some said – and to build a north aisle to accommodate boys from the newly-established Farm School. The chancel had become so dilapidated and dangerous that a curtain had been placed across the end of the nave some years before his arrival. The maintenance of the chancel was usually the responsibility of the Rector, but as his predecessor in office had spent so much money on improving the Rectory he may thus have avoided pressure to attend to the deterioration of the chancel.

The Reverend Joseph Cater (Rector from 1886 to 1895)

Cater is forever remembered for his gem of a book called 'Bisley Bits'. The few extant copies are so treasured that they are passed down through families as heirlooms. There is a photograph of him standing by the south wall of the church with an impressively large group of choristers, never since matched in number.

Highly decorated interior of nave and chancel. 1890s

Cater was responsible for the elaborate decoration of the walls of the chancel and nave, as portrayed in some photographs of the interior of the church. It is recorded that the task took five years to complete but it was not to the liking of his successor who removed it.

The Reverend John Gwyon, LD (Rector from 1895 to 1928)

The demise of the Revd John Gwyon and the annulment of his extraordinary legacy are covered in another chapter, but it would be unfair to create an impression of the man based solely on these events. There can be few better ways of describing village attitudes towards this strange person than by passing on this succinct commentary by an old friend of the author who knew him well and wrote[(15)]:-

When the Revd. John Gwyon came to replace Cater in 1895, there followed a ministry of 33 years of diligent and faithful service, during which he performed scrupulously and punctually at the statutory duties required of him. Unfortunately, he was by nature a recluse and a scholar, with a strong disposition to miserliness. This did not endear him to the parishioners, who mostly closed their doors when they saw him coming and pretended not to be at home. At the time I first knew him (from 1912) there were only three houses in the village where he was welcome to call for a cup of tea; and I am glad to say that ours was one of them. I think I should add in fairness to him, and as something in addition to the regular performance of his minimum duties redounding to his credit, that he was also instrumental in recovering some of the ancient documents which had gone astray and having them worthily bound at what must have seemed to him great expense for the benefit of posterity. The choir in his early years was, as I think it still is, a credit to the Parish. By the time I joined it in 1912, it consisted of 20 or more men and boys, among whom my brother was the principal soloist at the Festivals.

It is also recorded that Gwyon was fastidious in his attendance for morning and afternoon prayers each day at the village school. He was instrumental in making good the chancel, which had been so shoddily rebuilt just forty-five years before that it required his urgent attention. He pasted a hand-written note inside the front cover of the Register of Burial (commencing 1813) explaining at length how he had to carry out these urgent repairs in 1918 during the First World War when materials were hard to obtain. The expense of this remedial work, inflated by wartime conditions, must have been particularly perturbing to a man 'with a strong disposition to miserliness'. Nevertheless, these repairs have indeed stood the test of time.

Another of his notes, this time scrawled inside the front cover of a typewritten privately-published book[16], states:-

> This bound volume, containing the history of the Incumbents of the adjoining Parish of Pirbright, and matters pertaining to that Incumbency and Parish, with incidental relating to this Parish of Bisley and other neighbouring parishes, has been presented by the author to the present Rector of Bisley, and his successors, as an heirloom in perpetuity, to be kept in the iron safe at the Parish Church for that purpose. It will be noted that there are particulars in this volume giving additional information about the 'Parish of Bisley' not contained in 'Bisley Bits' written by my predecessor in this benefice – The

> Rev Joseph Cater, Rector from 1886 to 1895, which work is a history of the Parish of Bisley and its Rectors with incidentals, the chief additional items being those relating to the Manor of Cowshot, of which the Rectors here were Lords at one time.
>
> John Gwyon, L.D., Rector of Bisley, Surrey:- Since 1895, thus thirty years now.
>
> Doyen (Senior) Incumbent in the two Deaneries of Emly and Woking:- Since 1920, Surrogate for granting marriage licences, etc, etc, etc, etc. February 1st 1925.

The book is no longer kept in the church safe, nor has it passed through the hands of recent incumbents, because the Revd Peter Gotelee presented it to the author some years ago who now treasures it as much as any heirloom. The book contains a great deal of useful information not found elsewhere but disappointingly, so far as Bisley is concerned, only a limited amount is written about this village, and then only where it relates to the Parish of Pirbright.

Gwyon was certainly an eccentric character and in later life his mental health deteriorated. He committed suicide in the old rectory on 28th December 1928. It was claimed at the time that he had been the second Rector to take his own life; the first, name not now known, was said to have hung himself from the yew tree outside the church porch.

The rectory in which Gwyon tragically died was put up

for sale after his death and renamed Bisley House by Mr William MacQueen, its new owner. Its name was changed again in 1947 when the house was bought by Mr George Bogle, who named it Coombe Manor.

The Reverend Charles Montagu[(17)] Horley (Rector from 1929 to 1954)

Horley was the first Rector to take up residence in a new rectory in Clews Lane that had been built on the same parcel of glebe land as the former parsonage. Horley was regarded as a good preacher,[(18)] a kind personality and a well-loved man in the parish. The names of both his sons are inscribed on the tablet in the church to those who lost their lives in the Second World War.

Upon Horley's retirement, the Diocesan Pastoral Committee suggested that Bisley and West End should be amalgamated because of a shortage of candidates coming forward for ordination. The Diocese was keen to establish a United Benefice which would ease the manpower problem, allowing them to offer a better stipend while still reducing the overall cost, and enabling them to sell one or other of the two parsonage houses. Not surprisingly in those days, the proposal met with horror in both villages, and was strongly resisted. The scheme to amalgamate the parishes was shelved for the time being and the Vicar of West End was made 'Priest-in-Charge' at Bisley until a new Rector was appointed.

The Reverend Windsor Roberts.

The Reverend Canon Windsor Roberts (Rector from 1957 to 1962)

Throughout his incumbency at Bisley, Windsor Roberts remained Archdeacon of Dorking, there being no suffragan bishopric there at that time. He cut a formidable figure around the village, often wearing gaiters and a frock coat. He had five unmarried sisters all living at the rectory. He was a little aloof but kind-hearted and very pragmatic. On receiving the news that swept the village in 1960 that Bisley was to have a top security prison, he sought to reassure people who feared the worst and, having been a former prison chaplain, he said that the presence of a prison was not as terrifying as some people imagined.

The Reverend Peter Douglas Gotelee (Rector from 1976 to 1985)

The hitherto independent Ecclesiastical Parishes of West End and Bisley were amalgamated under Peter Gotelee who, on taking office, became the first Incumbent of the new 'United Benefice', assuming the title of Rector of Bisley and West End. Gotelee was scrupulously even-handed to the extent that he often said that it would be good to move the short distance to Newbridge where a new rectory would be mid-way between the two villages.

It would be inappropriate to mention by name or mark the achievements in this book of 'Clerks in Holy Orders' alive and well today who, at various times during the last quarter of a century, have been charged with 'the care of souls' at Bisley. However, it must be stated that all the clergy throughout history have shaped and guided the village in their respective ways to an enormous extent, and to them the community owes a great debt of gratitude.

---

(1) *The Victoria History of Surrey.*
(2) 'Dority Bray, baptised Maundy Thursday 1561'
(3) Private correspondence dated 21st June 1926 from John Cree to the Revd J Gwyon.
(4) *Curates and Vicars of Pirbright.*
(5) One of two documents in the possession of Albert Collins of Guildford shown to Curtis.

(6) Purchased by NRA in 1889: 'Glebe land: 9.471 acres. Price £475. Vendor: The Rev J Cater.'

(7) Concealment meant that part of the chantry revenue had been withheld pending a review of the due amount.

(8) *Antiquities of Surrey.*

(9) The Book of Common Prayer: Authorised by Act of Parliament in 1662 and had evolved from the first prayer book written in English in 1549 that for the first time set out forms of service for daily and Sunday worship.

(10) Both recorded by Lamont at the front of the 1673 to 1760 Register under a list of 'Benefactors to Bisley in Surrey'.

(11) *Bisley Bits.*

(12) *Christian Guardian.*

(13) *Cecil's Remains.*

(14) Cecil wrote the hymns 'I Will Arise' from Luke xv 18.19. Congregational Church Hymn Book, Anthem No.12, and 'At Thy Feet On Christ We Lay'. Methodist Hymn Book, No 933.

(15) Letter from Kenneth Beal to Revd Peter Gotelee. 10th April 1981.

(16) *Curates and Vicars of Pirbright.*

(17) *Montagu* (spelt without an 'e').

(18) *Woking Opinion.*

Chapter 5

BEATING THE BOUNDS

Beating the Bounds is a very ancient ceremony that was once of great significance but which became superfluous during the 1800s as large-scale mapping was carried out across the land using Jesse Ramsden's new accurate theodolite. The Board of Ordnance (the forerunner of part of the Ministry of Defence) was actually a civilian organisation that had been charged with undertaking a national military survey and, in 1790, it started mapping the countryside in Kent where there was an imminent threat of invasion by the French. In this part of Surrey the first Ordnance Survey map at a scale of 6 inches to the statute mile (I:10,560) was completed in 1871. For more than a century the need to periodically walk parish boundaries has been unnecessary, because the whole of Britain has been reliably mapped and widespread illiteracy is a thing of the past. The ancient ritual of Beating the Bounds is therefore no longer performed except in a few places, where it is done very occasionally just to satisfy an innate desire for maintaining traditions or to mark some special occasion.

The custom is said to have arisen in heathen times as an imitation of the feast of *Terminalia,* dedicated to the god *Terminus,* the guardian of fields and landmarks and maintainer of peace among men. The early Christians adopted it, as they did with many other pagan festivals, and added Christian meaning to the ceremony. They accompanied the bishop into the fields, where litanies were chanted and God's mercy was implored that He would turn away evils and plagues; that He would send good and seasonable weather, and would give in due season the fruits of the earth. Traditionally, though not invariably, Beating the Bounds took place on one of the Rogation Days – the Monday, Tuesday or Wednesday in the same week as Ascension Day (Holy Thursday).

In early times it was important to confirm parish boundaries because the relative size of rural communities influenced their religious, social and economic development. The extent of parishes was often disputed and, in an age when illiteracy was common, the ceremony of Beating the Bounds fulfilled three very useful purposes: It instilled in the minds of participants the extent of the parish, it identified the precise line of the boundary and it confirmed previously claimed territory often in the presence of neighbouring villagers. A group of parishioners, and perhaps observers from neighbouring parishes, would walk the boundary stopping every so often, usually at some landmark, to carry out the three traditional parts of the ritual. Firstly a short prayer was said, then one of the parishioners was bumped against a tree or on the ground sufficiently hard for that person to remember that precise spot, and then finally, before moving off, some lasting mark was made as an additional precaution against any subsequent disputes. The mark might be a cross cut in a tree trunk or post, or whatever else seemed appropriate at that spot.

The earliest extant record we have of the ceremony taking place in Bisley is for 1805 although, undoubtedly, it was performed here for many centuries before that. Here, as in many parts of England, it had become the means of handing down details of settlement boundaries from generation to generation and of conveying this information from parish to parish. The 'bounds' may generally have been beaten as regularly as every seven years in order to prevent surreptitious encroachments remaining unchallenged for too long.

A detailed description of the 1805 Beating the Bounds at Bisley was recorded in 'The Wardens' Book, 1776 to 1841' by a 29-year-old farmer called James Steptoe, and it reveals a considerable amount of information about local landholding and landmarks in the village. It was providential indeed that the Reverend Joseph Cater took the trouble to make a verbatim copy in his 'Bisley Bits'[(1)] since there is now no trace of the original. This is how Cater regarded Steptoe's report of the procession:-

> 'Of all the memoranda that has at any time been made in these books, by far the most important and the most valuable is *"a list of the parish boundaries made the 25th year* (sic) *of May in the year 1805"*. By way of additional security, as well as for the interest it bears, the description of the Bisley boundaries is here transcribed:-

Beginning first on Bisley Church Green at a mapel against Mr Collyer's called Barhan. Bareing to the south side of the green up Kill Lane to a cross of the south side of the lane in the corner against Kill Close.

Through the hedge into Clinton's fields into Hangmore Cops.

Over into Hall's Mead along into the bushes at the gate a cross in an oak, from that to Spong's yard in a elm, from that to the furst tree at the lane end a cross.

Keep a crost the Coman a little below Carmans to a cross.

Bare a long the south side of the hill to a cross.

Start to Hall's ground to a cross.

Under the Hedgen through the ground to a cross at the corner of Hall's against Roaks Mead.

Keep a long up the Mead to Water Lane end to a cross.

Start a long up to Towers mead a cross in a oak.

Another cross at the Sheep Wash at the further corner of the Mead.

Over the Witherack back.

Under the hedge a crost the Common to the Limekill a distance from the hedge a cross keep round under the hedge to the road that comes from pold oak to Cowshot Corner a cross.

Bare up the side of Gravel pit hill to a cross.

Keep along to a cross upon the hill.

Back down the side of the hill to a cross.

Down to pold oak a cross in the oak.

Keep along under the hedge to Godyhale Lane end, a cross.

Over the gate into Mr. Street's field down to the corner into the Cops to a crab between the furs field and the Cops to a cross.

A crost the Cops to the corner of the Sapite field in a oak a cross.

A long Mr. Street's Mead to the lane to a cross in a Crab.

Bareing to pingrove to a cross in a Crab.

A long pingrove into rogers field to a cross in a chery tree against Sarles Mead.

A long over the hedge into the lane to a cross at Brigses gate.

Keep round the Common to Truly water a cross.

Keep to the right hand of Neysmith's Mead to the corner of Trys Mead to a cross in a oak against Royers Mead to a cross at Truly house door against the yard.

Keep to the left hand of Royers field round to the gate to a cross in the lane.

A long the lane to Newbrige a cross.

Down old house lane to Trys Mead Gate a cross, into Chobham field.

Up the meadow piece into Little Burcet up under the hedge to a cross in a crab.

Keep a long into the other field down the road to the corner a cross in a crab.

A crost the Mead into Royers field to the left

> *hand hedge a cross in a oak, a long at the end of hill place field over the stile in the lane a cross, a long the lane to hostone gate a cross, up the lane to Cotts Barn Door a cross, down the lane to Clepitts gate to a cross, up the fields down into Bunans Lane to a cross at the corner of Friends field, a long up the lane round by hostone Gate up to hilplace.*
>
> *Seven Eakers Gate a cross, down the lane to the Stile round to the right of hillplace field, up under the Hedge into Old House field down into Church Lane.'*

Now two full centuries later it is still possible to recognise enough of these landmarks to plot much of the route from one point to another, although during the intervening period there have been so many changes on the ground, particularly with the fencing of property boundaries, that it has become virtually impossible to walk large sections of the circuit.

It seems that *Terminus* was not always very good at 'maintaining peace among men'. Beating the Bounds often led to angry confrontations, even violent exchanges. The parchment-bound churchwarden's book previously mentioned had two further entries concerning an ongoing dispute with Pirbright over land at Cowshot:-

> *June 9, 1841.*
>
> *Walked the boundary of Bisley parish against Cowshot, present*

Thomas Loveland, CW.
Jno Hill.
Jno Collier.
Jas Steptoe.
Wm Barnes.
Richd Martin.
Hen^{y} Hill.
Geo Collins, Game keeper to the Earl of Onslow.

On the part of Pirbright parish, Joseph Hodskins who objected to the boundary so walked by the above named individuals.

July 13, 1841

Walked the boundary of Bisley against Pirbright parish. Present

Thomas Loveland, CW.
Jno Hill, Sn^{r}.
Jno Collier.
Thos Martin.
Step^{n} Steptoe.
Geo Hill.
Jos^{h} Tedden.
Ja^{s} Hone.
Wm Hill.

Walked the part incroached by Pirbright parish and cleared the original bound marks out, and had refreshments at the Hen and Chickens, Bisley.

Collins, the gamekeeper, had obviously been invited along on the first occasion to add legitimacy to Bisley's claim to the disputed territory. Surely Lord Onslow would not have allowed him to accompany the party, and thus be seen as the representative of the Lord of the Manors of Cowshot and Bisley, had not the Earl himself believed Bisley's claim to be valid.

We have no details of the perambulation that took place in 1863 but news of the long-running battle with Pirbright had obviously attracted wider attention on the next occasion when, on Ascension Day in 1888, a national press reporter accompanied the beating party and brought along one of the country's foremost newspaper artists. Pirbright, however, declined the invitation to attend and that seems to have ended the age-old argument. The Bisley marks at Cowshot were dutifully renewed once more as the group walked that area. A brief report of the event was published in *The Graphic* a few months later, together with an excellent illustration of the Rector being bumped against the barn door at Scott's Farm in Bisley Detached.

A local historian(2) at Pirbright never mentioned the former dispute when writing to the Rector of Bisley on 24th September 1924 to enquire about the Bisley parish map:-

> Dear Sir, I have the pleasure of offering for your acceptance a copy of my Notes on 'Incumbents of Pirbright, Worplesdon, and other parishes or places in Surrey'(3) which I should like to think may become a sort of heirloom for successive Incumbents at Bisley.

A friend has lent me a copy of 'Bisley Bits', 1892, by your predecessor, as Rector, the Rev J Cater, who appears in an illustration from The Graphic of Dec. 1, 1888, 'Beating the Bounds'. In this, one of the people is seen carrying the Bisley Parish Map. I should be very glad indeed to have an opportunity of examining this Parish Map, and to compare it with one of the Parish of Pirbright made in 1805-7. Could you facilitate my so doing?

Very truly yours, Henry Curtis.

Beating the Bounds: The Graphic. 1888 (laterally inverted)

For some inexplicable reason,(4) the image in *The Graphic* was laterally reversed, and this error was repeated in 1892 when it was reproduced in 'Bisley Bits'. If the picture is viewed in mirror image, Bisley Church becomes instantly recognizable with the 1873 north aisle extension appearing correctly on the left-hand side of the west porch, and the artist's signature 'L Bogle' can be seen the right way round. (William) Lockhart Bogle[5] was an outstanding illustrator who made a living working for newspapers, magazines and book publishers. Bogle was one of a select group of artists on *The Graphic* during the 1880s and 1890s. He had considerable success as a portrait painter and his most notable commission was Disraeli, and this work now hangs in the National Portrait Gallery.

Beating the Bounds (Corrected illustration)

The bounds were beaten again in 1904, but there is no report of the event.

A local newspaper[6] reported several interesting matters about the beating of the bounds in 1922. It stated that a verse of 'O God Our Help in Ages Past' was sung outside 'The Garibaldi' pub, where the old doorstep on the corner of the building marked the parish boundary. The party then proceeded through the front door of Mr Tanner's (later to become Mrs Thoroughgood's) shop, opposite, and out through the back door, indicating the boundary actually ran through the middle of the premises. (This part of Bisley was lost under the Surrey Review Order of 1933 when most of the houses in Limecroft Road, together with some land at the rear and most of the common opposite, were transferred to the Urban District of Woking and added to the Parish of Horsell.) The group, guided by Stephen Steptoe, who had walked the route with his father (also Stephen) in 1863 as a nine-year-old boy, proceeded in a clockwise direction passing the Princess Christian Homes to Cowshot Common, where they 'followed across the ranges in direct line past War Dept stone 1073 to an acute point near Clock Tower'. The boundary was over target number 46 on the 200 yards firing range. The Constable accompanying the party had the range firing stopped while the party were crossing the boundaries here. When they reached Ford Road, they 'rested at noon for bread and cheese, etc, supplied by Mr Sturt of the Hen and Chickens Inn, and provided for by the Bisley Parish Council'. Mr W S Patey, Headmaster of the Bisley Boys School, had taken notes throughout the morning but had to leave at that point for another engagement. He had expressed the hope that Mr Steptoe would continue taking notes in the afternoon but it seems this wish was not fulfilled. Perhaps Mr Steptoe had availed himself rather too liberally of Mr Sturt's hospitality.

Mrs Thoroughgood and daughter.

On the next occasion, in 1930, Mr Steptoe was the oldest participant and Peter Fuller was the youngest. Aged 76 and 6 respectively, they both completed the walk, which took about seven hours. A photograph[7] was taken by the barn at Scotts Grove Farm in the part of the village called 'Bisley Detached',[8] a roughly triangular area of land completely isolated from the rest of Bisley. Scotts Grove House has its kitchen in Bisley while all the other rooms are in Chobham.

Stopping point at Scotts Grove Farm during the Beating of the Bounds. 1930
Left to right: *Edgar Hill (aged 11), Mr Francis Garner, Peter Fuller (6), Esmunde Sidery (8), Mrs Cis Fuller, Fred Hill (7), John Gosden (11), John Mepham (10), Ron Mansfield (11), Bill Hockley (11), Mr Stephen Steptoe, Tom Elliot (18), Tony Fuller (12), Alfred Hills (18).*

In 1945 a monthly magazine called '*Woking Review*' reported that Beating the Bounds would be undertaken in the spring, but the plans were postponed by the Parish Council 'until the conclusion of the war'. The Second World War ended later that year, but it would be another 38 years before the ceremony was revived.

Plans were made to hold the event in 1983, exactly 700 years after what was, at that time, the earliest known date in the history of Bisley when Thomas the Rector made his defiant stand. However, it soon became apparent that significant sections of the boundary would be inaccessible because secure protection against two-footed intruders had replaced fencing against four-footed animals in many places during the preceding half century. Circuitous deviations would have to be made here and there to avoid impassable obstacles.

Eventually a route was established and the necessary permissions obtained, and on Saturday 7th May, the day before Rogation Sunday, thirty-seven parishioners gathered at St John the Baptist Church for the start. Thirty-one people went the whole way round and another twenty-three participated just in the morning or the afternoon. Notes (**Appendix C**) were made at each stopping place by one of the churchwardens.

The event was repeated in the year 2000 and some of the parishioners who had walked the boundary seventeen years before took part once again. The route was virtually unchanged this time and the proceedings were recorded on video film for posterity (later to be transferred to a more modern recording medium). Rather fortuitously the party had been invited to make use of some sturdy Scout tents pitched in a field at Bullhousen Farm, where it was planned to stop for lunch. As everyone sat down inside to eat, there was an exceptionally heavy shower of rain that finished as quickly as it had begun, just as everyone was ready to continue the walk. Peter Fuller joined the party at the lunch stop, thus maintaining the continuity linked by just four individuals all the way back to 1805 that spanned almost 200 years.

---

1) *Bisley Bits.*
2) Henry Curtis, Consultant Surgeon to the Metropolitan Hospital, London, lived at Furze Hill, Pirbright.
(3) *Curates and Vicars of Pirbright.*
(4) The British Library, Newspapers, has checked the illustration but cannot offer an explanation for the mistake.
(5) Coincidentally, another Bogle, George Cranston Bogle, moved to Coombe Manor in 1947 but to his knowledge he was unrelated to the artist.
(6) *Woking News & Mail: 1922.*
(7) The names and ages of the participants in the Beating of Bounds can be found in the caption for the photograph on page 69.
(8) The explanation for this unique detachment may be found in Chapter 15 on page 70.

Chapter 6

THE HOLY WELL

Taking the public footpath across the fields from Clews Farm towards Bisley Church, one soon passes a very unusual Grade II Listed building. At the foot of a large oak tree, there is a spring called the Holy Well of St John the Baptist from which flows iron-rich clear water that has never run dry or frozen up. This ancient well has provided a continuous supply of drinking water for centuries and was mentioned more than 300 years ago by John Aubrey,[(1)] who wrote 'Near the Church is a spring called St John the Baptist Well. The dedication made me curious to try it with galls,[(2)] which turn it a purple colour. It is colder than other water in summer but warmer in winter.'

It is very likely that the remote location of the nearby church was chosen centuries ago because of its proximity to this spring. The church was established long before the sparse habitation of the area could be called a village and, indeed, it remains to this day completely separated from the settlement area of Bisley. The spring itself may even have been the centre of pagan worship, as so many were, dating back to the Dark Ages or the Roman occupation before the arrival of Christianity. The sight of clear water emerging from the depths of the earth must have seemed quite miraculous to early local people; all the more for being cool in the heat of summer, yet remaining unfrozen throughout the winter. Such phenomena were quickly sanctified and accredited with all manner of healing properties and magical powers. In today's society, where we have drinking water piped directly into every home, the importance of a dependable local supply of uncontaminated potable water has largely been taken for granted. Clean water, after all, brings essential sustenance to life itself, cleanses wounds and washes the body, all seemingly very sound reasons for our ancestors who lacked the rationality of modern science to infer that natural wells and springs were put there by some deity, or were even the actual dwelling place of a supernatural being. Little wonder then that early Christians had great difficulty in dispelling nature-based beliefs, legends and customs that had all developed around these supposedly sacred geological features. In a few cases springs were covered over and forgotten, but generally Christian missionaries soon realised that the myths associated with these shrines were far too entrenched to be overcome by persuasion alone, so instead of trying to eradicate the heritage of pagan traditions and practices, they absorbed them into their own religion by dedicating the water source to a Christian saint. Surely there could be no better choice than Bisley's Patron Saint, John the Baptist, who had baptised Jesus Christ in the River Jordan, an act of outward cleansing with water symbolising inward purification. However, pagan and Christian practices co-existed in strange juxtaposition for centuries in rural England. Even today, ancient rituals associated with springs, and having no Christian connection whatsoever, are sometimes observed on certain days of the year, though nowadays simply to perpetuate tradition and provide entertainment.

There is no way of knowing whether or not a simple pagan shrine or a pre-Saxon place of worship existed beside the well at Bisley, or a short distance away, where the present-day church was built, but these possibilities should not be dismissed. There is evidence(3) from the Pyrford Charter Bounds (AD 956) suggesting that a church was located close to the well, possibly on the same spot as our present church, this perhaps being the earliest date that can be established with reasonable accuracy for its religious connection.

The crystal-clear spring water issuing from the Holy Well has a distinctive taste as it contains a significant amount of dissolved iron(4) and traces of other minerals. A glassful left standing in daylight for just a few days, soon appears undrinkable as it starts to develop a ferruginous sediment and jelly-like brown globules in suspension. Henry Lawson formerly owned the land where the spring water surfaces and leaves unmistakable brown discolouration on the ground from where it drains away into a nearby ditch. Nevertheless, this did not deter him from drinking a fresh glassful of the liquid every day, frequently quoting a long list of ailments for which it is supposed to have beneficial qualities. Nobody has tested the reputed healing powers of the water with such enthusiasm as Henry, who lived healthily into his 90th year. Water from the Holy Well is still regularly used at baptisms at Bisley Church – very freshly-drawn, one hopes.

Who would dare use stale water and risk leaving brown stains on baby's head and garments, incurring mother's wrath for good measure?

The man-made structure of the well above ground has a cyclic history of falling into disrepair followed by various sorts of restoration. In 1892 The Revd Joseph Cater, Rector of Bisley, wrote[5] 'St John the Baptist's Well is now neglected, choked with weeds, unhonoured and unfrequented.' His successor, the Revd John Gwyon, who arrived in 1894, arranged for a simple but practical wooden cover, comprising four posts supporting a pitched roof of wood and tile, which was erected in 1897. The design of this structure was typical of so many up and down the country, and not unlike a rather more substantial one constructed over a 'Holy Well' at Dunsfold in Surrey, close to the Parish Church of St Mary and All Saints. Dunsfold's well is also believed to be the reason for the church being established next to it which, like the one at Bisley, is some considerable distance from the village centre. Gwyon's well cover at Bisley, being poorly-designed and rather flimsy, collapsed thirty years later. All we have now are sketches taken from one long-lost photograph.

The cover of the well was restored twice by Mr Lawson, firstly in 1938 and then again in 1947 following vandalism. After he died in 1956, it was capped with a crude concrete slab that looked as if it had been cast *in situ* above the stonework. A picture was published in a local newspaper[6] in 1970, under the heading 'Facelift for ye olde well', showing this unsightly slab. The county antiquities department was keen to improve the overall appearance of the structure which was still owned by the Lawson family, who were reluctant to do anything to it that might attract further vandalism. Many years later Henry Lawson's daughter, Helen, made it known that she would bequeath the Holy Well to the Church and, in 1989, the little piece of land containing the spring was duly acquired by the Parochial Church Council. No further restoration work was planned until June 2003 when a more permanent solution, approved by the Surrey County Council Historic Buildings Advisor, was undertaken by a small group of volunteers.[7] They removed the slab of concrete, added additional courses of stonework and fitted a removable stainless steel grill. The water is now maintained at a constant level just above this grill by means of a small outlet pipe, from which the water issues into an open ditch. There is a small notice affixed to a post close to the footpath where passers-by can read about the history of this Grade II Listed building.

---

(1) *Antiquities of Surrey*.

(2) Probably cherry galls used as a primitive test for acidity, though numerous superstitions and magical powers were ascribed at that time to many types of galls.

(3) *Early Medieval Surrey*.

(4) The rufous-coloured insoluble jelly-like ferric iron deposit found around the well is the result of oxidation of soluble ferrous iron compounds by bacteria.

(5) *Bisley Bits*.

(6) *Woking News & Mail. 1970*.

(7) Mike Hammett, Norman Holden, Tim Price, Ron Spradbery & Gordon Sutton.

Chapter 7

GOD'S ACRE AND ALL THEREIN

'For anyone whose soul is stirred by the thought of old England, the little parish church of St John the Baptist, Bisley, stands in the most beautifully obscure setting they could hope to find. One is enveloped in an atmosphere of timelessness, and of being lost in the heart of the country.' This eloquent description[(1)] applies as much today as it did almost half a century ago.

A set of heavy wooden oak gates was erected in 1948 at the main entrance to the churchyard in Church Lane. It comprised a pair of large gates for vehicular access together with a smaller pedestrian gate on one side and a matching fixed panel on the other, all set back about 25 metres (82′0″) from the road in order to provide a small parking and turning area. These entrance gates were donated by the late Henry Lawson in 1948 in memory of those from Bisley who died serving their country in the two World Wars. The two large gates were inscribed 'God's Acre', a commonly used expression to denote a consecrated churchyard regardless of size. About ten years ago these two heavy gates were damaged by a vehicle and had to be replaced, though the newer ones soon needed reinforcing as their joints began to loosen as a result of shrinkage.

Spaced along the gravel path are five imposing Victorian-style lamp posts erected within the last five years to illuminate the long driveway at Evensong on dark winter evenings. Each post bears a small inscribed brass plaque. On reaching the burial ground about halfway up the path, the churchyard opens up to the left where a familiar assortment of gravestones mark the final resting places of generations of former parishioners. Tradition has it that the most God-fearing sort would normally be buried on the south side of churches but at Bisley nearly all the churchyard is on the north side!

These days memorials are usually made of natural stone, marble or occasionally slate, and generally take the form of an upright headstone or an inclined tablet that is often shaped like an open book. Kerb edging around graves became popular in early Victorian times to which was usually added marble chippings or paving to fill the enclosed area. Kerb sets are no longer normally permitted as they impede the use of grass-cutting machinery. Some other forms of grave-marking were quite popular in former times. Small cast-iron Celtic crosses or plain crosses (sometimes called Roman or Latin crosses) became readily obtainable from hardware stores in the Victorian era. Some of these had a rail in which a short name or initials could be inserted, while others just had a space for the deceased's name to be painted. Examples of the former type still exist in Bisley churchyard. Another method of marking a grave was to construct a half-rounded covering in brickwork along its length. Bisley used to have a good example of this very near the yew tree beside the porch.

One of the simplest memorials was the 'head-to-toe' board or 'grave rail', comprising two short wooden posts, one at each end of the grave, connected by a horizontal wooden rail on which details of the departed would be written. A few examples of these grave-boards still survive in other Surrey churchyards but not, unfortunately, at Bisley where none remained[(2)] in 1950.

Typical grave marker board.

The burial area on the north side of the church has been expanded twice in just over a hundred years, and now there is a pressing need to extend it yet again. The first enlargement used a modest amount of the adjacent glebe land, known as Church Barn Field, and was consecrated by the Bishop of Winchester on 2nd May 1900. According to the then Rector, it was the first time the size of the churchyard had been increased in over 800 years. A slight difference in ground level is just discernible each side of the original hedge line where the last of three lime trees still stands. The other two limes were felled in the late 1960s when they became diseased. The second extension enclosed considerably more of the glebe field and was consecrated on St John the Baptist Day 1930 by the Right Reverend Cyril Golding-Bird, Suffragan Bishop in the new Diocese of Guildford that had been founded three years earlier. The enlarged churchyard reached the corner of the bell-mouth at the end of Kiln Lane, formerly a large grass triangle known as Church Lane Green. It also incorporated the site of a dilapidated old tithe barn that had been blown down in a bad storm in the winter of 1884/5. The barn would have partly obscured the view of the church as one approached along the main path. Cater, writing in 'Bisley Bits' in 1892, stated that it had frequently been asserted that there was formerly a parsonage house in Church Barn Field but the only reference that could be found was in an undated terrier of glebe property, a scrap of paper about eight inches square and signed by two churchwardens who held office from 1712 to 1714. This mentioned 'a house and barn' but Cater was unconvinced, adding, 'Beyond this there is not a scrap of evidence to show that there ever was a glebe residence. In all probability, the house mentioned in the Terrier was but a small brick erection adjoining the old Tithe Barn… affording protection for cows, but scarcely calculated to meet the requirements of a gentleman's family.' We can now throw some light on this issue. The barn had been quite close to the church but there had indeed been a very small old dwelling as well, known as Church Cottage, some distance away on the north side of Church Barn Field adjacent to Church Lane, where two bungalows now stand. It had never been intended for use as a parsonage, merely a charity cottage or parish house. The cottage was 'end-ways on' to the road and it had charming little gothic windows.

Some folk have asked why no trace of the tithe barn has ever been found when digging graves. In fact there has – though very little. According to William Sidery, a former organist at Bisley from 1943 to 1950 and schoolmaster at Knaphill School, 'a few old bricks were unearthed in 1948 when new graves were dug for the remains of Mr Chas H W Hill and Mr Henry Walter Cheeseman adjoining the north side of the churchyard in the portion last consecrated.' The tithe barn probably had no more a course or two of brick foundations, protecting the timber structure from damp arising from the ground beneath, that probably would have been taken up while removing the rest of the barn. An old land drainage system, found during grave digging in the 1980s, was not thought to be associated with this building. The clay drain pipes themselves were quite interesting as they were not round, like modern ones, but 'U' shaped and laid with the opening facing downwards. Each one had been stamped before firing with the word 'DRAIN' in capital letters, which immediately indicates the period of manufacture. A tax was imposed on all bricks and tiles in 1784 but, after much protest, the government of the day exempted field drains in 1826 provided they were clearly identified as such. The tax was abolished altogether in 1850 and so these land drains must have been made sometime between these two dates.

The two oldest memorials in Bisley Churchyard.

To find the oldest headstone in the churchyard, one has to walk round to the south side of the church where John and Elizabeth Hone were laid to rest. It is now almost impossible to read their inscriptions which have deteriorated markedly during the last half century. Furthermore, the last few lines on Elizabeth's stone recently became hidden as the memorial unexpectedly sank into the ground and tilted at an angle. It was found to have been broken above the bottom line of text. It has now been re-set in an upright position, which unfortunately could not have been achieved without permanent loss of a few lines. Repair was not an option, and the only other alternative was to lay the pieces horizontally, whereupon the whole inscription would have weathered more rapidly. The full inscription, recorded here for posterity, includes a strange reference to 'Lavender', which has resulted in much speculation:-

'Here
Lyeth ye body of
Mrs Elizabeth Hone
wife of Mr John Hone.
She was daughter of
Mr Wm. Batt of malding
in Surrey cousin jarmyn to
Mr Thos. Carter of Denham in
Bucks. Who was the Grandson to
Sir Wm. Bowyer of the same
place, Bart. She died Nov.
the 12th 1739 aged 61.
Here
also lieth the body of
the above John Hone whose
ancestors has enjoyed Lav-
ender early in King Edward
the third's time. He went into ye
Excise 1703 served in divers
posts of trust and left it.'

Quite why there has been so much conjecture about the inclusion and meaning of this odd expression '… enjoyed Lavender', written on this tombstone, is a little surprising, since the Will of Isabella Campion, of which the English translation was widely known, explicitly stated in Latin that John Hone lived in a free tenement called Lavender. Furthermore, this assertion was corroborated, albeit unintentionally, during a fireside conversation at Bullhousen Farm by John Gosden, the Street's elderly tenant farmer. He mentioned the name 'Lavender' in passing when talking about a supposedly Tudor farmhouse that had been bought in the 1860s by the National Refuge for Homeless and Destitute Children and demolished because it was too small and dilapidated for their requirements. It had been replaced more or less in the same place by the new Farm School house in 1868. Assuming the headstone inscription is accurate, and there is no reason to suppose it is not, then the Hones must have been living there from the first half of the 14th century 'early in King Edward the Third's time', as recorded on the epitaph, long before the Tudors. There again, the original house may have been rebuilt in Tudor times. Further evidence of its existence is provided in the Will of another John Hone, which states '… to the said estate called Lavender, which estate has been in my Family for several ages…' The farmhouse was not far from the former public house named 'The Yew Tree' that stood beside the Guildford Road, nearly opposite the junction of Ford Road.

Next to the weathered gravestone of John and Elizabeth Hone stands another one of similar size, but with a slightly more ornately-shaped top. The epitaph for this member of the family states:-

'Here
Lies the Body of
John Hone Junr Esq
Barrister at Law and
Member of the Middle
Temple London. He
died April the 7th 1755
Aged 27 years.'

If one were to make a list of all the memorials, or a thorough search of the burial records, the name Hone would appear more frequently than that of any other Bisley family.

Traditionally, the Canadian shooting teams visiting Bisley Ranges in July come to St John the Baptist to pay their respects to two Canadian marksmen who died over here. The first has his grave marked by a rectangular monument with a ridged top. The main inscription gives no indication of the circumstances of his demise:-

'Sacred to the memory of Major Henry Fullerton Perley.
Born 5th of March 1831 at St. John NB Canada.
Died 15th of July 1897 at Bisley Surrey.'

However, a small plaque, subsequently affixed to one side, reveals more details of his death and commemoration:-

'In memory of Major Henry Fullerton Perley.
A member of The Dominion of Canada Rifle Association
who gave his life to the construction of
the MacDonald Stewart Pavilion at Bisley in 1897.
This plaque is placed here by the
members of the DCRA
in Honour of the 100th Anniversary. July 13th 1997.'

The Canadian Hut,(3) as it was formerly called, was started in March 1897 with Major Perley as project manager and construction foreman. He was working under tremendous pressure to complete it by July when the shooting teams were due to arrive, but the strain proved too great and he collapsed and died just before completion. He was given a full Military Funeral and buried in Bisley Churchyard.

Thirteen years later another Canadian died here and was also interred on the eastern side of the churchyard. He has a conventional headstone with this inscription:-

'In
Memory of
William Henry Greet
Member of the
Canadian Bisley Team.
Born in Dublin Ireland
January 19th 1883
Died at Bisley
August 2nd 1910. Aged 28.

DEAR IS THE GRAVE WHERE OUR LORD IS LAID
DEAR IS THE MEMORY WHICH NEVER SHALL FADE
SWEET IS THE HOPE THAT AGAIN WE SHALL MEET
KNEELING TOGETHER AT JESU'S FEET.

Erected by the Queen's Own Rifles of
Canada Chapter of the Imperial Order
of the Daughters of the Empire.'

In days before the 'Middle Sunday' of the Imperial Meeting in Bisley Camp was filled with competitions, the Canadian visitors would always come to Matins at Bisley Church. To the great pride of the visiting party, 'O Canada' would be sung at the end of the service, after which the congregation would file outside to the two graves where prayers would be said.

Close by, there are a pair of identical granite crosses, one of which marks the final resting place of George and Mary Smith. They were the parents of the Reverend Walter Landon Smith, who was Rector from 1881–86, and they all lived at the rectory.

'In memory of
George Pyemont Smith, M.D.
who died at Bisley Rectory
May 5th 1888. Aged 67.

Also of Mary Elizabeth
widow of the above
who died July 10th 1897.

Wait patiently for Him'

The other cross intriguingly states:

'In Loving Memory of MARY
the beloved wife of The Revd. Richard Chambers, M.A.
who entered into rest Sept. 5th 1885.
Also, The Revd. Richard Chambers, M.A. aged 58 years,
husband of the above who died Sept. 27th 1888.'

The circumstances of how this 'man of the cloth' and his wife came to be buried at Bisley are not recorded. He never held the living of Bisley, but it is believed that the couple resided at Knaphill possibly after his retirement as a parish priest.

Perhaps one of them was related to the Smiths, or maybe he officiated now and again at St John the Baptist Church.

Finally, but by no means least, is a recent addition to the churchyard, a stone commemorating those from the well-known military rest home at Stafford Lake that was run so efficiently throughout the twentieth century:-

'To the memory of
the many ex-Service men and women
who worked in Lord Roberts' Workshops
and resided in SSAFA Forces Help's
Princess Christian Homes
Stafford Lake, Bisley
From 1900 to 2000
And of those who cared for them.'

Fifty-three plaques are arranged in lines on simple structures on each side of this stone, each one bearing the name, date and, where applicable, the former regiment of all of those who have been associated with the Homes and have died since 1991. Their names are listed in **Appendix D**.

One should not be surprised at the absence from this churchyard of any magnificent or imposing memorials standing as silent sentinels high above the graves of people of great wealth or stature in the community. Bisley has never had a great manor house nor country estate of significance and no wealthy parishioners with which one might associate such grandeur or extravagance. The unadorned simplicity of Bisley churchyard is part of its charm and a Springtime visit, when primroses and cherry blossom catch the sun, will not disappoint.

---

(1) *Woking Review.*

(2) Confirmed by William James Sidery.

(3) Renamed the Macdonald Stewart Pavilion in 1975 in memory of Walter Stewart who had dedicated much time, effort and financial support to the DCRA and the renovation of the building.

Chapter 8

ST JOHN THE BAPTIST CHURCH

Turning one's attention to the church itself, one is struck by the peaceful isolation of this building and the quaint rusticity of its porch, overshadowed by the almost obligatory churchyard yew tree. A former Rector is reputed to have committed suicide by hanging himself from this very tree, but there is nothing to substantiate this story which could well be just pure fabrication. Being a little too close to the porch, the tree has an overbearing and forbidding appearance that fits well with this gruesome tale. Mature yew trees were greatly valued when the longbow was the primary weapon of war. No other wood performs so well. In villages such as Bisley, the churchyard was often the only enclosed land where the poisonous yew could be grown without risk to livestock. Yew trees are renowned for extreme longevity, but the fact that the girth of this particular specimen has increased by such a significant amount in the last hundred years, from 88 to 114 inches (2.25 to 2.90 metres), indicates that it has not yet attained full maturity.

Bisley Church has a 14th century porch[(1)] that is typical of the period, with timber panelling beneath a low sill with equally spaced hollow-chamfered mullions above. In contrast to the unspectacular size of the side panelling, the impressive entrance is formed by two massive pieces of timber each 42 inches across at the top, where they form a pointed arch. They are opposite-handed sections of oak riven lengthways from a single tree. Aesthetically correct proportions for this imposing entrance are maintained by the use of thick cusped bargeboards on the open gable end and a heavy oak tie-beam. The roof rafters are a comparatively recent replacement even though some of them have signs of re-use. An illustration of the porch at the Church of St John the Baptist, and a plan of the sections of timber used in its construction, were published in 1927 in 'The Charm of Old Surrey'[(2)] by Henry Alderman, who was a master carpenter and a talented artist who produced many sketches for *'The Illustrated Carpenter and Builder'*. Nearly all his sketches are excellently executed but unfortunately the perspective of the porch roof of Bisley Church is noticeably incorrect. That apart, he does capture the rustic charm of the timber structure.

The York flag-stone flooring inside the porch was laid in 1989 over rather incongruous red and black Victorian quarry tiles, in order to hide them as well as to serve the important purpose of raising the sunken floor to improve accessibility. The quarry tiles, hideous as they are, have a protective membrane sandwiched between them and the new layer of flooring above. We are told that the body of Isabella Campion lies beneath the porch. The instruction in her Will of 1506 stipulated that 'My body to be layd in the Porch of the Parish Church of St John the Baptist of Busley', though the only documentary proof is a much later plaque inside the nave testifying that her wish was granted. Long widowed, she died in 1517, and in all probability the terms of her Will would have been fulfilled, particularly as she made a very generous bequest to the church – a field[3] at Pennypot known as Broachmead, just three-quarters of a mile from Scotts Farm, her sizeable home in Bisley Detached.

The west wall of the church has roughly squared blocks of 'sarsen stone', sometimes called heathstone, which occurs locally as isolated boulders on the Bagshot Series of Sands, and was used for structural strength in many buildings of importance. It is workable when green, but rapidly hardens on exposures to the elements, and is found in many local churches, the walls of Windsor Castle and locks on the Basingstoke Canal. Smaller pieces of sarsen stone were often collected by householders for use as path edging and thresholds. Wide use was made of another local material – a dark iron conglomerate, a type of 'puddingstone', that was used extensively in the south wall of Bisley Church. Its formulation appears to be principally iron pan with a small amount of silica, cemented with naturally-occurring oxides that have been fired to produce relatively soft ferruginous blocks. These blocks possess tremendous inherent compressive strength similar to that found in modern proprietary thermal construction blocks and are therefore perfectly suitable for wall construction. However, by far the most interesting walling materials from the historical point of view are the thin courses of tile and isolated pieces of brick, incorporated here and there in the walls of the church, that may well be Roman in origin. Reclamation and re-use of building materials would have been an important consideration in this area because of the dearth of natural stone and difficulty in transporting heavy materials. A good example of early recycling was the removal of almost every fragment of Chertsey Abbey, which was taken for re-use elsewhere after it was destroyed in the 16th century during the dissolution of the monasteries.

On entering the nave through the west door, which is much newer than its 13th-century style suggests, one finds a small nave and belfry measuring just 37′6″ x 18′2″ (11.43 metres by 5.5 metres). The nave is probably 13th century but so little of its early English character can be seen within, that it is virtually impossible to estimate its age with accuracy. Standing beneath the bell tower, the visitor can see two wooden pillars and truncated beams where there was once a small 'singing gallery' that would have been used by musicians, had the village been so fortunate as to have any. A fixed wooden ladder behind the font leads to an intermediate floor in the bell tower, which is of cross-braced timber construction that has modern reinforcement and weather-board cladding. Above this is the bell-cot itself, containing the three ancient bells fitted to an old timber bell frame, all protected by a relatively modern, oak-shingled broach-spire.

The eye is soon drawn to the left-hand side of the nave where two chamfered arches, each having a span of almost 11′6″ (3.5 metres), are supported centrally by the moulded capital of a pillar, so large in diameter (24″ or 600mm) yet so short in height that one scarcely notices the narrow north aisle beyond. This imposing feature was necessary to support this side of the nave when the original wall was removed in 1873 during the construction of the north aisle extension. Before most of the north wall was demolished, it had a small arched doorway which can be clearly seen in old illustrations. Most early churches had a north door, known as the 'Devil's Door', which was left open during baptisms so that the evil spirits in the child could escape during the christening ceremony. The door was also important in medieval services, as those taking part would process out into the churchyard and back in through the west door. The original north wall also contained a very old single-light lancet window and two other windows of which little is known other than they are depicted in old illustrations that show one of them as being the largest window in the church.

The wall on the south side of the nave inclines outwards at the top, as does what little now remains of the original north wall. Both of these are over 3′ 3″ thick (1 metre) at ground level. So much the pity then that no records were made during the formidable reconstruction of the north side as, in all probability, we would now be able to learn so much more about the character of the main body of the church. It was traditionally said[(4)] that the time 'for elevating the Host at High Mass was dependent upon the moment at which a sunbeam shining through a south window reached a particular spot on the north wall of the nave'. One wonders through which of the two windows the light had to shine in order to fall upon the critical point, and whether there was some particular mark or feature at that spot?

There is a good description of the roof in Mrs Rosemary Cooper's excellent booklet[(5)] where she states that:-

> Inside the nave can now be seen the braced rafter roof where the collar beams are stiffened by diagonal struts; the inner ends of the sole pieces are tenoned into inner wall plates from which vertical ashlar pieces rise to support the rafters. This single framed roof was formerly ceiled, as can be seen by the batten and nail marks on the rafters, and would then have given the appearance of a barrel roof. The central massive tie-beam is heavily cambered, and the belfry is ceiled at the west end of the nave by original close studding.

The chancel measures 20′10″ x 13′8″ (6.35 by 4.16 metres) and was rebuilt in 1873 by Mr Evan Christian under the direction of the Revd Walter Eaton. It replaced a 15th chancel which had become so unsafe that it could not be used and was shut off from the nave. Excellent sketches were drawn by Edward Hassell[(6)] in 1830 and copied in Cater's book[(7)] showing the side and end views of the Tudor chancel which had typical timber and brick infill walls.

With the exception of certain parishes in which responsibility for maintenance of parts of the church was written in legal agreements, traditionally the parishioners had to look after the nave and the priest was responsible for the upkeep of the chancel. It is very likely that the progressive deterioration of the chancel at Bisley had occurred during the tenure of several rectors, each of whom was loath to halt the decay that had developed during previous incumbencies. The Revd Walter Eaton had obviously been chosen as the very man to face this daunting challenge, which had become no small embarrassment to the bishop. In Eaton's own words (the Bishop had) 'urged on one the necessity for immediate restoration'. Eaton seemingly took this task upon himself with great enthusiasm because immediately upon his Institution, he set about the task of raising funds. He secured £800, including a loan against the collateral of Broachmead, which was sufficient to commence the substantial restoration the following year. Not only did he attend to the complete rebuilding of the chancel, he removed the superfluous singing gallery that may have also become unsafe and he constructed a north aisle to increase seating capacity within the church. The Rt Revd Samuel Wilberforce, Bishop of Winchester, officiated at the re-opening ceremony, as the church was part of that Diocese at the time.

Unfortunately, the new chancel had been built upon the original foundations that later proved to be inadequate for the greater weight of the new structure. A hand-written note[(8)] from Gwyon, found pasted inside the front cover of the Register of Burial (commencing in 1813), reads:-

> Owing to the very unsatisfactory state of the foundations of the Chancel of the Church here serious cracks revealed themselves in the walls, of such a nature as to make the whole chancel dangerous to the public within the meaning of the late various new Acts of Parliament empowering the Surrey County Council to inspect and if necessary to condemn and close the chancel to the

public, as rector within the powers conferred by the 'Ecclesiastical Dilapidations Act 1871' on the Winchester Surveyor, I was obliged during the year 1918 and in the midst of the great world war then raging, with its terrible slaughter, and at greatly enhanced prices, to practically rebuild the structure of the chancel at a cost, estimated by the above named official surveyor, of five hundred pounds. Four new buttresses with best bricks and material, embedded in specially good Portland cement had to be erected, the foundations underpinned with specially prepared concrete, the brickwork of the walls and plaster made good where defects in last material and workmanship, the whole of the roof removed and replaced with practically new woodwork and tiling, in most cases replacing very rotten old material, as far as woodwork was concerned especially. The chancel is now in very good structural repair, and will not require, it is to be hoped, any further substantial repairs[9] for many years to come apart from occasional attention to minor requirements such as falling tiles, etc.

January 1st 1919. JOHN GWYON, Rector of Bisley, Surrey:- Since 1895.

Future Rectors were absolved of further liability for chancel repairs under the Ecclesiastical Dilapidations Measure of 1923, which was just as well because settlement cracks soon appeared on the outside of the brickwork. These have been monitored at successive quinquennial inspections, but fortunately no undue movement has been detected and the building is now said to be stable. The interior of the present chancel had exposed rafters until the 1970s when a plasterboard ceiling was added to lighten the appearance.

A vestry was built onto the side of the chancel in 1918 to replace an improvised area within the north aisle, separated by a curtain and used for changing and keeping vestments. However, most of the vestry was occupied by an organ donated by the Ellenborough family in 1929 to replace an earlier one(10) situated in another part of the church. This organ had been made by Roy Huntingford & Co in 1889 and rebuilt for Bisley by Smith & Foskitt. It was dedicated on 1st September 1932. The remaining space in the vestry, small as it was, had a wooden partition separating it from the organ chamber. A lever protruded through a slot in this partition for pumping the organ by hand until 1959, when the organ was fitted with an electric blower. In 1977 and 1978 a firm of organ builders from Edgware, called B C Shepherd & Son, fully restored the instrument (**Appendix E**), increasing its capacity as well as improving the quality of sound. A list of organists from the mid-1800s to the mid-1900s is shown in **Appendix F**. The vestry has been extended twice – in 1955 and then again in 1980 – but one wonders how the Revd Joseph Cater, together with his impressive choir of 32 men and boys, ever managed without any proper vestry at all.

Bisley Church Choir. 1962
Left to right (rear): Richard Clifton, Shirley Wagstaff, Michael Bayliss, Pamela Bailes, Brian Howarth, Roger Richards, Bert Henbest (Verger), Walter Ellen (Churchwarden), Kenneth Ouin (Churchwarden). (front): Kathleen Wagstaff, Claire Ouin, Josephine Coxon, Norman Nicholas (Lay Reader), Revd Winsor Roberts (Rector), Margaret Ellen, Hugh Thrift, Frank Fertig, Frances Fertig (Organist).

An ancient piscina**(11)** carved from a block of chalk is built into the south wall of the nave forming a small trefoil niche, measuring about 13″ x 9″ (320 mm x 220 mm). It was rescued from beneath the ruins of the Tudor chancel and may have suffered the same fate as a tablet in the nave with a Latin inscription which was torn down during the Reformation, a time when anything that seemed to have a connection with the Church of Rome was abhorred. Alas, there is now no trace of the marble tablet which read:-

Hic tumulata jacent Isabellae Champion ossa,
Ossa deaurato marmore digna tegi,
Ecclesiam hanc prato donavit nomine Brachmead,
Sanctae et Catholicae Religionis opus,
Et moriens dixit, conanti infringere donum,
Coelestis vitae portio nulla cadet!

Roughly translated this states:- 'Here entombed are the bones of Isabella Campion, bones deserving to be preserved in costly marble. She gave to this church a field named Broachmead, for the benefit of the Holy and Catholic Religion, and on dying said, whosoever infringes this gift, shall fall from his portion in everlasting life.' Though it is no substitute for the missing tablet, there is a brass plaque inside the nave, near the chancel arch, commemorating this benefactress in English as follows:-

In sacred and grateful memory of
ISABELLA CAMPION
who A.D.1517 gave the meadow called Broachmead
for the sole use and benefit for ever of this
Church of St. John the Baptist
at Bisley Surrey. This charitable
endowment greatly aided towards the
restoration of the church A.D. 1873.

No-one knows what became of a large framed board with black and white lettering that hung for fifty years or more, firstly in the chancel, then in the vestry. The inscription reproduced in 'Bisley Bits', and again here, is now the only extant version of Mrs Campion's Will translated from Latin:-

In the name of God. Amen.
I Isabella Campion als Champion in Busley in the county of Surrey, Widdow being of sound mind and memory doe make and ordaine by these presents my Testament or my last Will in this manner. Firstly I give my Soule to Almighty God thro' Jesus Christ my Saviour. My body to be layd in the Porch of the Parish Church of St. John the Baptist of Busley aforesayd. Item. I give and bequeath all that my Mead called Brachmead lyeing in the Parish of Chobham to John Hone who dwells in a free Tenement called Lavender and to his heires for ever. Under this Law and Condition nevertheless that the aforesayed John Hone and his heirs for ever with two other approved Men one whereof is to be chosen by the s^d John Hone and his heires the other by the honest parishioners of Busley $afores^d$ and they to be Feoffees of and in my meadow $afores^d$ called Brachmead soe y^t y^e $afores^d$ John Hone and his heirs and two other Feoffees soe to be chosen as $afores^d$. The whole commodityes and proffitts from the aforesaid meadow arizeing yearely be given and delivered to the Churchwardens of y^e $afores^d$ Church to the use and profitt of the s^d Church for ever. Provided that the $afores^d$ Feoffees of me and my heires pay or cause to be payd to

the Chiefe Lord of the Fee thereof the rents and other services thereof due and of right accustomed and that they keep this my Will and Testament. The rest of my goods and chattels I give and bequeath unto John Hone my faithful Executor. In testimony whereof I have put my hand and seale to this present Testament the 15th day of the month of September in ye twenty-first yeare of the reigne of Henry ye Seaventh.

Witness to this John Hone, Wm Whager, Alono Leigh, Robert Cobbett and others. And so the Lord have mercy on my Soule.

Translat ab origine Testament in latino. H. Hyde.

To the Rev. John King, Rector, the Churchwardens and Parishioners of Bisley in Surrey, this transcript of the will of their Benefactress is presented by their faithful, obedient servant,

James Holland, Essex Street, Strand.

Mary Bainbridge, another benefactress who contributed towards the rebuilding of the National School and provided an incentive for good attendance, has a brass plaque in her memory affixed to the south wall of the chancel near the altar:-

... To the Glory of God
in affectionate remembrance of
MARY BAINBRIDGE
of Chobham in this County
Died Augt 15th 1877
Aged 97 years.
This Reredos has been given by her nephew
RICHARD PERCIVAL DANIELL.

There is one more brass plaque and that is on the west wall, the text being cast in relief:-

In memory of
Lance Corporal Robin Kitchin
2nd Batt. Lincoln Regiment
Died at Gibraltar 13th February 1912
Aged 20 years
This Tablet was erected by
The National and Military Services of Gibraltar.

There are two marble plaques mounted side by side on the south wall of the nave, in memory of those who died[(12)] during the two World Wars:-

To the Glory of God
And in grateful memory of
those of this Parish.
who sacrificed their lives in
the Great War 1914 - 1918
Robert Bradford
Fred Ferdinand Collins
Edwin George Daborn
Horace Daborn
Wilfred Walter Henbest
Arthur Jack Hills
Frederick Honer
John Mason
Thomas Harry Newman
Leslie Robert Petrie
Richard Batty Pollard
George Arthur Smith
Edwin Suter
George Whitehorn

'Faithful unto Death'

In grateful remembrance of those whose names are
inscribed below and laid down their lives during the
Second World War 1939 - 1945

P. A. St. John Brown	M. Bernard Horley	Allen E. Shackleton
John M. Burton	J. Michael Horley	John A. Shorter
Kenneth E. Corrie Thomas	F. Johnson	Charles J. Smith
Alfred E. Cox	Edward Purdue	George A. Towne
Kenneth B. Dowe	Patrick L. Puxley	Daniel Walkinshaw

In their memory the Oak Gates were erected at
the entrance of the Churchyard.
They shall not grow old as we that are left grow old.

The window behind the altar is a stained glass, triple-light lancet, showing the Crucifixion in the centre, with St John the Baptist on the left and St John the Evangelist on the right. The set of three leaded lights were commissioned 'In memory of Anne Iddins. Fell asleep, 16th Sept^{r}., 1870'. She was the sister-in-law of the Revd Walter Eaton. The Revd Joseph Cater observed[13] somewhat dismissively that 'neither the drawing nor colours bear a close inspection' but few church-goers nowadays seem to share this opinion. Most people generally find this depiction aesthetically pleasing, with a good balance of colour, attractive design and good detail. One wonders if Cater had been comparing this window with his more agreeable mental impression of the exquisite stained glass in a side window, of which he wrote[14]:-

> 'On the north side' (of the derelict Tudor chancel) 'was a window of stained glass, the colouring of which is said to have been very rich; it represented a figure in dark blue garment, with hands uplifted as though in the act of prayer. The hands were not joined; there was no beard, and the hair was of a golden yellow colour. Of this window not a scrap remains.'

Arguably the finest stained glass in the church at the present time is seen in a modern window on the north side of the nave. It comprises a set of three panels together illustrating 'Suffer little children to come unto me…'[15] and was given by Henry Lawson of Lynbrook as a memorial two years after the death of his wife Edith, who died in 1951, aged 76.

There is a 500-year-old square-topped window in the south wall. Close inspection reveals that the mullions and simple geometric tracery are not original but, despite this re-working, the effect does not appear contrived. It has three trefoiled lights of stained glass showing 'the feeding of the five thousand'[16] and was commissioned just over sixty years ago, also by Mr Lawson. He died on 10th October 1956.

There used to be another 15th century window in this wall which was removed and discarded along with the ancient features of the north wall during the restoration undertaken by the Revd Walter Eaton in the late 19th century. It is such a pity that the preservation of these important features was not considered desirable in those days, the south wall window being replaced with a modern one of no particular historical or architectural interest.

This very year, a window in the small east wall of the north aisle has been removed in order to construct a doorway into a new extension currently under construction outside the north wall of the chancel. This window was similar in size and shape to the one at the opposite end of the north aisle, but contained stained glass marked simply 'In memory of H.S.I.' Could this be another Iddins? And just who were the couple commemorated by the huge Latin cross next to the path in the churchyard that is simply inscribed 'In Memoriam: C.F.I. 1848 & R.I. 1875'? Intriguingly, the name Iddins is not listed on the Bisley Census records for 1841, 1851 or 1861, nor is there, for that matter, any other surname beginning with the letter 'I'. So who were they all? One may reasonably conclude that, like the larger triple light in the chancel, this little window was also commissioned in memory of one of the Iddins family. As for 'CFI 1848' and 'RI 1875' on the stone cross, the latter obviously died during Eaton's incumbency and they may have been his father-in-law and mother-in-law. It is also interesting to note that the Revd Joseph Cater's 17-month-old daughter, Violet, was buried beneath this large cross, suggesting the 'CFI' and 'RI' were related to the Caters.

There are two framed embroideries hanging on the north wall, salvaged from a damaged altar frontal at St. Anne's Church, Soho, which was destroyed by bombing in 1940 during the Second World War. These embroideries have hung at Bisley since 1966.

A large oil painting once hung on the wall at the back of

the singing gallery of 'Elijah's glorious ascent into heaven in a chariot of fire'[17], the ceiling above being painted with angels and clouds for good measure. Perhaps it is just as well that all this had been removed before Joseph Cater took office, as he certainly would not have approved. The fate of this picture is not known.

While on the matter of paintings, many an artist has chosen Bisley Church as a subject to portray, perhaps because of its timeless charm and leafy rural setting. The author possesses three fine watercolours, two by John Cooper painted in the 1980s and another dated 1912 and signed by L R Motram, an artist unknown in this village. We must, however, mention certain individuals who regarded the expression of their respective talents as being less of a pastime and more of a duty to make a permanent record for posterity. C T Cracklow was one such person. He was a London architect and surveyor whose 'Views of Churches and Chapels of Ease in the County of Surrey' – all 156 of them – was published in the 1820s. The author has one of the few original coloured lithographs made by Simonau, using the new lithographic printing process that had recently been brought to England from Bavaria. 'Bisley Church SW' is written beneath the main picture, with a small sketch of the ground plan. Cracklow's illustration is architecturally accurate and clearly shows, beyond the yew tree and the porch, a head-to-toe grave board in the churchyard and farther still the wooden side and part of the roof of the old tithe barn.

Bisley Church (chancel) by Edward Hassell.
Copyright British Library

John Hassell (1767-1825)[18] made a very large number of watercolour paintings of Surrey churches, including Bisley Church, but his artistic talent did not match the superior expertise of his son, Edward (1811-1852), who also painted Surrey buildings but in a very different style, concentrating more on their interior. Edward's legacy for Bisley includes two beautifully-executed watercolour images of the outside of the church and three sketches of the inside. His illustration, entitled 'Bisley Church, North Side. E Hassell. 1830',[19] shows a black chimney emerging from the side wall of the old chancel which corresponds exactly with the position of a stove and chimney shown in one of his interior views. The scene depicted in his 'Bisley Church, East end', drawn in 1828, is partly sketched and partly detailed, yet the whole picture imparts a wealth of information not seen elsewhere. Firstly, the heating stove is not tucked away in some inconspicuous corner or even against the wall. It stands almost in the centre of the chancel, partly obscuring the view of the altar from the nave; its chimney rises in front of the east window before changing angle to exit through the side wall. Just why it was put in such a prominent position in front of the focal point of the church remains a mystery. Other interesting details include the large window recess in the north wall, the former position of the pulpit; the shape and size of the chancel arch before enlargement; the box pews each side of the wide stone flag central aisle through the nave, and two large tablets above the arch and between what appears to be a royal coat-of-arms. One of Edward Hassell's other sketches shows the west end viewed from inside the chancel, looking through the rood-screen that is little more than a simple framework with double doors, seemingly without any form of embellishment whatsoever. Its simplicity is matched by that of the gallery at the west end of the nave with its two intermediate supporting posts and a low rail. Another sketch, also signed and dated 1828, merely shows the detail of the sanctuary: a very small altar, the plain east window and the altar-rail that has a central gate with turned balusters matching those under the fixed rails on each side.

*Bisley Church (north side) by Edward Hassell.
Copyright British Library*

The Jacobean pulpit, raised upon a stone base incorporating a short flight of steps, has delicately carved oak panelling and fret work, typical of the early 1600s, arranged in three equal sections forming half a hexagon. It is much more ornate than the pulpit shown on the opposite side of the chancel in Edward Hassell's drawing, and therefore must have been relocated from another church and installed at Bisley some time after 1828. The finery of its panelling is quite unlike anything else inside St John the Baptist Church, thus adding more weight to the likelihood that it was made for some other church.

The font is probably 14th Century and is reputed to have originated from Evesham Abbey, but for many years it was used as a bird bath in a garden at Chobham, the home of Major-General Percival Napier-White, CBE, CB, who gave it to Bisley Church in 1965.

In 1930 the floor of the nave was relaid to which new ash pews were attached. These were very similar in size and design to the ones they replaced. Chairs with rush seats were put in the north aisle, and oak panels were installed in the chancel where new choir and clergy stalls were fitted.

After years of procrastination, the Parochial Church Council eventually agreed to replace the antiquated central heating system in 1992. The decision was eventually hastened, not by the inconvenient positions of the old radiators, nor by the inefficiency of the finned pipework beneath the floor grating, but by the increasing risk of bodily injury as the grating panels along the centre of the nave began to give way and had to be hurriedly patched. Dirt and dust accumulated on the 2″ (50mm) bore finned pipework, which emitted almost no noticeable heat, and here and there a few coins, no doubt once intended for the collection plate, lodged out of reach beneath the grating. There was a very bulky free-standing cast-iron radiator positioned oddly in front of the font, and another in an equally awkward place on the other side of the main aisle, restricting the seating area and the passage to the north aisle. Inconspicuous pipework now interconnects the replacement radiators arranged along the walls in conventional fashion, and the floor trench has gone. So too has all chance of an unwary bride suffering the indignity of catching the heel of her shoes in the grating or experiencing the embarrassment of literally tripping up the aisle.

A formidable wooden eagle lectern with a broken beak arrived from St Mary's Mission Church at Send in 1965, but it was restored very professionally by Frank Fertig and proudly placed at the side of the chancel arch where it now glowers menacingly at the faces of the seated congregation.

The church possesses some valuable communion silverware that is kept in a bank for security and therefore rarely used. A silver cup bears London hallmarks for 1570 and has a cover with hallmarks for the previous year. A silver paten was given by the Reverend John King, Rector, in 1813 and was hallmarked in London in 1795. A silver paten made by Edward Charles Brown has London hallmarks for 1872.

Other belongings held elsewhere for safe-keeping include several very old registers, the oldest being a vellum book, entitled:-

> *The Register booke of the parish Churche of bisley in ye countie of Surrey, newly written in the yeare of our Lord God 1598 and in the fortieth yeare of the raigne of our most gracious Sovraigne Ladie Elizabeth by the grace of God Queen of England France and Ireland, Defender of ye Antient Christian Catholic Faith &c. wherein is contayned all christeninge, weddinge, & burialls commanded by her Matie to be made for Diverse good causes & considerations.*

The entries commence 37 years earlier with the baptism of a child, Dorithy Bray, on Maunday Thursday 1561. The earliest book of church accounts starts at 1673. Another book contains burials from 1678, briefs from 1683 and churchwardens' accounts from 1692. All subsequent obligatory records are preserved together with tithe rents, rails and wardens' notes, and together they provide a most valuable account of social history showing how the moral tone, customs, welfare and village life have changed through the course of time. Many interesting entries in these registers are noted in Chapter 18.

---

(1) Stated as being 12th century by Cater in *Bisley Bits.*

(2) *Charm of Old Surrey*

(3) Field No.6937. 3.195 hectares (7.90 acres) O.S. Grid Ref: SU 967614

(4) *Victoria History: Surrey.*

(5) *St John the Baptist Church: A Guide and Short History.*

(6) *Surrey Arch. Coll. Vol.75*

(7) *Bisley Bits.*

(8) *Parish News. July 1992*

(9) The Dilapidations Measure of 1923 exempted the Incumbent and his successors hereafter from future repairs.

(10) This was certainly not the first organ as the Rector paid £4 0s.0d. for 'revoicing and retuning the organ' on 21st April 1889 and A Cheeseman was paid a quarterly fee of 12s.0d. for blowing the organ in 1890. However, some of the 'organists' dating from 1865 may have played the harmonium mentioned on 26th July 1886.

(11) A stone basin, with a drain into the churchyard, for the priest to wash his hands before celebrating Mass and for washing the vessels afterwards.

(12) These names are repeated on the War Memorial in the centre of the village.

(13) *Bisley Bits*

(14) Ibid.

(15) Andrew presents the boy with the loaves and fishes to Jesus. John VI v9.

(16) Jesus said, 'Suffer little children to come unto me, and forbid them not: for of such is the kingdom of God.' Luke XVIII v16

(17) *2nd Book of Kings v11*

(18) *Surrey Arch. Coll. Vol 75*

(19) British Library: Extra-illustrated copy of Antiquities of Surrey with over 6,000 prints and drawings collated by Percival.

Chapter 9

BISLEY RANGES & NRA

Some excellent books have been written on the establishment of rifle shooting at Bisley and the history of the National Rifle Association, but this one brief chapter endeavours to portray Bisley Camp and Ranges as one might see them from the village perspective. Consequently, some major events are covered only to the extent to which they pertain to matters of parochial interest, or where they have had a significant impact beyond the boundaries of the shooting complex.

Bisley is a name known in almost every corner of the world because of its long-standing association with rifle shooting, yet few who live in the village or who travel thousands of miles to compete on the ranges in the summer know how, or why, this particular stretch of Surrey heathland became the international centre for dedicated marksmen from around the globe.

A hundred and fifty years ago Great Britain lived under a perceived, if not real, threat of invasion by the French and there was a pressing need to encourage civilian volunteers to train as marksmen in case of emergency, reminiscent of the much earlier days of compulsory archery practice throughout the land.

A Volunteer Force was formed in 1859, comprising small informal groups and rifle clubs all over the country. Such was its popularity that volunteers joined in their thousands and Lords Lieutenant were quickly instructed to organise these bands into formal county Corps to co-ordinate and lead the volunteer movement. One particularly fervent supporter of the Volunteer Force and promoter of a national association to hold an annual rifle-shooting event was Lord Elcho(1). The National Rifle Association was duly established under his chairmanship by the end of that year and the first national shooting competition was held on Wimbledon Common the following summer.

Queen Victoria was invited to mark the opening of the competition on 3rd July 1860 by firing the first shot. Thoughtfully, the rifle had been well-fixed in a purpose-made mechanical rest and carefully aligned so as to avoid the Queen having to test her skill or, worse still, missing the target altogether to the acute embarrassment of the assembled dignitaries. On pulling a silken cord attached to the trigger, the gun fired and the bullet struck within a quarter of an inch of dead centre at a distance of 400 yards. That original steel target is now one of many fascinating exhibits on display in the NRA Museum above the NRA Offices in Bisley Camp. Her Majesty graciously consented to give a prize of £250 (a huge amount in those days; easily enough to buy a house) for the best individual marksman. The NRA added their own gold medal and gold badge for the Queen's Prize. The monetary amount has remained unchanged to this day but the prize remains the most prestigious award in the world for rifle shooting.

In the years that followed the first meeting, the NRA grew in strength and reputation and the competitions became hugely popular. Nevertheless, all the equipment and buildings had to be dismantled at the end of every meeting, as the Association were permitted to close only a small part of Wimbledon Common for just a few weeks every year. However, it was not so much the inconvenience of the upheaval before and after the meeting but the need to improve safety in the late 1880s that became the driving force to find a permanent home for the event.

Finding a suitable location proved to be surprisingly difficult, even though there was no shortage of advocates spread around the southern half of the country eagerly promoting their favourite site. There was, of course, considerable prestige and no little financial reward to be gained. Suggested sites included Richmond Park, Staines and Pirbright in Surrey, Compton Downs in Berkshire, Cannock Chase in Staffordshire, Dunstable in Bedfordshire, and the South Downs near Brighton in Sussex. The chosen site had to be readily accessible by train from London and close enough to avoid excessive travel costs. Remember that in those days there were no private cars, only the rich could afford to travel by coach and horses, whereas the railway could transport people by the hundreds, quickly and in comfort. The new venue would have to be large enough to ensure complete safety and also to accommodate the sizeable infrastructure. Once re-erected, the buildings became permanent fixtures. Ranges offering a choice of distances would have to be constructed and equipped with stop butts and proper marking systems. Large expanses of open ground would be needed for the multitude of competitors living under canvas and, finally, there would have to be even more open ground to increase the size of the danger area behind the ranges, where stray shots over the stop butts would lose velocity and fall harmlessly.

The search involved a good deal of work but it was not without its own rewards, as reported at the time[2] '... the task was congenial, and entailed acquaintance with interesting persons, visits to agreeable houses and even a little rook-shooting'.

Initially Bisley was not even considered and, even when the Association vacillated between the merits and disadvantages of a few areas with the greatest potential, Bisley had not been included on the shortlist. Almost unexpectedly, and as time was running out for further use of Wimbledon, Bisley became the preferred option, as one person[3] on the NRA Council, who had seen it several times, managed to win over his fellow board members with persuasive reasons for choosing it. In the end the decision to move to Bisley Common had been largely influenced by the cheap travel and other concessions offered by the railway company, and to some extent by its proximity to Aldershot which would enable closer liaison between the Volunteer Rifle Corps and the Regular Army. The War Office and the Commander of the Aldershot Division were favourably disposed towards the proposal to move the ranges to Bisley, aware of the potential benefits for infantry training. When help was sorely needed, both the railway and the military responded magnanimously with generous offers of assistance.

The term 'Bisley Common' was loosely applied to this site, since much of the new range area lay in what was then the West End part of Chobham Parish. West End is now a separate civil parish and has kept the name, despite retaining the implied association with an adjoining community. The heathland site was already owned by the War Office, which was prepared to offer the use of it to the NRA. However, still more land was required in order to establish a permanent camp next to the ranges. This was achieved by purchasing part of the Manor of Cowshot in the Parish of Pirbright, most of which was owned by Lord Onslow. The NRA had to pay a heavy price (£12,232-14s-3d) because the whole site was a good deal larger than the Association actually needed. It comprised several landholdings extending to a total of 80 acres (about 32 hectares), but the owners were not prepared to relinquish valuable parts of their farmland by selling small parcels of land, and insisted that the Association had to buy the lot. This large investment almost exhausted its reserves, but fortunately the military authorities and the railway company came to the rescue by offering considerable practical assistance which was gratefully accepted by the Association. Contingents of Royal Engineers from Aldershot formed working parties to level the ranges, construct the butts for catching bullets and build the mantlets where target markers would be fully protected while shooting was in progress. The London & South Western Railway was on excellent terms with the NRA and, seeing the potential for lucrative passenger business, built a single line spur as far as the Basingstoke Canal entirely at its own expense, provided all the materials for the Royal Engineers to continue the line into Bisley Camp and, as additional incentive, gave the princely sum of £1,000 to defray other expenses. The railway spur had to be finished in time for the opening ceremony at the July meeting in 1890 but, with only twenty months from start to finish, it seemed an almost impossible task. This was achieved, however, by building it as a light tramway and by pressing ahead with the work at remarkable speed, and by not waiting for completion of all the legal formalities. Apart from the limitations that applied to street tramways, largely restricting the speed of locomotives that could be operated upon the line, it would, in every other respect, be a conventional railway.

Initially the plan was to design the ranges for shooting more or less westwards, but it was soon realised that boggy ground at Cow Moor and to the east of High Hoglees could not be avoided and, worse still, shooting would be hampered by the evening sunshine. Once dry ground had been identified on which the two main ranges, Stickledown and The Great Butt, could be orientated in a generally north-westward direction, it was not difficult to position the smaller ranges for shooting in more or less the same direction. Two more 'permanent ranges' were established north-east of The Great Butt, beyond the belt of woodland known locally as Polledoak Slade. These became known as Short Siberia and Long Siberia (a witty connotation with the Russian federal district that is known for its remoteness from the hub of activity).

The overall layout of the camp and ranges serves as well today as it did originally more than a century ago. Many changes have occurred in the meantime but not to the extent that Victorian or Edwardian marksmen would lose their way, were any able to return today.

Bisley Camp: The Graphic. 1907

The opening ceremony at this new venue was held on 12th July 1890 and, in similar fashion to the first shot fired at Wimbledon thirty years earlier, was marked by firing a fixed rifle. Though not a pretty device, the iron contraption holding the gun at Wimbledon in 1860 had performed admirably and so a very similar one was constructed for firing the first 'official' shot at this new venue. On this occasion it was the Princess of Wales, later to become Queen Alexandra, who pulled a silken tassel attached to the trigger. Bisley Ranges were open for business. The link with the monarchy, established all those years ago at the first Wimbledon meeting, was to remain unbroken – many members of the Royal Family have paid regular visits to

Bisley Camp, including Her Majesty Queen Elizabeth II, who is Patron of the National Rifle Association.

Within a few years of the first Imperial Meeting at Bisley, the facilities had to be increased both within the Camp and out on the ranges, such was the popularity of the sport. In 1904 Queens Road had to be diverted[(4)] at Wisdom Corner, at a cost of £59-1s-6d, when a 300 yards stretch of road had to be re-aligned in order to make room for extra firing points on the Great Butt which was aptly renamed Century Range once it had 100 targets, since increased to 108. Stickledown Range had to be enlarged in capacity to meet the growing demand for yet more firing points and extended shooting distances. These requirements were met by doubling its width to provide 50 targets and lengthening it from 1100 yards to 1200 yards, a formidable shooting distance of two-thirds of a mile. Meanwhile, it was decided to add 200 yards to Long Siberia, but there was a problem. The range already sloped downwards towards the targets, and at a distance of 800 yards the targets would be out of sight. The solution was to form a high earth bank with a flat top on which to place the line of firing points. However, it seems that the elevated embankment was rarely used for shooting and soon fell out of use. During the 1950s and 1960s, local children frequently played on this grass bank which they called 'Green Hill' and which has since become enveloped in scrub and woodland. The remaining part of Long Siberia Range ceased to be used for target shooting in 1972. The shooting distance on Short Siberia was subsequently reduced from 300 to 200 yards for safety reasons and, later still, the conventional target frames were replaced by a new cantilever design.

Right from the outset, a number of Bisley residents have derived various benefits from the presence of the Camp located on the edge of the village. Some villagers have been directly employed on the estate or in the club-houses, others have provided goods and services, such as supplying daily milk or accommodating visitors during the busy July period. These long-standing arrangements have been mutually advantageous and have generally operated extremely well. However, things have not always gone smoothly and on one occasion Major Charles Etches, OBE, the Secretary of the NRA, had to write to Mr William Hawkins of Wisdom Corner, who had been permitted to graze cattle within the Camp. His typewritten letter, dated 13th January 1933, stated:-

> Dear Sir,
> I have received a complaint from the Steward of the Honourable Artillery Company Hut that your Cattle have strayed into the enclosure and, besides other damage, have eaten up the wallflower plants. I would suggest your seeing him with a view to offering some compensation.
>
> I must again request you to see that your Cows are kept under control, and until you are able to find someone who can be depended upon to do this it would be better to keep them outside the Camp enclosure.

For good measure, and before signing off 'Yours faithfully, etc' in the customary way, Etches added in his own hand:-

> 'They have also been in my garden more than once.'

The availability of the ranges for military, as well as civilian, use was fostered by the long-standing co-operation between the military authorities and the NRA, though additional accommodation had to be provided outside the confines of the Camp for the overwhelming number of infantrymen in training. Every year overspill areas on Cowshot Common and Sheets Heath were crammed with army tents pitched in neat lines, with simple brick buildings with corrugated iron roofs here and there affording primitive facilities for basic needs. These toilet and ablution blocks were taken down after National Service ended in 1960, though some of the concrete bases were left in place. The uneven stony track that dissected the tented area on Cowshot Common was not levelled and surfaced with asphalt until long after the end of the Second World War and, until this was done, Queens Road was not regarded as a 'through road'. Those who did drive along it, needed to be alert to the potential danger at the unprotected level crossing but, ignoring the flag man's signal one day in the late 1940s, a van driver drove into the path of a train and was lucky to escape with only minor injuries.

The unusual spectacle that greets the visitor on first arriving at Bisley Camp has inspired many eloquent descriptions over the years, not least among journalists. One portrayed it[5] as 'a small self-contained Empire', looking 'like a Victorian Western', sounding 'like the battle of

Waterloo' and inhabited by 'a race so picturesque and individual, so fascinating in their behaviour, that it is a matter for surprise that anthropologists ever trouble to go abroad. As does not always obtain in remote territories, the people are very gentle and hospitable and go out of their way to make the conversation intelligible to the stranger.' The unique qualities of Bisley Camp have been given a stamp of approval by the Local Planning Authority, which has designated almost the whole complex a Conservation Area because of the unusual ambience imparted by the colonial design and construction of many of the buildings. Some remain in their original Wimbledon form while others have extensions or other alterations, and there are also modern replacements that reflect some of the historic architectural style. The expanse of open ground on the ranges has been designated by Natural England as a Site of Special Scientific Interest for its ecological value and diversity of wildlife.

The first impression of the Camp is that of a Victorian-cum-Edwardian time warp, comprising an odd blend of colonial elegance with military functionality: attractive wooden clubhouses furnished with large verandahs sit in strange juxtaposition with standard military-pattern billet huts.

Two notable ex-Wimbledon demountable buildings are the clubhouse of The Muzzle Loaders' Association of Great Britain and the 'Fulton Block'. The Muzzle Loaders' establishment is to be found next to the road leading to Stickledown Range and, for many years, was called the Exhibition Hut. It was described(6) in 1960 as once having been the NRA Members' Club 'a spacious, well-lighted building with a lounge, writing room and gun room', to which was added the somewhat dismissive remark 'whilst in the rear portion were the Ladies' Club rooms'. Typical of so many clubhouses, this one has a capacious verandah that extends around three sides. A short distance down the hill is a single-storey wooden building that is best known for being the shop, armoury and workshop of G E Fulton & Son. It does have other occupants and once housed the NRA until its new headquarters were built alongside in 1902. Fulton's building is unique insofar as it is the largest portable building in the country and it appears to have been erected 'inside-out' – frame outermost and clad on the inside. In fact this was done intentionally as all four walls are fully protected from the elements by the wide overhang of the roof.

The first Pavilion at Bisley Camp

It is such a pity that the original Pavilion, which commanded a central position in the Camp, was in such decay that it had to be taken down in 1922. The wildly extravagant embellishment of its façade was so much more interesting than the comparatively dull exterior of its replacement.

The most famous landmark on Bisley Common is without doubt the white Clock Tower. It has often appeared in publicity material and articles on shooting, and it stands in splendid isolation on the highest point in the camp, Hog Lees, overlooking vast tracts of heath beyond the ranges. On a clear day the clock tower could be seen some distance away in the opposite direction from the top of Reidon Hill at the far end of the village. This viewpoint is now obscured by a belt of trees that has developed along the edge of the common. The iconic square-shaped clapboard tower was erected in 1934 to replace the one from Wimbledon, which had a tapering cross-braced frame and was fitted with a chain-and-weight operated clock movement. Alongside, a drum was hoisted daily on a signal pole and a cannon boomed out to indicate the start and finish of firing. In 1921 the cannon was replaced by a loud horn, still in daily use. The 1943 *Spring Journal* of the NRA stated that there were once plate glass windows at the foot of the tower and that 'the glass having been broken by bullets, it was decided in 1901 to remove the glass and protect the works with a steel shield; at the same time, the open sides of the structure were closed by a wooden lining. As several bullet holes were found also in the clock faces, one wonders if the damage was caused by very "stray" bullets or by highly illegal deliberate shots directed by that same mistaken sense of humour which impelled certain "young bloods" to scale the tower and tamper with the hands of the clock.' Unfortunately, this steel protection did not prevent the theft of the 'works' and two of the hands on Boxing Day in 1980. Replacement parts, including an electrically-driven movement, were soon installed but more serious problems arose almost thirty years later. A thorough inspection recently revealed considerable decay in the wooden structure requiring etensive, and costly, remedial work which was completed in 2010.

The Canadian Clubhouse, built for visiting Canadian teams, has been renamed the MacDonald Stewart Pavilion after the foundation that generously covered most of the cost of refitting it in 1975. It has a cedar, shingle-clad, mansard roof with a lower catslide section extending over the wide verandah and is said to be made entirely of timber imported from Canada. A member of the Dominion of Canada Rifle Association, who was overseeing its construction in 1897, died before it was finished and is buried in Bisley Churchyard.

Entrance gates to Bisley Camp.

A magnificent set of wrought-iron gates and pillars were erected at the entrance to the Camp in 1904, but the metal-work was removed in the early 1940s and melted down for the war effort. The road between the pillars is now the exit in the 'one-way' traffic system by the entrance.

In 1987 the journalist Susie Cornfield thought that the fabric of the Camp was past its best when she wrote[(7)] 'the face of Bisley, in post-war years, has changed. Time has not dealt kindly with some of its clubhouses, whilst disease has stolen trees from the lines of chestnut, lime and maple.' She was not alone in this analysis and a programme of substantial investment was embarked upon to reverse the deteriorating situation. The facilities were sympathetically refurbished, upgraded and augmented, and nearly all the buildings and surrounding gardens have now been restored.

Beautifully-mown expanses of green lawns, skirted by lines of fine trees, provide an aesthetic backdrop to the neo-colonial development throughout much of the camp. Halfway up the long avenue of lime trees, through which one passes on entry to the camp, is an avenue of Canadian maple trees branching away to the right to provide a fitting approach to the Canadian Pavilion, which is sometimes affectionately known as the 'Canadian Palace' since it is arguably the finest clubhouse in the camp. A row of mature sweet chestnut trees along Club Row, together with the limes, were chosen specifically because they blossom in July when the Annual Meetings are held.

The National Small-Bore Rifle Association moved its headquarters to Bisley on 5th February 1980 with the opening of new premises very close to the Camp entrance, named Lord Roberts[(8)] Hut, in honour of 'Bobs', as he was affectionately known by his closest friends. In 2002 the NSRA moved within the camp into a magnificent new multi-purpose building built for the Commonwealth Games that year, and which is by far the largest building on site, transferring the name which evolved into the Lord Roberts Centre.

Internationally-accepted electronic targetry has been introduced on the new 300 metres Olympic-type range and a wide spectrum of full-bore disciplines is available at Bisley. Facilities for small-bore (or rim-fire) shooting, air-rifles and muzzle-loading guns are now well established.

There has been a considerable expansion of sporting clay pigeon shooting during the last decade under the control of a commercial organisation, Bisley Shooting Ground, with numerous types of 'clay' shooting on the recently named Cottesloe Heath. The whole establishment has fully regained its former splendour and now offers the widest range of shooting sports in the world. Bisley is rightly called the National Shooting Centre.

The premier event in global shooting circles remains the Imperial Meeting, in which a great many competitions are crammed into the middle two weeks of July. So tough is the most prestigious competition of all – HM the Sovereign's Prize – that it was not until 1988 that a perfect score was attained. This is how it was reported in the national press:[(9)] 'Philip Bennison did the seemingly impossible at Bisley on Saturday when he won the Queen's Prize by putting every shot into the bullseye during the second and final stages of the event. He is the first man in the 137 years of the competition to win the highest possible score of 300, with 40 of his 60 shots landing within the small central V-bull.' This outstanding achievement was to be repeated just seven years later by a Canadian J A M Paton who, incidentally, scored the same number of V-bulls. Winning the Queen's Prize at Bisley is the highest achievement in rifle shooting to which a marksman, male or female, can aspire.

George, Arthur and Robin Fulton.
Photo: Felicity Cavey

Whilst on the subject of the Queen's Prize, or King's Prize as it became between 1902 and 1951, one of the most remarkable achievements has been the success of the Fulton dynasty. George Fulton won it in 1888, his son Arthur won it three times in 1912, 1926 and 1931, and grandson Robin also won it in 1958. Arthur Fulton's prowess as one of the finest rifle shots of all time was duly recognised when he was awarded the MBE in 1959 for services to shooting. He had previously won silver medals in the 1908 and 1912 Olympics, and had been awarded the DCM[(10)] for gallantry during World War One. George Fulton set up in business as a gunsmith upon winning the prize of £250, which was a considerable sum in those days. Both Arthur and Robin took over the family firm in their turn, and it is still trading very successfully as G E Fulton & Son, although no longer with a Fulton at the helm.

Interviewed for an article in the illustrated monthly periodical *Windsor Magazine* in 1909, the then Chairman of the NRA, Earl Waldegrave,[11] said in quaint language of the day 'originally the national wapenshaw covered a week only, but now it takes a fortnight, and the double period is quite needed for the competitions. Years back, the Queen's Prize was decided several days before the meeting closed – really about the middle of it. No doubt the main purpose of this was to allow men from the country to finish up and go home, but the result was that the latter part of the meeting lost in interest. More recently, the Queen's Prize has not been decided until the last day of the meeting, the interest being thus maintained. Moreover, there have been various radical changes from year to year in reference to the conditions governing the shooting for the great trophy. When Wimbledon was still the infant prodigy, it was a case of forty survivors firing for the Queen's Prize; then the number was raised to sixty; and finally to a hundred – the Queen's hundred. There have been proposals that the meeting should be held at a date other than July but they have come to nothing, and I imagine we are always likely to begin operations on the second Monday in July. If we were to meet earlier we should interfere with the hay harvest, and if we were to meet later we should come into conflict with the wheat harvest and the moors.'

Very strict safety laws have been enforced on the ranges right from the outset. There have been very few shooting accidents in over 100 years at Bisley, but there was a fatality when someone ignored warning signs and deliberately climbed through a safety fence. Since then, a much more substantial high fence topped with razor wire ominously delineates the boundary of the whole of the ranges and the range danger area. This stretches from Pirbright Camp in the south to the mortar ranges at Greyspot Hill and Hangmoor in the north, and from the Chobham Ridges in the west to Priest Lane on the outskirts of West End in the east. No-one can claim to have crossed this perimeter fence inadvertently or unwittingly.

Automatic and semi-automatic military rifle fire at Pirbright and discharges on the high-explosive ranges to the north produce considerable noise, for which Bisley is often mistakenly blamed. Visitors to the village of Bisley and neighbouring communities, and also people who have recently moved there from outside the locality, tend to be very conscious of the background sound when shooting is in progress. Residents who have lived there for years have largely grown accustomed to the background crackle of gunfire, but the irritating high frequency component of the sound of each shot can be very acute where there is no woodland between range and recipient to soften the sudden unexpected noise. The NRA and Ministry of Defence are well aware of the muffling effect of trees and woods, which reduces the sharpness of gunfire, and have allowed the natural colonisation of woodland on areas once kept open.

An incident that caught the attention of a national daily[12] was the last wishes of a shooting devotee who, having been called by that great scorer in the sky and, like football fans who have their ashes scattered in the penalty box of their favourite football ground, wanted his ashes scattered at Bisley. He arranged for them to be put in a 'socking great' firework rocket and launched with great ceremony over the ranges. So he's out there somewhere..!

Full-bore target shooting cannot be described as a particularly spectator-friendly sport because there is no competition rivalry, for each individual endeavours to secure the maximum score largely at his or her own pace. Onlookers are therefore unable to keep track of shot-by-shot progress, as the line of competitors can be strung out up to a quarter of a mile along the firing points. Without good eyesight or a telescope at hand, it is difficult to see the result of each shot indicated by the marker at the far end of the range. Each person is almost oblivious to his, or her, surroundings; so intense is the level of concentration while shooting that all thought of fellow participants is forgotten until the final count of scores. Needless to say, the sport attracts very little by way of sponsorship. Notwithstanding this state of affairs, which in many other sports would be regarded as little short of disastrous, shooting can boast 'the finest collection of silver and silver plate that can be seen together at any one time in any one place',[13] ranging from the enormous China Cup and the National Challenge Trophy, both of which require four men to carry them, to hundreds of smaller trophies, some just a few inches high yet just as exquisitely fashioned. The magnificent array of trophies is no longer put on display during the Imperial Meeting in the Exhibition Hut, as these priceless prizes are now carefully arranged in The British Pistol Club Hut.

Open Days are now frequently arranged to encourage people to try their hand at the various types of shooting on offer, and special non-shooting events, held at times to avoid disruption of the shooting calendar, produce much needed revenue. The one which drew the largest crowds was the one-day Country Sports Fair on 20th September 1970, organised by the British Field Sports Society. During the preparation for the gundog trials on Stickledown Range, a quantity of wartime mortar bombs and hand grenades were discovered(14) partially buried in an old trench.

Ashburton Shield and some of the other trophies on display.

Of the countless trophies, perhaps the most notable is the Elcho Shield. Lord Elcho persuaded his friend, the great Victorian artist George Frederic Watts, to design a prize for a long-range shooting competition. Watts decided that it would take the form of an iron shield. Lord Elcho wrote to him saying, 'I wish to leave the conception as well as the drawing of our shield entirely to yourself.' The design was done within months but it would take years before the trophy would be finished. It was presented for the first time in 1865 as the award for the oldest international shooting competition, initially between England and Scotland, a long-range competition first held in 1860. What a magnificent trophy it was: a masterpiece of delicate *repoussage* (a process of carefully raising the design in relief by beating out the back). The shield measured 6 feet by 3 feet (1.8m x 0.9m) and was described[(15)] as being 'divided into compartments, in the most prominent of which Britannia, armed and erect, is represented, with the sea in the distance, and in the foreground her attendant handmaids. A medallion, exquisitely drawn, of the Queen's head, separates the allegorical from the historical part of the shield, where miniature groups suggestive of Bannockburn and Flodden, Tilbury and Wimbledon, are introduced. Just above the point of the shield stand two figures, a Highland and an English Volunteer, shaking the right hand of good fellowship. In one corner, it must be noted, into the design has crept a small spider which is, according to tradition, the creature whose persistence inspired a dispirited Robert Bruce to victory against the English at Bannockburn in 1314.' Lord Elcho was delighted with the shield, stating[(16)]

'No finer specimen of modern repoussé metal work is to be seen.' G F Watts was renowned for his allegorical paintings and, being an enthusiastic shot and, having his own rifle range at his home at Compton, near Guildford, was the natural choice for this commission. Watts also designed the target for the Running Man Range at Wimbledon, as well as the NRA Queen's Medal which was sketched on the back of an envelope. It features an archer and a rifleman, linking past with present, and includes the NRA motto.

Medal depicting the NRA logo.

The National Rifle Association can be justly proud of its remarkable history, three decades at Wimbledon and 120 years or so at Bisley – *Sit perpetuum*[17] (Let It Last Forever).

(1) The Rt Hon Francis Richard Charteris, born 1818 and died 1914, was known as Lord Elcho between 1853 and 1882 and later became the 10th Earl of Wemyss and the 6th Earl of March, GCVO.

(2) *History of the NRA, First Fifty Years.*

(3) Hon Thomas Francis Freemantle, later to become 3rd Baron Cottesloe and Chairman of the NRA Council (1931-9).

(4) *The Story of Bisley.*

(5) Eric Keown writing in Punch. 13th July 1949.

(6) *Story of Bisley.*

(7) *The Queen's Prize.*

(8) Field Marshall Frederick Sleigh Roberts VC, 1st Earl Roberts of Kabul and Kandahar, 1832-1914, Commander-in-Chief of the British Army 1901-1904, a staunch supporter of rifle shooting.

(9) *Daily Telegraph.* 1998.

(10) Distinguished Conduct Medal, the second level military decoration after the Victoria Cross, and the Distinguished Service Order were replaced by the Conspicuous Gallantry Cross in 1993.

(11) William Edward Seymour Waldegrave, 10th Earl Waldegrave (1882–1933)

(12) *Daily Telegraph.* 2002.

(13) *Story of Bisley.*

(14) *Story of Bisley – Part 2.*

(15) *The Queen's Prize.*

(16) *The Three Elcho Shields.*

(17) *Sit perpetuum* (Let It Last Forever or Let it Stand Forever) is the motto of the NRA and appears on the

NRA logo, together with a medieval longbowman and a rifleman standing together with the dates 1300-1500 shown next to the former and 1860 beside the latter.

Chapter 10

THE RAILWAYS

The "Bisley Bullet"

People still talk about the legendary train from Brookwood Station to Bisley Camp, affectionately known as the 'Bisley Bullet', as if there was just one single engine. In fact there were around twenty-four steam locomotives that were used on this branch line during its sixty-two years of existence. No doubt an aficionado would have immediately recognised the different wheel configurations, the class to which this or that engine belonged, and so on, but rarely did the casual observer notice anything other than the familiar old 'Bullet' had arrived on time.

The generous terms offered by the London & South Western Railway to provide a passenger service all the way into the camp from London, was undoubtedly one of the main reasons that Bisley Common was chosen by the National Rifle Association in preference to several other potential sites as the location for the new permanent ranges. The management of the L&SWR had been determined to ensure that the lucrative business should not be lost to a competitive company. It is apparent from contemporary correspondence between the General Manager and the NRA Council that a close working relationship was cultivated and maintained[1]. This resulted in an agreement that the railway would make a significant reduction in the fare for passengers travelling from Waterloo Station, and also lay a branch line out of Brookwood Station running due west for half a mile (800 metres) to a point on the side of the canal[2] from where the Royal Engineers would continue it northwards into the new camp. Who today can possibly imagine, in our present cost-conscious era, that a railway branch line would be planned and built for use for just one month of each year, no matter how popular the event? What was particularly remarkable was not so much that the deal had actually been struck, but more the speed at which the single-line spur was started and finished once the ink was dry. By the time the line was operational, some of the legal formalities had not been completed. The necessary Board of Trade licence was not obtained until a month later and it took even longer to finalise the War Department lease, which had to be backdated when it was eventually signed four months after the official opening of the line. The L&SWR took the unconventional step of constructing the branch in accordance with rules relating to street trams[3] in order to avoid the more demanding and more costly regulation that applied to railways. This unusual strategy also ensured that it could be completed in time for the start of the 1890 meeting. These regulations restricted the speed of locomotives using the line, but this was of little consequence as the overall length of it was so short. In almost every other respect, the so-called tramway was a conventional railway. The Light Railway Act would have been more appropriate, but this was not put on the statute book until six years later.

More than half the branch line, and much of its associated civil engineering work, was undertaken by the Royal Engineers who were also busily deployed within the camp levelling the ranges and making high banks as stop butts behind the targets. A considerable amount of infrastructure had to be put in place along the 1¼ miles (2 km) of track: a siding at Brookwood Station, widening of the embankment at Pirbright Arch with a small bridge over the road, a girder bridge over the Basingstoke Canal where the line swung northwards towards the camp, a third bridge and a cutting under Cowshot Road (because the Board of Trade refused to allow a level crossing at this point[(4)]), two level crossings – one on Cowshot Common and another in the camp – and finally a small station with a passing loop inside Bisley Camp. All this was completed in time for the first train carrying the Prince and Princess of Wales[(5)] to travel direct from London into Bisley Camp on 12th July 1890. The Prince formally opened the branch line and the Princess fired the first shot on the new ranges.

Once the service was up and running, the fare to and from Brookwood was 3d. Those travelling third-class from Waterloo had already bought their return tickets for 1s. 6d. while the NRA Council and staff, who travelled first class, were charged 3s. 0d. return. The journey time from London was about an hour, including six minutes for the train to make its way gently from Brookwood to the camp because the line was restricted to a maximum of 10 miles an hour, slowing to just 5mph at the un-gated level crossing on Cowshot Common, where the engine had to blow its whistle to warn of its approach. There were originally two camp stations, one located just inside the camp complex, comprising little more than a platform for ease of access to the ranges, and the main station near the Pavilion. The latter was used only for the first season and was rebuilt in time for the start of the 1891 meeting, a short distance back in the direction of Brookwood on the opposite side of the camp level crossing. The station building was[(6)] 'a modest timber built affair resembling more a cricket pavilion than a railway station and comprised an office, booking hall, and waiting room' and was later converted by the Lloyds Bank Rifle Club for use as a clubhouse.

'Bisley Bullet' arriving at Bisley Camp Station.
Copyright: Lens of Sutton Collection

At the outbreak of war in 1914 Bisley became an important centre for small arms training and the train service operated throughout the year. The line was extended in 1916 by German prisoners-of-war, who constructed an additional three miles of track westwards with stations at Pirbright Camp[(7)], the new camp at Deepcut and another at Blackdown. This extension was opened the following year by King George V and Queen Mary but it closed in 1918, just after the end of the Great War and was lifted in 1929. Even the line to Bisley was put under threat of closure during the 1930s, but the outbreak of World War Two ensured its continuation throughout hostilities when Bisley Camp was again put at the disposal of the War Department for military training. The Pirbright extension was reconstructed during the Second World War, but the section from Pirbright to Blackdown via Deepcut was never reinstated.

When bodies of American servicemen at Brookwood Cemetery were exhumed in 1948, and laid in formal rows on Cowshot Common under heavy guard to await removal by rail and repatriation to the USA, a temporary platform was put up just inside the camp entrance where there had been a platform for just one year – during the very first Bisley Meeting in 1890[(8)].

Train leaving at Bisley Camp Station. 1948
Copyright: Lens of Sutton Collection

Though the train service was used extensively during both World Wars, it never seemed to operate profitably after World War I, and payments to the NRA stopped when the L&SWR was absorbed into the Southern Railway in 1923. Running costs and maintenance of the line became more and more burdensome for the new operating company and, in May 1952, the inevitable announcement was made by British Railways Southern Region, as it had by then become, that the Bisley branch would close at the end of the Imperial Meeting in July that year.

The *Woking News & Mail*[(9)] reported:

> Tomorrow the service comes to an end. The last train ever to run will leave Brookwood at 7.28pm and return from Bisley at 7.37, and it is hoped that the two red coaches and the 0-4-4 tank engine will be suitably decorated. Since the war the train has not been well patronised. The fare of 5½d. for a single journey, although high, is not economical, and next year it has been arranged to carry passengers by bus.

The final public service run of the Bisley Bullet is fondly remembered by many, both villagers and shooters, and is aptly described in The Story of Bisley[(10)]:-

> The last journey out of the Camp was in the evening after the final of the Queen's Prize, and this was conducted with great 'mock' ceremony. The Band marched slowly down to the station playing solemn and mournful music. Leading the procession were certain 'duty personnel' – a 'banner carrier', 'medal carrier', 'undertaker' and 'pall bearers'. They were followed by an increasing number of 'mourners'. Down to the station they went, where a large crowd was assembled. The last train was already crowded, but more and more climbed aboard, standing on the running boards and the carriage roofs, and on the sides of the engine itself, which

> was decorated with flags, and on the front, crossed rifles over a target. At last the train was ready to move, but its departure was held up by someone pulling the communication cord, and then the frequent and prolonged pulling of the whistle had lowered the steam pressure so much that the power was insufficient to start the overladen locomotive and carriage. After some delay the train eventually began to move slowly away from the Camp. A firing party of the Gloucestershire Regiment fired volleys in farewell, and the line was well primed with fog signals. The last public train to leave Bisley Camp puffed away amid cheers and shouts, its progress round Cowshot cutting to Brookwood being marked by a series of explosions as it detonated the fog signals along its route.

A local newspaper reporter among the assembled throng at Brookwood, could plainly hear the detonations and wrote(11):-

> Crowds waiting on Brookwood Station traced the progress of this last journey by the noise of the explosions as the train passed over them. The noise of the fog signals was almost deafening and as the train crawled to the platform at funeral speed the pipe band on the platform struck up a mournful lament.

'Bisley Bullet' on Cowshot Crossing. 1952
Copyright: Peter Fidsczuk

Actually, the same train (push-and-pull set no. 734 with M7 class 0-4-4T no. 30027) made its final appearance at Bisley Camp Station on an altogether more tranquil occasion, when members of the Railway Correspondence and Travel Society commissioned a special excursion on 23rd November 1952. The engine was eventually taken back to the locomotive sheds at Guildford and the carriages were last used in the West Country.

Within eighteen months of closure much of the track had been dismantled, and a decade later the bridge at Pirbright Arch was taken down. However, the NRA were unable to relinquish responsibility for the bridge at Cowshot Road until 1966 when terms were finally agreed for it to be transferred to Surrey County Council.[(12)]. The Council demolished the bridge, infilled just enough of the cutting on which to construct the connecting piece of road and footpath, though railing had to be erected beside the footpath where the made-up ground dropped away sharply. Finally the girder bridge over the Basingstoke Canal, the last remaining item of infrastructure, was removed by British Rail in 1979.

Bisley branch line railway bridge across the Basingstoke Canal

In 1988, some thirty-six years after the closure of the line, the *Woking News & Mail* wrote[13]:-

> For 62 years the Bisley Bullet served the NRA's Camp but there is little today to remind us of this unique service. Tracks have disappeared beneath housing developments and vegetation and the route is almost impossible to follow. The remains of

> the bay and short unloading platform can be seen at Brookwood Station, and the platform and buildings at Bisley Camp Station now house the Lloyds Bank Rifle Club.

Not long afterwards Lloyds TSB Rifle Club, as it is now called, bought a railway sleeping carriage for use as additional dormitory accommodation for its members. It was delivered in its original British Railways two-tone livery of carmine red and cream and transported through the village by road on a low-loader vehicle. On arrival at the camp, it was lowered by crane onto a short section of rail beside the platform where it remains to this day, though now repainted green.

There were two accidents on the Bisley branch line during its 62 year existence. The first occurred on 11th April 1898 at Bisley Camp Station, while the engine was manoeuvring around the loop to take up position at the other end of the carriages for the return journey. The engine reversed into the carriages, shunting them back almost 40 feet (12 metres) with such force that about 130 soldiers of the 15th Middlesex Regiment were hurt,[14] 23 seriously, their heads receiving cuts and injuries as rifles flew out of the luggage nets. The second accident happened on 4th July 1947 when a Woking Gas Company van failed to stop at the un-gated Cowshot level crossing, despite the flag man's signal which the driver later claimed was confusing. The van was struck by a train, sending it 50 yards (46 metres) along the line towards the camp. The van was completely wrecked and the two occupants were fortunate to escape with only minor injuries and shock. In those days, unlike today, Cowshot Common was almost completely devoid of trees from one end to the other, with heather and grass being the predominant vegetation. A train approaching the camp from the direction of Brookwood would have been very conspicuous to anyone on the common as it neared the level crossing but, conversely, would have been difficult to spot behind a thick belt of trees from vehicles travelling in the opposite direction. A man with a red flag and a green flag was put on duty at the level crossing during busy periods, and, at 3.37pm on the day the accident occurred, gave an unambiguous 'red flag' signal to the van driver.

Shooting folk and locals with long memories still recall with some affection the Bisley Bullet running between Brookwood Station and Bisley Camp. Some remember using the service regularly each summer while others recollect just that last memorable journey on a July evening, now more than half a century ago.

The 'Wharncliffe'

It will surprise some people to learn that Bisley Camp and Ranges were once served by another three railway systems, or tramways to be precise, of which one is of significant historical interest.

A quaint little box-like locomotive had been used for twelve years at the former site of the ranges on Wimbledon Common, conveying people in small open cars between the camp and the outlying firing points. It was extremely well utilised during the shooting competitions in July, but as soon as each annual meeting was over all the track and rolling stock had to be removed together with the temporary buildings, shooting equipment and other paraphernalia, and put into storage until the following year. Though no doubt inconvenient, the land had to be restored at the conclusion of events in accordance with terms under which the National Rifle Association had been given temporary exclusive use of the common. Having tried unsuccessfully to have Wimbledon Common enclosed, Earl Spencer, the owner, handed control of it to the Conservators in 1871.

The use of a small tramway to transport competitors, officials and spectators to and from the Wimbledon Ranges was first tested in 1864, when the 3′6″ gauge temporary line was put down and used for the whole of the July meeting that year. Competitors and visitors paid 2d to ride back-to-back in a horse-drawn train of four simple open cars that were totally devoid of any comfort or safety. Apart from a few minor incidents at the beginning, mostly resulting from the lack of safety, the new means of transport was found to be a great success. Two additional cars were added in 1877 that were built with inward-facing seating and guard rails, but still without any form of springing or any other concession for comfort. Soon afterwards the four original cars were modified to this safer design.

In 1877 Merryweather & Sons, a firm manufacturing steam fire engines at Greenwich that had recently started making light steam locomotives primarily for use as street trams, saw a good opportunity to promote these new machines by offering to supply one to the National Rifle Association for trial use as a replacement for the horse on the existing tramway. The offer was accepted upon the assurance that it would operate sufficiently quietly so as not to upset the concentration of competitors nor alarm the many horses within the camp. A report on the initial test stated[16] that '… it has worked in a very satisfactory manner all day. It makes no smoke, and absolutely no noise, and runs at a very respectable speed over the slightly laid road on the common.' In fact, it was deemed necessary for the driver to blow a whistle now and again to warn of its approach.

Following the successful performance the previous year, a new steam tram was purchased by the NRA from Merryweather in 1878 at the concessionary price of £331-2s-0d. The locomotive was again a boxed-in type, measuring 8 feet (2.4 metres) long by 6 feet 6 inches (2.0 metres) wide, weighing 4 imperial tons (4.06 tonnes) and being specially designed to suit the original track gauge of 3′6″. It must have been no less successful than the one used on test because within a year it had been named 'Wharncliffe' after the then Chairman[17] of the NRA. While Merryweather had secured an agreement to maintain the machine and move it in and out of storage every year for the annual competitions, another company, John Aird & Sons, was given the responsibility of laying the track and then taking it up again each year and, when necessary, replacing sleepers and sections of rail. The John Aird firm took some pride in having completed the new permanent line for the range tramway at the new Bisley site in 1890 a full month before the Bisley Bullet line was ready for service. However, soon after the relocation from Wimbledon, both Aird and Merryweather lost their respective service contracts to the London & South Western Railway, which had developed an extremely good working relationship with the NRA partly as a result of the mutual benefit derived from the branch line from Brookwood. Not only did the L&SWR take over the running and maintenance of the little line, they even provided engine drivers to operate 'Wharncliffe'. The L&SWR also linked a shed to the line to protect the engine but not the tramcars, it seems, which remained outside exposed to the elements.

'The Wharncliffe'. c.1913

In 1893 the 'Wharncliffe' had to be dismantled for extensive repairs. As this could not readily be done on site, the tram was taken to the L&SWR works where the job was completed in time for the start of the 1894 meeting. By this time the original Wimbledon track was virtually worn out and was eventually replaced a few years later. Two smart new tramcars, each designed to carry 42 passengers, were bought in 1899 but 'Wharncliffe' was just not powerful enough to pull a full load so it had to be taken away yet again, this time to the Merryweather works, for fitting a new upgraded boiler that would produce more pressure.

This tramway ran behind the 600 yard firing points of what was called the '90 Butt' or Mid-Ranges (later Century Range) proceeding north-eastwards to the end of the firing points near Wisdom Corner where it turned northwards to the 200 yard firing points of the first group of Permanent Ranges (Short Siberia Range), a total distance of about half a mile. The far end of the line was extended northwards up to the butts of the farthest Permanent Range (Long Siberia Range) where it ran beside the markers' mantlets.

The camp end of the tramway was re-routed several times. The terminus of the 'Wharncliffe' line during the very first Bisley meeting had been adjacent to the platform on the 'Bisley Bullet' line near the camp entrance, but the following year it was cut back a short distance to just behind the first firing point of Century Range. Then in 1898 it was extended north-westwards as far as the Bazaar Lines inside the camp complex. Yet another change was made in 1900 when it was moved into the heart of the camp next to the camp station.[18] Each new termination point at the Camp had been regarded as permanent, but this time it really was to be so. This latest extension had been made at the behest of the Incorporated Soldiers and Sailors Help Society with, at the very least, tacit approval of the military authorities who had a vested interest in the opening of new homes for disabled ex-servicemen to be built at an isolated location not far away from the ranges. A temporary light spur-line also had to be laid at the same time so that the 'Wharncliffe' could turn away from the ranges at Wisdom Corner, cross what was then the end of Queens Road and continue more or less in a straight line over War Department land directly towards Stafford Lake some 650 yards (600 metres) away to where the homes[19] would be built. This temporary extension probably lasted no more than a few months but provided a very convenient way of delivering the construction materials to site by means of rail freight, using the camp station sidings for transferring the goods relatively easily between trains. The additional rails, procured by the NRA from Devonport,[20] were merely loaned for the duration of the project and had to be given back to the NRA[21] for use within the camp as soon as they were no longer needed for the Princess Christian Homes, as they were to become known and which are the subject of the next chapter.

A plan was conceived to make the tramway go right through the camp up to the 'Long Range' (Stickledown) but the scheme was never implemented for financial reasons. Another idea that was never pursued was to lay two sets of rails with two trains going to and fro in opposite directions more or less continuously, thus providing a more frequent service and supposedly doubling the income.

The 'Wharncliffe' line was always a highly valued part of the camp infrastructure, never more so than in the middle of the day when, as Colonel Cole[22] noted: 'The immediate pre-lunch break journey always caused a minor sensation, for the tramway then transported far more passengers than ever it was designed to carry, with men in varied uniforms clinging on, in precarious positions, to the sides of the already crowded passenger accommodation.' If the numerous individuals who regularly jumped on and off the open carriages along the route while the tramcar was in motion had duly paid the one-way fare of a penny (1d) and, as was expected of honest passengers and those who had a ticket meticulously tore it up at the end of the journey, it is doubtful, even then, whether the takings on the Range Tram would have been sufficient to cover costs. However, at least one person did not subscribe to this view because in a letter imploring the NRA Council to reinstate the tram service long after it had ceased to operate, a familiar figure of advancing years who bemoaned the absence of transport reasoned that if the charge of 'one penny per trip, any distance, could be collected by the driver or postillion, the finances of the Association would benefit overwhelmingly.' Nevertheless, it has never been explained why the fare at Bisley had been fixed at only half the amount of that charged a quarter of a century earlier at Wimbledon.

Hiring drivers from the London & South Western Railway company had proved to be an expensive choice and a cheaper option was soon found. A local man, Charles Ginman,[(23)] who described himself as a blacksmith and locomotive engine-driver, and who had been employed as a train driver by L&SWR at Guildford, was engaged by the NRA in 1900 primarily as a blacksmith but also to be the permanent driver for the 'Wharncliffe' tram during the July Meetings and on Saturdays throughout the shooting season. Ginman was still living at 2 Springfield Cottages at West End at that time, but later moved with his family to 'Sunny Bank' in Guildford Road, Bisley, which is nearly opposite Port Way. He was allowed to leave the engine each night at the end of the line closest to home. Consequently the daily timetable oddly showed the first train journey starting at the ranges and travelling into the camp, but it is very doubtful whether any passengers were carried on this trip. It appears that Ginman was paid to run a Saturday service from spring until early autumn, except during the busy July meetings when he ran the 'Wharncliffe' continuously every day. Evidence of the supplementary Saturday service is to be found in correspondence dated Thursday 18th April 1912, when Ginman was laid up with a poisoned foot and signed off work by Dr Stanley Nix, MD, of Urtica Villa, Knaphill. The NRA Acting Secretary hurriedly had to send a letter to the Locomotive Superintendent at Guildford requesting a temporary driver to report for duty that Saturday, though just how promptly a substitute engine-driver was deployed is not known. One might presume that the absence of further correspondence on this matter tends to suggests that short notice had not been a problem.

Christopher Bunch, who has painstakingly researched the history of the 'Wharncliffe' and Bisley's other railways, notes that boys from local schools were employed during the Annual Meetings for various tasks around the camp, some of whom acted as attendants on the range tramway. These were pupils at the three local boarding schools in Bisley and West End – the Shaftesbury School, the Farm

School (as it was called prior to 1919) and the Gordon Boys' Home. At the request of Princess Alexandra, lads from the Gordon Boys' Home had the honour of being paraded before Their Royal Highnesses, the Prince and Princess of Wales, who attended the meeting in 1900.

The 'Wharncliffe' was probably never taken out of its storage shed at any time during the First World War. The army had verbally expressed an interest in using it at Blackdown Camp in 1917 and were formally offered terms to hire it, but there is no confirmation that the offer was accepted. The locomotive was steamed in 1919 for a boiler test, possibly with the intention of resuming the service to the Siberia Ranges, though this did not materialise and the little steam tram never ran again.(24) Its shed was virtually demolished in a gale in 1929, and the following year the NRA took the decision to sell the engine, tramcars and rails to a scrap-metal merchant. The sale price was £95-0s-0d, which was put aside to offset the cost of the impending diversion of part of Queens Road to extend the firing points on Century Range.

Ticket issued in 1952.

One of the original Wimbledon tramcars ended its days outside Brookwood Station with a makeshift roof and was used by the station taxi drivers as a waiting area between fares. This was no isolated example of re-use of obsolete items put to some ingenious purpose by resourceful locals; there were certain other pieces of equipment – even portable buildings – that found their way from time to time into nearby gardens, farms and nurseries after the respective management of Bisley Camp, Brookwood Hospital and other local establishments had no longer needed that these redundant assets were no longer needed.

The Butts Tramway

There were other tramways which operated on the ranges at Bisley, the largest was generally known as the Butts Tramway which had been constructed solely for the purpose of conveying targets back and forth from the target sheds to three of the ranges.

When the ranges were built in 1890 the main target sheds were erected close to the stop butts on Century and the Siberia Ranges, almost half a mile from the main body of the camp. It was important to locate the sheds as near as possible to the rising frames by the markers' mantlets, because the shooting targets that sit in the frames need frequent renovation and replacement. In 1893 the repair yard was equipped with a 20″ gauge track (approximately 500mm wide) running through some of the sheds from where it branched in two directions – left to Century Range and right to Short Siberia and, at a later date, to Long Siberia beyond. Most of the bulky targets were, and still are, about 6′0″ (1.8 metres) square and so they were stacked on low trucks which were then pushed by hand to their destination.

There used to be a dwelling originally called Range View, and later renamed Bolling House, situated somewhat incongruously right alongside the target shed yard and surprisingly close to two of the ranges. It was owned by the NRA for letting to an estate worker. Mr & Mrs R Ratcliffe and their daughter Mary were there for a long time but they must have suffered more than they were prepared to admit with the noise of rifle fire such a short distance away. Mrs Ratcliffe, a familiar figure around the village during the 1950s, and rarely seen without her bicycle, was asked about this one day at the Fox Garage where she worked in the canteen. She replied without hesitation that she never took any notice of the noise from the ranges but 'simply could not abide the racket from Fox Engineering next door'.

Two diverging rough stone tracks opposite Loampits Farm in Queens Road led down to the Siberia Ranges; the one on the left also led to Range View where it veered sharply right across the front hedge of the property and then left into the target shed yard. As the use of cars increased, a patch of open ground in front of the house became an informal parking area for Short Siberia. The proximity of this car park to the line of fire on Short Siberia was never considered to be a serious safety risk in those days, and indeed there is no record of any mishap. The house has now been demolished and, following planning permission in 2004, a new link road was made interconnecting

Century and a second car park at the side of Short Siberia.

The rails for the butts tramway were replaced in 1960 but soon afterwards the gauge was widened[25] to 24″, when a second-hand Lister diesel engine already built to this gauge was acquired to pull the target trucks. The branch to the Siberia ranges was never altered since presumably this stretch had already become obsolete.

The sheds and workshops in the maintenance yard were simple, timber-framed structures with corrugated-steel sheet cladding, perfectly adequate for the purpose even though they were heavily used throughout the year. The first peace-time Annual Meeting after the end of Second World War was covered by *Picture Post*[26] and which stated '… some 10 cwts.[27] of low grade flour is used each year for patching the targets. About 30 cwts. of distemper is used every year to colour the canvas targets, and a thousand yards of canvas is needed.'

Though the target sheds contained nothing of significant risk of theft, their remoteness certainly rendered them vulnerable to vandalism. An arson attack occurred in the late 1980s, completely destroying all the sheds and their contents and severely damaging the tiny Lister engine. By that time the internal road system was well developed, and targets could be stacked on the back of a pick-up truck or Land Rover and transported to wherever they were required. As the Butts Tramway was no longer needed, the NRA disposed of the rolling stock and rails.

The increasingly ubiquitous use of cars during the inter-war years necessitated restrictions on vehicles driving on to the ranges, and roads had to be improved around the camp. Cars were blame for the decline in evening social events for visitors who 'scattered to the winds and the neighbouring villages in search of entertainment'.[28]

The Running Deer Tramway

This device presented competitors with a moving target, in the form of a silhouette of a deer mounted on a small carriage travelling a short distance on a 34" gauge track across an opening between two banks. It was pushed into view by a small team of people, the momentum carrying it across to the other side where a second team was waiting behind the other protective bank to rotate it on its built-in turntable and send it back again. The first Running Deer was made from a sheet of iron, and the second was steel, but when steel-tipped bullets replaced lead in 1897, canvas was used thereafter and the Running Deer lost its fine antlers. The two metal deer are now displayed as bullet-pitted sentinels outside the main door of the NRA Offices. They were copies of a full-size drawing of a red deer stag, drawn at the request of Lord Elcho by Sir Edwin Landseer in 1864. He was one of the most famous artists in the Victorian era and his popularity has never waned. In Manson's biography[29] of Landseer, he remarks, 'How many volunteers, one wonders, knew when they were peppering the iron deer, that they were firing at what was practically the handiwork of Sir Edwin Landseer?'

---

(1) *Tramways of the NRA.*
(2) Chris Bunch – personal communication.
(3) *Tramways of the NRA*
(4) Chris Bunch – personal communication.
(5) Later to become HM Edward VII and HM Queen Alexandra
(6) *Bisley Camp Branch Line.*
(7) Pirbright Camp had been established in 1881
(8) Chris Bunch – personal communication.
(9) *Woking News & Mail*. 18th July 1952.
(10) *The Story of Bisley*. Cole
(11) *Woking News & Mail*. 25th July 1952.
(12) Chris Bunch – personal communication.
(13) *Woking News & Mail*. 12th May 1988.
(14) *Branch Lines from Brookwood.*
(15) Chris Bunch – personal communication.
(16) *Volunteer Service Gazette* (published weekly as 'The Official Organ of the Volunteer Force').
(17) After Edward Stuart-Wortley, Baron (later Earl of) Warncliffe. 1827-1899. Chairman of the NRA 1875-79.
(18) *Tramways of the NRA.*
(19) Off-cuts of rail found at the Homes by the author in 1970s, provide strong evidence of the existence of this branch.
(20) *Branch Lines from Brookwood.*
(21) Chris Bunch – personal communication.
(22) *The Story of Bisley.*
(23) Charles Ginman, born in Chichester, married Mary Ann Timlick and had four children. He died in 1931, aged 67.

(24) Chris Bunch – personal communication.

(25) *Branch Lines from Brookwood*.

(26) *Picture Post*.

(27) 10 cwt. = 10 hundredweight (508 kg).

(28) *Queen's Prize*.

(29) *Landseer*. Manson.

Chapter 11

THE PRINCESS CHRISTIAN HOMES

The following article by Major Moffatt[1], published in the (Bisley & West End) *Parish News* in August 1985, provides an excellent insight into the running of the Princess Christian Homes:-

> If you turn off the Guildford Road just by Bisley Common and drive or walk up Stafford Lake the noise of the traffic recedes in the distance and suddenly you come upon some old Edwardian buildings. This is Princess Christian Homes built in 1902 and given as a gift by the Building Trades Federation on land donated by Lord Pirbright to the Incorporated Soldiers and Sailors Help Society, as it was then called, now The Forces Help Society and Lord Roberts Workshops.[2] Originally built as four separate homes (hence the plural in the title) the buildings were later joined by covered corridors to make one, albeit spread out, unit. The name derives from the President of the Society at the time, The

Princess Christian of Schleswig-Holstein, a daughter of Queen Victoria.

As well as being a 'Home of Rest' for discharged Servicemen a workshop was established and 18 disabled men were employed, largely on basket making. Little is known of the activities of the Homes between the wars but after the Second World War training was given in basket making, clock repair, clock assembly and invisible mending. Thankfully the need for training maimed ex-Servicemen decreased over the years and one by one these activities ceased; basket making continued until last December (1984) when sadly our last basket maker died on Boxing Day. The baskets found a ready market in the Society's showrooms in Brompton Road and members of the Royal Family were regular customers.

Twenty-two men from three Services now find a home here and the policy is to make it more of an 'extended family' than a 'residential care' home. Financial contributions from residents are small, representing only about a third of true costs with the balance found from Society funds (no State help of any kind) and everybody does whatever he is able to keep the place running smoothly. Ages range

> from 65 to 89 and the 'youngsters' can be found gardening, window cleaning, running the laundry, looking after the aviary, maintaining the machinery, cooking breakfast, washing up, decorating or more sedentary occupations; in fact doing what any senior family member might do in his own home. Those too old for active chores can enjoy a well earned rest with books, television, playing snooker or just sitting in the sun, when available. All have sufficient pocket money to live a full life and none need feel that he has been put away on the shelf.

Major Moffatt had been appointed to oversee a substantial programme of refurbishment and alteration which he undertook with relish. He was a very self-motivated individual and just the right person to take charge of the extensive refitting and new building work that upon completion was officially opened by Queen Elizabeth the Queen Mother. Little did he, or anyone else, suspect that the establishment would be shut down and sold within two decades, following the amalgamation of Forces Help with another charity.

The original scheme to construct a purpose-made home for wounded soldiers, where they could either stay during convalescence or live out the rest of their lives and also work within their respective capabilities, was a novel concept in the Victorian era but it quickly garnered public support and substantial donations, especially with the backing of Princess Christian[3] and Lord Roberts[4] who was at that time Commander in Chief of the British Forces in South Africa. These two very influential people had both lost a son in the Second Boer War (1899-1902) and became closely involved with the plight of wounded men returning from Africa, setting up the charity to provide several homes with workshops for disabled ex-Servicemen.

The land at Bisley was donated by Lord Pirbright and a small dilapidated dwelling had to be demolished to make way for the homes. Designs[5] for the project were invited by The Building Trades Federation which provided the buildings entirely at its own expense, though a significant amount of practical help was given by the local military command with the approval of the War Department. However, the site was rather isolated and so a half mile long single-track road was laid across the common from Reidon Hill to Stafford Lake to facilitate access. It was surfaced with the latest tarred macadam but passing places were obviously not regarded as necessary, and none was provided. For much of its length the road ran alongside and almost parallel to an existing unmade track that soon fell into disuse and of which there is now virtually no trace. In order to align with the front boundary of the new buildings, the otherwise straight road turned slightly on approach, crossing a pond pretentiously called Stafford Lake. A bridge would have been rather costly so a solid crossing was made that incorporated two culverts below water level connecting each side of the newly-bisected pond. Brick parapets with chains and railing were added for safety, together with metal plaques on each side proclaiming 'STAFFORD LAKE

1900'. The road was constructed more for future access than for transporting building materials which could be brought to site more easily by alternative means. At the request of the Society, a temporary railway track was laid by the Royal Engineers for transporting heavy construction materials by rail via Brookwood and Bisley Camp. It was connected to the Bisley Ranges tramway behind the firing points of Century Range near Wisdom Corner, a distance on not much more than 675 yards (620 metres) from the Homes running across level ground all owned by the War Department. The camp terminus of the tramway had to be altered to facilitate loading at the goods yard in the Camp Station. The temporary line was required for less than a year and so the Wisdom Corner branch was quickly removed just before the official opening of the homes by Princess Christian in 1902. The only recent evidence of the existence of this line was some discarded 'off-cuts' of railway line found next to the Princess Christian Homes in 1979.

Princess Christian Homes. 1905

Close ties with the National Rifle Association were maintained as overseas visitors were given accommodation at the Homes when there was spare capacity during the Imperial Meetings. Little else is recorded about the early years of the establishment except for an incident recalled by a Norfolk resident whose family had lived at Knaphill for generations and who stated in a letter in 1981 that his paternal grandfather had worked on the ranges when they were being built, and also at Princess Christian Homes 'until the Secretary ran off with the funds'. The first Warden at the Homes was Major Kitchen, whose son Robin died at Gibraltar in 1912 and in whose memory a commemorative plaque is to be found in the nave at Bisley Church. The first Matron at the Homes was Sister Candy; there is a photograph showing her seated in the church porch.

One local person, George Fry, was given a place at the Princess Christian Homes in 1991 where he lived happily for nine years. Apart from wartime service with the Royal Electrical and Mechanical Engineers, he had worked at the Knaphill watch-making firm of W W Boorman & Son from 1931 until his retirement in 1985.

Though not a local man, by far the most notable resident was Colour Sergeant Alfred Richards,[(6)] who had been severely wounded in 1915. He was making toys for children while convalescing at the Princess Christian Homes when, unexpectedly, he received the news that he was to be awarded the Victoria Cross. A journalist eager to meet the gallant soldier was surprised on arrival to find that '… before you get through the waiting room you can hear the men singing at their work: One-armed Tommies cutting out toy patterns and jig-saw puzzles… one-legged Jack Tars deftly engaged in basketwork, and heroes of both services assembling parts of forts, men-of-war, field guns, villages and farmyards.' When interviewed, Richards replied modestly, 'I am proud to learn that my comrades chose me as one of three of the bravest, but we all did our duty even though luck may have helped some to more noticeable acts. I don't know how the vote was taken, but had it been a comrade instead of myself I should feel just as proud.'

Those villagers old enough to remember the 1950s may recall one fellow who had been unable to walk since the war and who used to go up and down Stafford Lake Road in a black invalid tricycle. One day he sneezed and inadvertently drove into the ditch with a lurch, whereupon he found he could move his legs and very soon he was able to walk again.

The saddest story witnessed by the author was of another old soldier, Scottie, as he was known, who always wore a tartan beret and shuffled up and down Stafford Lake Road. He would not speak to anyone and, though I saw him many times, I never bothered to speak to him, presuming he was just a rather unsociable character. One day, while working in the field next to Hassells, I heard a funeral cortège proceeding along Stafford Lake Road, led by a piper playing the lament 'Flowers of the Forest'. Scottie had died. Soon after I was to learn that while in Burma he had been captured and tortured, and his toes and half his tongue had been cut off.

In 1948 the Incorporated Soldiers, Sailors and Airmen's Help Society, as it was then called, decided to start a market garden in the 1¼ acre (0.5 hectare) field on the other side of Stafford Lake Road directly opposite the Homes. The Comptroller sent a letter to Jim Hill of Strawberry Farm, explaining:-

> Dear Sir,
> I am writing with regard to the fields which have been leased to you for some years, which belong to the PRINCESS CHRISTIAN HOMES and for which there is no lease operating. I have been in communication with the Society's Solicitors regarding a new lease, and they are prepared to grant one from year to year. Owing to the fact that the Princess Christian Homes are now a centre for the training and rehabilitation of severely disabled men, it is proposed to take one of the fields into use for further cultivation in order that these men may be employed. Therefore, in the near future, we shall take over the field in question. I shall be glad to hear from you as to whether you are agreeable to an agreement on a yearly basis, with six months' notice on either side to terminate it or to vary it.
> Yours truly, Miss E M Acton CBE

A slightly larger field at the side of the Homes, once crossed by the temporary railway line, was used for growing withies for basket-making. The remaining fields owned by the charity, situated towards Grindstone Handle Corner and which had been cultivated during World War Two, became hay fields in post-war years.

One wing of the Homes became the convalescent home of the Queen Alexandra Hospital in 1914 for serving and recently discharged women military personnel, remaining open until the early 1960s.

Just two years after the amalgamation in 1997 of the Soldiers', Sailors' and Airmen's Families Association and The Forces Help Society under the new name of SSAFA Forces Help, the charity decided to close the Homes within six months, moving the residents to other parts of the country. The news came as a bombshell to the old boys, some of whom had lived there for decades. Tears welled up in their eyes as they passed on the news to walkers on the common that they had befriended over the years. It was very hard for them to come to terms with the changing situation, and by June 1999 the place was empty.

Upon closure of the Princess Christian Homes, a memorial was erected in the churchyard at St John the Baptist Church, flanked by three lines of plaques on each side bearing the names of individuals associated with the Homes who have died since 1991. The full list of names is shown in **Appendix D**.

The buildings, often claimed to be situated in Knaphill but actually located within the Parish of Bisley, remained unoccupied for some years while the charity investigated the possibility of redeveloping the site. Green Belt planning restrictions prevented this, as they had done some years earlier when a scheme to build a block of self-contained flats for ex-service personnel on the withy field had been turned down.

Ironically, the site was bought in 2005 by a private company, Nellsar Homes, that runs a number of residential homes for the elderly, mostly in Kent. The firm has completely renovated the buildings, provided sympathetic alterations and replaced the antiquated interconnecting passages between the buildings to form a homogenised unit. It opened in 2009 as Princess Christian Care Centre, a modern residential care and nursing home for the elderly, and for dementia sufferers, equipped with 96 bedrooms all with en-suite facilities.

---

(1) Major T E Moffatt, (Royal Engineers), last Commandant of the Princess Christian Homes.

(2) Re-named 'SSAFA Forces Help' in 1997.

(3) HRH The Princess Helena Augusta Victoria (1846-1923), fifth child and third daughter of Queen Victoria, married Prince Christian of Schleswig-Holstein in 1866.

(4) Field Marshall Frederick Sleigh Roberts VC, 1st Earl Roberts of Kabul and Kandahar, 1832-1914, Commander-in-Chief of the British Army 1901-1904.

(5) *An unsuccessful design* by Edwin O Sachs was published in the American Architect & Building News in 1900.

(6) Sgt A J Richards, VC was one of the famous 'six VCs before breakfast' at Gallipoli in 1915. After his death in 1955, his Victoria Cross was sold for £110,000.

Chapter 12

SCHOOLS

The Farm School & Shaftesbury School

In order to understand why Bisley was chosen in mid-Victorian times as the place to set up a remarkably innovative project to train and educate orphaned and destitute boys from London, it is necessary to understand the almost indescribable deprivation and squalor that was taken for granted in the city at that time, and life-changing incidents experienced by two people who resolved to improve the lot of these unfortunate wretches.

Appalling conditions existed in parts of London around the first half of the 19th century, where an all-pervading foetid atmosphere emanated from open sewers and dunghills, and horrendous overcrowding occurred in filthy dwelling places wholly unfit for habitation. Outbreaks of disease and persistent ill-health were commonplace, and crime, cruelty and debauchery were rife. The worsening situation was eventually tackled head-on and, in some ways, so successfully that some of the systems put in place during the Victorian era still serve as well today as they did then.

A young solicitor's clerk by the name of William Williams, who had suffered a crippling accident as a boy, was travelling to the West Country by train in 1843 when he heard a commotion in the carriage next door. Upon investigation, he was appalled to discover a dozen young gutter-snipes, handcuffed and manacled together, destined for shipment from Plymouth to Australia as punishment for petty crimes they had committed. Williams was deeply affected by this scene and the 'miseries of children condemned through poverty to live as the dregs of society'.[(1)] Recognising that their plight had been caused by the appalling conditions in which they lived, their lack of education or family support and their struggle for survival which led them to a life of pilfering, he gathered together a group of friends and founded one of the first Ragged Schools in a hayloft above a backstreet cowshed in a disgusting part of St. Giles-in-the-Fields known as the Rookery. The Ragged Schools provided a refuge to any young street urchin who came to the door and gave sustenance, comfort and education but, above all, they showed these children that someone cared for them and gave them hope for the future.

When Antony Ashley Cooper, later the Seventh Earl of Shaftesbury, was a boy at Harrow School he witnessed a pauper's rowdy funeral procession at which the drunken and staggering pallbearers upset the coffin, tipping the deceased onto the street and, amidst guffaws of laughter and ribald remarks, the body was recovered and carried noisily and unceremoniously along its way. He was horrified by the experience and resolved at that moment to devote his life to relieve the suffering of the nation's poor. Lord Shaftesbury was already well-known for his tireless efforts to stop the exploitation of children in mills and mines by the time he came to hear of William Williams' work, whereupon he offered immediate support and became closely involved with the project. Shaftesbury had been born into the nobility yet had suffered a very unhappy childhood and well understood Williams' concern for these unfortunate boys. Mustering some additional help, they opened the first 'Refuge' (home) for these poor wretches who had no families and nowhere to live. From its humble beginning in 1852, this venture grew quickly and, with Lord Shaftesbury's close involvement, it attracted influential attention and funding to enable more refugees and Ragged Schools to be opened.

Encouraged by the boys' overwhelming support for Lord Shaftesbury's idea of a big training ship, it was not long before the suggestion was put into practice and the opportunity arose to buy two old frigates from the Admiralty, which had started to dispose of wooden-hulled sailing vessels. The second of these acquisitions was 'HMS *Arethusa*', the fourth naval ship to be named after this mythological Greek water nymph, which had been built in 1849 and was the last ship to go to war entirely under sail. It had been badly damaged in the Crimean War[(2)] and towed to Malta for repair before sailing back to Chatham in 1860 to be lengthened and fitted with engines. The Society took possession of the *Arethusa* in 1874 and moored it further up the River Thames at Greenhithe for 250 boys to learn various trades or to be trained for the Navy.

The founders' next scheme was to search for a place in the country to get as many children as possible away from the filthy London environment and into fresh air and healthy surroundings. They sought to acquire a farm of 60 to 100 acres, ideally with a sizeable house that could be adapted to suit their needs. They found one for sale at Bisley which was cheap, well-located and had 88 acres of good workable land for mixed farming, but the dilapidated old farmhouse was neither large enough nor suitable for conversion. They bought the farm for £4,725, leaving sufficient capital for a large purpose-made residential school to be built on the site of the old dwelling. A national newspaper report of the newly-completed school began 'Those who know the out-of-the-way village of Bisley, with its wretched-looking cottages, will be surprised when they again visit the place to see the handsome and imposing structure which fronts the Green…'

The Farm School.

Another contemporary account of the project[3] stated that the style was:

> '… a sort of Gothic, with bands and patterns of coloured bricks, and walling of red bricks,' and that 'the building consists of a centre and two wings, connected together by corridors. The Centre contains a committee room, store rooms, living room for the master, and separate infirmaries. The left hand wing contains workshops for several departments, and a broad open dormitory over having an open timber roof. The right hand wing contains the dining room, with a similar spacious dormitory above. In the rear the kitchen and proper offices are erected as separate buildings; and again in the rear of each of the wings are swimming baths and lavatories. The total frontage of the buildings is about 160 feet, and the entire cost £5,775. Young and weakly boys from London will be transferred there from the London Refuge for Homeless and Destitute Children so that they may be trained to look after cows and pigs, grow vegetables, till the land, and thus be fitted for service at home or in the colonies. To so good an enterprise we wish the best success.'

The new Refuge Farm School was completed in 1868 and within a year 100 boys from London had taken up residence to start a new life in the country learning carpentry, tailoring, shoe-making, bread-making and working on the farm under the guidance of Alexander Mitchell, the farm manager. There they looked after cattle and pigs, tilled the ground, grew vegetables and learnt valuable horticultural skills from Anthony Waterer from Knapp Hill Nursery who was a great supporter of the school. Some of them also became proficient in bee-keeping because Robert Roberts, the mathematics master and Mitchell's son-in-law, kept hives in the grounds. Produce from the farm was more than enough to satisfy the needs of all the pupils and staff and so the surplus was sold to local residents. Music was an important part of school life from the outset and a brass band was formed in 1869 under Mr Prosser, producing many talented young musicians, some of whom went on to join regimental bands.

Mr Robert's gardening class.

A second school, even larger than the first, was built in the grounds about half a mile away in 1873. It was named the Shaftesbury School and opened with 57 boys and would soon house almost 200, a few of whom could not adjust to the new rural environment, or the strict regime, and were sent back to the London Refuge.

Shaftesbury School.

In the space of less than 30 years the humble 'ragged school' in a hayloft above a cowshed had developed into a nationally known and respected Society that would surely have failed, had it not been for the tireless work of William Williams, its far-sighted founder, and the influential support and commitment of Lord Shaftesbury. This success was all the more remarkable for having been achieved against a background of general public apathy and criticism.

Meanwhile, the Rector of Bisley, the Revd Walter Eaton, realised that more pew space was needed in the village. However, either he was unaware that another school was soon to be opened or he hopelessly underestimated the combined requirements of these two establishments. Having come to Bisley only the previous year and having just completed extensive renovations at St John the Baptist Church, he wasted no time in adding a north aisle. Sadly, this extension was far too small and to his astonishment and great annoyance, he found that the church would not be needed at all because an imposing school chapel was to be put up in 1874 close to the Farm School. The chapel was built by George Augustus Calder entirely at his own expense on land donated by Lord Pirbright and, not only was it large enough to accommodate the pupils and staff from both schools, it even had a separate room in which villagers could buy a cheap cup of tea and meet friends,[(4)] an added touch that really must have rubbed salt into the wounded pride of the Rector. In 1901 the Bishop of Winchester visited the chapel to confirm a number of boys from both schools.[(5)]

History does not record any lasting bitterness within the rectory evoked by Calder's generous benefaction, save for the briefest mention of the chapel some eighteen years later in 'Bisley Bits' when Cater wrote somewhat dismissively that '... it is the only Nonconformist place of worship in the parish'.[(6)] Nor does the book have much to say about the schools themselves, which are covered in just two short sentences, even though they obviously had a marked impact upon the life of the village and had saved many a boy from a life of poverty.

Jess Stevens and his kitchen staff.

A few years later the school chapel was enlarged to provide a vestry and a sanctuary[7] but as it was easier to build the new chancel at the southeast end of the nave,[8] the interior layout had to be re-orientated when the altar was moved from one end to the other. Unfortunately, much of the original embellishment that adorned the outside of the chapel, so typical of the era, was removed at the same time, apparently without good reason since it did not interfere with the extension.

A new sanatorium was built in 1896 in which contagious patients could be isolated from those with lesser ailments. In those days scarlet fever, consumption and diphtheria were commonplace as well as being serious notifiable diseases. The 'Bungalow Hospital',[9] as it was known in the village, was situated beside the main road opposite Wilcot House and replaced a smaller infirmary constructed thirteen years earlier which was converted to flats for staff. Additionally, several new houses were put up here and there around the village for the increasing numbers of people employed at the schools.

'The Bungalow Hospital' (with Wilcot House behind). 1920

New education laws in 1919 forced the two schools to combine, whereupon the Farm School became the Lower House and the larger one in Shaftesbury Road became the Upper House of Shaftesbury School. In 1920 the name of the Society changed from the National Refuge for Homeless & Destitute Children to the Shaftesbury Homes and Arethusa Training Ship, later to be shortened to the Shaftesbury Homes and Arethusa, the name by which the organisation is known today.

Still more reorganisation was needed after the Second World War as a result of further changes in educational and welfare requirements for children. A new headmaster by the name of T T Barnes was appointed in 1948 and proved to be just the right person to carry out this important task and the school went from strength to strength. Exam results were excellent; and music, art and drama became more and more important in school life.

The school band with Mr Prosser.

Unfortunately the demise of the establishment was not far off, because the endowment was dwindling as wealthy patrons died one by one and costs were rising at an alarming rate. In 1957 the difficult decision was taken to close the school at Bisley at the end of Summer Term on 25th July 1959. It must be said that not many boys had enjoyed life at Shaftesbury School. It had been a very tough regime by today's standards, but it had provided them with 'a chance of a lifetime', the phrase used as the title of Marion Bailey's book[10] about the development of the Society and its establishments. It has been said by some with first-hand knowledge that she paints a rather benign and nostalgic picture of life at the school that not all former pupils would recognize.

The Society wasted no time in disposing of the estate. A few of the staff houses and the chapel were sold privately and the rest of the school was put up for auction on 10th November, scarcely three and a half months after its closure. The sale was held at The Albion Hotel Woking and conducted by Alfred Savill & Sons. The auctioneers' description of the lots, land sizes where specified in acres, rods and perches, the order of sale and the prices achieved, were as follows:-

Lot Nos.			
	1	Grayswood, 3 School Close	£ 2,400
	2	Stanmore, 4 School Close	£ 2,450
	3	No1 Chapel Cottages	£ 1,700
	4	No2 Chapel Cottages	£ 2,050
	5	The Senior School with playing fields 30a. 2r. 38p.	£14,500
	6	The Headmaster's House	£ 3,000
	7	Freehold land (in Shaftesbury Road)	£ 900
	8	The Lodge	£ 2,000
	9	The Hospital, Port Lane	£ 4,700
	10	The field behind the Hospital 2a.2r. 0p.	£ 1,900
	11	No1 The Laurels	£ 2,000
	12	No3 Memorial Cottages[11]	£ 1,800

13	No4 Memorial Cottages	£ 2,200
14	No1 Belper Cottages	£ 1,650
15	No1 The Firs, Port Lane[12]	£ 1,550
16	No2 The Firs, £ 900	
17	No3 The Firs, £ 1,700	
18	The Refuge Farm School	
	11a. 3r. 4p.	£10,500
19	Freehold land (in School Close)	
	0a. 3r.20p.	£ 1,150

The auction realised a total "hammer" price of £59,050 with most lots fetching around the pre-sale estimate. The Lower House, which the auctioneers called the Refuge Farm School, was pulled down and replaced by a small private residential housing estate called Cedar Grove.

Memorial tablets bearing the names of former boys (**Appendix G**) who had died in the two World Wars were carefully removed from the walls of the chapel and taken to the society's headquarters in Shaftesbury Avenue in London.

All the staff dwellings, bar one, are now privately owned. The gymnasium, hospital and chapel are still recognisable from the outside but have been converted internally for alternative uses.

Standing in the derelict school hall of the Upper House (Senior School) shortly before it was demolished in 1964, Mr Barnes, the former headmaster who had just become head of Knaphill County Secondary School, confessed that he found it bizarre to 'stand amid this scene of desolation'.

The 7th Earl[13] of Shaftesbury was arguably the greatest

philanthropist of all time, justly earning the nickname 'Prince of Philanthropists'. He is commemorated with a massive memorial in Piccadilly Circus, which was erected in 1893 and is surmounted by the 9 feet high (2.7metres) aluminium statue of the Angel of Christian Charity popularly, if mistakenly, known as Eros.

Bisley National (or Village) School

Following the amalgamation of the Farm and Shaftesbury Schools, the new enlarged establishment was commonly referred to as 'Bisley School'. This misleading term incorrectly implied that it was the only place of education in the village when in fact a National School for local boys and girls pre-dated the Farm School by twenty-one years. On the 19th January 1847 the Earl of Onslow,(14) Lord of the Manor, gave an acre (0.4 hectare) of land to the Rector, Churchwardens and neighbouring clergy 'as a site for a school for poor persons of and in the Parish of Bisley and for the residence of the Schoolmaster and Schoolmistress of the said school or for either of them and for no other purpose whatsoever'. The full text of the Grant **(Appendix H)** clearly states that the children were to be educated according to the principles of the established church and 'to be always in unison with the Incorporated National Society' which was founded by the Church of England; in other words the place was to become what is now commonly known as a church school.

We do not know the size of the first building, what it looked like or whether its construction was funded by the National Society for Promoting Religious Education, an organisation keen to see a church school in every parish. The only information we have is that the school was in use before the end of 1847 and was 'quite small'. Whatever its shortcomings, it was pulled down in 1860 and completely rebuilt. The design of the replacement National School is typical of the mid-Victorian period and, like many others of its type, may well become 'listed' in due course because of its architectural merit.

Children at Bisley National School were rewarded with certificates for good attendance, the very best being given the handsome sum of 5s 0d which was paid out of interest from a bequest of £4 10s 0d from Mrs Mary Bainbridge of Chobham, who died in 1877 aged 97. Mrs Bainbridge was a great supporter of both the school and Bisley Church and is commemorated with a plaque in the chancel of the church. A few of these certificates survive and are treasured by great-grandchildren, or great-great-grandchildren, and there are samplers made by young girls embroidered with the name Bisley National School dating from the 1880s.

Meanwhile, Board Schools were established by the government in 1870 to provide a truly national system of schooling particularly for young children in towns and cities where there were fewer National Schools than in rural communities. To avoid offending the church and secular groups which, by that time had established many local schools of their own, government grants were increased to ensure these existing schools became part of the new educational structure. The new Board Schools were paid for out of local rates and were governed by elected school boards which still upheld Christian principals yet were forbidden to apply denominational formularies such as the Church of England catechism.

From 1876 it became compulsory for children to attend school, and it was made illegal to employ children under the age of 10 years.

For some unexplained reason, Bisley National School was taken over by a school board in 1893 and enlarged. This take-over may have been for the good reason that this was the only way of funding the much-needed expansion. In the event the new governance would be short-lived, because on 16th June 1899 the land and premises were vested in the Official Trustee for Charity Lands with the management of the school reverting to the Church of England. Although the church did not own the school, the Rector made absolutely sure that not one child would fail to appreciate the involvement of the Church of England and to understand the teachings of the church. To this end the Revd John Gwyon meticulously attended both morning and afternoon prayers at the school and every young lad with a promising voice was soon inveigled into the church choir. The choir did not admit girls in those days.

The Headmaster, Mr Edmund Asplet, was assisted by Elizabeth Young and his wife, Edith, who taught the Infants. Following his untimely death in 1902 at the age of 37, Mr SG Russ was appointed as his successor and became the organist and choirmaster at Bisley Church for the next ten years.

School boards were abolished in 1902 and state schools became the responsibility of county councils and a few large borough councils. These new education authorities were charged with the provision of both primary and secondary education, a system that continues to this day.

Bisley Village School. 1905

A photograph of around 40 pupils, taken in 1905, confirms that the school catered for all ages, as one little girl looks scarcely five years old while a tall boy with a watch chain upon his waistcoat appears to be at least fifteen. One of the boys is holding a slate marked 'BISLEY No. 2' but, with ages ranging so widely, surely not all of these pupils were in Class Two.

In 1921 the Chertsey Rural District Council's Sanitation Inspector reported: 'At Bisley County School there was an epidemic of Mumps and Measles during March and April. This affected attendance to such an extent that by the end of April only 29 children were present out of 73 on the books.'

Attendance would be severely depleted again at various times during the next quarter of a century when these and other contagious diseases spread rapidly through the school, usually during winter months. All the children were inoculated against diphtheria when the vaccine became available halfway through the Second World War.

Mrs Moulding.

Mrs Moulding, whose daughter still lives locally, succeeded Mr Russ as Head Teacher, and held this post until 1937 when she retired and Francis Arthur Garner was appointed Head. Mr Garner, who lived in Belgarvie in Church Lane, once told the children that if anyone came to his front door singing carols at Christmas time, he would throw a bucket of water over them from his bathroom above. Bisley Church of England School ceased to be 'a full range school', as Mr Garner recorded in the School Log, at the end of the Winter Term in 1937. From the beginning of the Spring Term, children aged eleven and over attended the Knaphill Council Central School, and Bisley became a 'Junior and Mixed Infants' School'.[(15)]

The outbreak of war in September 1939 delayed the start of the new school term by ten days. Children and parents were instructed in the procedures to be implemented in the event of air raids, and the youngsters were shown how to put on and adjust their gas-masks. It is recorded that air raids did indeed disrupt the school day sometimes, and a disturbed night was blamed on one occasion for pupils being late the following day.

Bisley Village School. 1930
left to right: (back row) Cecil Underwood, Albert Wye, Reg Daborn, Reg Underwood, Kitchener Barnes, Reg Gosden.
(row 2) Joyce Henbest, Bob Wylie, George Perdue, Jack Gosden, Joe Patterson, Tony Graham, Eddie Hill, Toby Hockley, Ivy Butler.
(row 3) Lil Westerman, Flo Westerman, Audrey Hewitt, Grace Wheeler.
(row 4) Molly Ash, Maud Burgess, Joan Stevens, Elsie Cheeseman, Mary Henbest, Joyce Hayward.
(front row) Sid Hill, John Mepham, Len Hewitt, Alan Harrington, Reg Lear, Ron Mansfield.

Mr Garner retired in 1941 and Miss Florence Liming was appointed Headmistress. She was assisted by Miss Clayton and Mrs Linger who taught the Infants. To the dismay of some of the children, the milk would be placed in front of the stove in the winter to warm it; a practice which was discontinued when the next Head Teacher, Mrs Hilda Handford, arrived in 1951. Eleven years later Mr Redman took over upon the retirement of Mrs Handford.

By the late 1950s the classrooms were becoming too cramped for the growing number of schoolchildren and the facilities were insufficient to meet increasing educational requirements. A new school was planned in connection with proposed residential development at Elm Grove Farm. Yet again, this would be publicly funded, but governance was to be allowed to remain with the Church of England.

The plan took shape in January 1961 when Surrey County Council acquired two large parcels of land[16] on which to build a replacement school, to be called the Church of England Voluntary Aided Primary School which opened in 1967. Orchard House, which had a large garden, was purchased for £5,000 and demolished so that it could become part of the playing field of the new school, but the school building was constructed in the far corner of the adjacent field that hitherto had been part of Elm Grove Farm. This was to avoid having an entrance directly connected to the potentially dangerous A322. The main entrance was located at the end of Hawthorn Way, one of the small roads on the residential estate built by the Woking building firm of Walter Deakin in 1962/3. This resulted in a problem, common to many schools, but unforeseen at the time, in that considerable congestion occurs twice daily near the entrance as most children are now taken to school, and collected, by car.

The Victorian former school building next to the Recreation Ground was then taken over by the County Council for use firstly as a remedial school, later as a teacher-training satellite and now for several mixed uses, the main one being a district Youth Centre.

---

(1) *The Chance of a Lifetime – The Story of The Shaftesbury Homes and Arethusa.*

(2) Ibid.

(3) *The Builder.*

(4) *The Chance of a Lifetime – The Story of The Shaftesbury Homes and Arethusa.*

(5) *Bisley Parish Magazine*. December 1901.

(6) *Bisley Bits.*

(7) *Kelly's Directory*. 1938.

(8) The school chapel had been orientated NW-SE, probably to suit the shape of the plot of land.

(9) The Bungalow Hospital may be found in Guildford Road almost opposite Wilcot Gardens.

(10) *The Chance of a Lifetime – The Story of The Shaftesbury Homes and Arethusa.*

(11) In memory of William Williams (1818–92), the co-founder and Secretary of The Shaftesbury Homes & Arethusa from 1843 to 1891.

(12) Port Lane is now called Guildford Road.

(13) Anthony Ashley-Cooper, The 7th Earl of Shaftesbury KG (1801-1885).

(14) Arthur George Onslow, 3rd Earl of Onslow (1777 –1870)

(15) Log Book of Bisley Church of England School.

(16) Both situated between the houses now numbered 229 and 259 Guildford Road.

Chapter 13

COLDINGLEY PRISON

After the closure of Shaftesbury School, and increasingly after disposal of the estate, there had been much speculation about the future of the main site – the Upper House, or Senior School, as it was sometimes known. Nobody had any doubt that the old Victorian pile was in poor condition and would almost certainly be pulled down, but there remained the hope that another school might be built on the same spot, particularly as there were 23 acres (9.3 hectares) of playing fields and other grounds attached to it that could readily be brought back into usable condition.

Events unfolded on 6th September 1960 when the Prison Commissioners announced that the former Shaftesbury School in Bisley had been acquired as the site for a new Category B top security prison. A double security fence would enclose 30 acres (12.1 hectares), a third of which would be the prison block and two-thirds would be used for recreation and market gardening. Outside the fence, to the north east, 65 new houses would be built for prison officers and their families.

When the plan was announced that the school would be replaced by a large prison, there was widespread horror and dismay in the village which was soon followed by anger and resentment that a school, of all places, should become a high-security jail. An enormous campaign was mounted to oppose it and there was an immediate demand for a Public Inquiry. While the Public Inquiry was being held, *The Daily Telegraph* carried half page reports of the daily proceedings and it was front page news in the *Surrey Advertiser*, the *Woking News and Mail* and the *Camberley News and Bagshot Observer*. However, the campaign was of no avail and a few months later it came as no surprise to many people to learn that the Appeal against the prison development had been dismissed, particularly as the telephone cables were already being laid while the Inquiry was taking place.

The *Surrey Advertiser*(1) reported local reaction to the news:-

> Mr A G Martin, Vice-Chairman of Bagshot Rural District Council declared 'This will come as a bolt from the blue to many of the councillors. Certainly it is a bombshell so far as I am concerned. There had been proposals for institutional use of the school since it was vacated, but these had been turned down.' The Rector of Bisley, the Ven Windsor Roberts, archdeacon of Dorking and a former prison chaplain commented 'It is probably a shock to everyone. I imagine that most of the people of Bisley will object. There are many reasons, and those of the womenfolk will be especially strong.

> Having had a certain amount of experience, I can say that it is not as terrifying as people imagine. At the same time, the news will come as an emotional shock, and I am sure there will be a strong demand for an inquiry. The natural reaction is to be horrified, but on the other hand we have a duty to show a Christian outlook on the matter. If this is, in fact, the best place for the prison, then I hope the village as such will co-operate.'

Within days, the Home Secretary, Mr R A Butler, announced that a Public Inquiry would be granted if one were to be demanded. Indeed one was, and within seven days 607 electors out of 725 residing in the Parish had signed a Petition calling for one. The Inquiry opened on 12th September 1961 in the main hall of the Shaftesbury School, which was packed with local people. It was at times acrimonious and emotional, and continual protests at times drowned the speakers. Evidence presented showed that that there was enormous local opposition. *The Daily Telegraph*[(2)] reported the proceedings each day in detail. An expert witness in town and country planning, speaking for Bagshot RDC, said, 'There is overriding objection of a major intrusion into the Green Belt, contrary to the careful and consistent policy of the planning authorities over the last five years, which the Minister has always upheld on appeal.' Mr A F Coxon, Chairman of Bisley Parish Council and a resident for 41 years, reaffirmed the objection of the villagers, stating 'Since the census[(3)] of local opinion was taken, nothing has happened to make us think differently. Indeed, what has emerged at this inquiry must confirm and strengthen our opposition.'

The press reported[4] that a Post Office[5] engineer, called as an additional witness by the Prison Commissioners during the Inquiry to answer questions about telephone cable being laid in advance, admitted under cross-examination that a pipe had been laid from Guildford Road to the site into which a cable could be put if required, and that the Post Office had 'initiated' a plan to lay a 75 pair-cable along Shaftesbury Road, reducing to a 50 pair-cable near the entrance to the site. This revelation cemented local opinion that the Inquiry was just a sop and a charade and the result had been pre-determined.

The Inquiry dismissed the local objections and approved the plans for the £850,000 jail. The first building contractor went bankrupt halfway through construction and the prison was not completed until May 1969.

The new institution, named HMP Coldingley after the ancient name for Colony Bog on Bisley Common, opened with just 50 male prisoners[6] transferred from several London jails, but it soon reached its design capacity of 300 inmates. It was a flagship prison modelled on Blundeston in Suffolk, which had incorporated several innovative work-related systems. Coldingley became Britain's first fully-industrialised prison, having three small internal factories: a metal shop making road signs; another fabricating shelving systems; and a commercial laundry for hospital linen. Prisoners worked a five-day week and received a small wage with which they could buy more goods and privileges than were available at other jails. These incentives created much demand for transfer from other institutions but only inmates within two years of release were given the opportunity of a place, and no remand prisoners were sent there at all.

In 1993 the prison was re-designated as Category C, meaning that those held were at lower risk to the public. Its operational capacity has recently been increased to 500 and many other substantial changes have occurred over the years, some better than others, but it is now even more focussed upon resettlement and training.

The avenue of trees was retained after the school was replaced by the prison.

Until very recently, the roadway from Shaftesbury Road leading to the front entrance of Coldingley Prison was lined by an avenue of trees, one of the few features still recognisable to old boys from the former school. One such character paying a nostalgic visit and seeing the formidable scene at the end of the avenue quipped 'nothing has changed'.

One may be forgiven for thinking that the next matter has been inserted merely to spice up the story. While there is no denying that it does add a touch of light-heartedness, it is absolutely true even though it has no direct relevance to HMP Coldingley. In typical Victorian style, a well-engineered sewerage system was installed as part of the infrastructure for the former school. It comprised a pumping-chamber at the Upper House, three-quarters of a mile of underground pipe that crossed the A322 and Church Lane with connections along the way from the Bungalow Hospital, the Farm School and several school houses, and an enormous septic tank chamber at the far end, situated in the middle of a field not very far from where the Trulley Brook runs close to Oldhouse Lane. The system remains *in situ* and the tank is still visible in the field close to Public Footpath No. 134. In fact one of the special conditions of sale of properties put up for auction by Alfred Savill and Sons in November 1959, when the site was purchased by the Home Office, was that the system would continue to be pumped until 29th April 1960 by which time all properties connected to it had to make alternative arrangements for sewage disposal. However, the only indication of the presence of the very deep pipe is a manhole cover in the front garden of a house since built directly over it beside Guildford Road. The cover was lifted in the 1970s, revealing a vertical access shaft with several climbing rings.

Banish the thought that the disclosure of this ready-made tunnel might lead to some mass break-out by individuals residing at 'Her Majesty's pleasure'. One trusts that their end of the pipe was well-sealed during the construction of the penal institution, but there again...

---

(1) *Surrey Advertiser & County Times*. 10th September 1960.

(2) *The Daily Telegraph and Morning Post*. 15th September 1961.

(3) A census paper opposing the prison was completed signed by 607 of the 725 electors in Bisley.

(4) *Surrey Advertiser & County Times*. 16th September 1961.

(5) General Post Office, responsible for telephones at that time.

(6) *Woking News & Mail*. 23rd May 1969

Chapter 14

VILLAGE HALLS

There have been three village halls in Bisley, or Village Institutes as they were formerly known. Mr W B Wakefield[(1)] of Wilcot House erected the first of these at his own expense in 1912, in the village sports field between the house and his miniature rifle range. The short track leading to the hall no longer exists and has been subsumed within the cutilage of 221 Guildford Road.

One of the last public shows to be held in the Institute was a performance of Dick Whittington' on 12th February 1921, held to raise funds for a Maternity Home at Woking. The cast comprised: Mary Arnold, Hilda Baker, William Burdett, Veronica Clark, Hilda Gills, Phyllis Groom, Ernest Hooper, Annie Kettridge, Leonard Oliver, Eileen Parsons, Mabel Robinson, Maggie Seppings, William Stevens, Primrose Watson, Eileen Wharf, Beryl Wright, Mabel Wright and Nancy Wright. The musical accompanists were Mrs H Cole, Dorothy Hill and Ted Oliver. The following year there was a mishap with an oil-lamp and the wooden building was burnt to the ground. By the time a fire engine arrived from Chertsey, it was too late to save anything.

The first Bisley Village Institute

The second Institute was a second-hand wooden YMCA hut from Inkerman, just a few miles away. One should not be churlish about such a generous gift but it is fair to say that it was not in the best of shape when it arrived. By the early 1950s it had become so dilapidated that people used to joke that when dances were held, the rats under the floorboards skipped around rather better than the people above. The Honorary Treasurer of the Institute, Walter Cundy, appealed for funds for refurbishment in a letter to all households:-

> This Institute has been of invaluable benefit to the people of Bisley for many years, the only hall available for public meetings, socials, youth movement, Women's Institute, etc. The income from letting just covers overhead charges: No profit is made by any individual or the Committee, and much of the upkeep is by voluntary effort. Until some hall or community centre is available, which, owing to priority building, must be many years yet, the Institute must continue to function. We have utilised so far all our funds in having our roof repaired and reproofed and installing new heating and cooking apparatus. Cloakroom re-planning, external and internal repairing, stage and floor repairs and other alterations are BADLY NEEDED. The Committee has authorised me to launch this appeal to raise £300. Several sums, ranging from £10, have been promised. We need much more and no donation is too small. Please help all you can and whatever you give will be gratefully acknowledged.

The *Woking Review*[(2)] reported in 1957:-

> Through the generosity of the late Mr Wakefield, the hut, the site and a sports field adjoining were leased at a peppercorn

rent. The continuity of this privilege has been made possible by the present owner, Mr Rodney Clarke – well known as the designer of the famous Connaught racing car – who has made it possible for the use of the hall and field to continue until the new hall is erected.

Bisley Cricket Club (in front of the second village hall).
Left to right (rear): Robert Roberts, POD Green, Albert Henbest, P Daborn, Horace Cheeseman, Bill Prosser, Harry Hone, G Cheeseman, G Bond.
(middle): Arthur Clifton, KP Repton, HE Guildford.
(front): H Cole, William Ashcroft, A Daborn, AE Mansfield, Albert Hone, W Newman, R Fish, W Stevens.
Photo: Jim Henbest

Plans for a third hall had already been drawn up in 1955 'to replace the present tumbledown shack'. It was to be a new building situated on the common just off Shaftesbury Road, behind the former Church of England School. A large noticeboard was put there proclaiming 'Site for the BISLEY NEW VILLAGE HALL', but it was a project that would never materialise. A committee was formed representing all village organisations (British Legion, Parochial Church Council, Fire Service, sports clubs, the WI and the two youth clubs) under an independent Chairman (George Bogle) and Treasurer (Walter Cundy), with the purpose of raising £4,500 to build this new hall. The fund had been started with £170 from a Bisley War Memorial Hall Fund that had been dormant since the end of the Second World War. House-to-house collections, carol singing, jumble sales, bazaars, dances, wastepaper collection and other money-raising events were organised over the next few years. A series of very large country fairs, incorporating dog shows and gymkhanas, were planned as the primary fundraising events to be held at two-yearly intervals. The first Country Fair was held on Saturday 22nd June 1957 in the field adjacent to Wilcot House, known as Bisley Sports Ground (neither the present Recreation Ground nor the large open of land on the opposite side of the A322 were suitable as venues for such an event at that time, being largely covered with scrub growth). Over 2,000 people attended the Country Fair which was opened by the actor Ian Carmichael, who also presented the prizes for the various competitions. The next Country Fair was held on Saturday 13th June 1959 in the grounds of the Shaftesbury School, but the event was tinged with more than a little sadness as the school had just closed down. The third and last Country Fair took place on Saturday 24th June 1961 on the 'new Bisley Recreation Ground'[(3)], now cleared of scrub, with many stalls and sideshows including several unusual attractions such as 'Crazy Bikes' and the 'Flying Witch', and there was even a four-mile road race from Woking. The mammoth event attracted almost 3,000 people, including the Bishop of Guildford, and considering that the population of the whole village was less than half this number, that was quite an achievement. The Village Hall Fund had grown to £700 in the first 2 years, £1,300 a year later, £2,000 by 1959 and just over £3,000 after the third Country Fair.

The governing body of the Shaftesbury Homes offered the freehold of the redundant school chapel to the village for £3,500, which at that time seemed an enormous amount. The offer was reluctantly turned down as it would have been beyond the capabilities of the fund, taking into account the additional cost of around £6,000 to convert it into a village hall. To everyone's surprise, the governors responded with a very generous gesture by offering the chapel for a mere £500 prior to the imminent auction at which whole of the estate, apart from a few parts already sold, would go under the hammer on 10th November 1959. The Committee jumped at the offer and the deal was struck. Months of detailed planning and hard negotiating with architects, builders, the Local Planning Authority and Government departments ensued. Then another stroke of luck occurred. The Ministry of Education agreed to make a grant of one-third of the cost of purchase plus one-third of the cost of conversion work. The estimated total amounted to £6,750, though it was said at the time that it would have cost at least £26,000 to construct a similar facility from scratch.

Shaftesbury School Chapel (Later converted into the third village hall).

Details of the conversion from chapel to hall were well described in the local press[4]:-

> The previous softwood floor, which was rotten in places, was removed and 70 tons of hardcore were laid as a foundation for the new floor of Canadian maple by the two local youth clubs[5] working under the supervision of Mr Coxon. That, said Mr Bogle, saved £156 on the contract. The same two youth clubs saved about £100 by voluntary

> work on the car park, and the parish council gave £65 towards the cost of other materials. Although the stage curtains were made professionally, all the others throughout the hall were made by the Women's Institute. Apart from this the Institute also raised £178 14s. 5d. The drive was laid by Mr Coxon and volunteers, and the paving stones were presented by friends in Guildford. What had come to look like a rubbish dump outside suddenly became a garden when Alistair Patterson and the whole of the Goff family descended on it. The building contractor was A Cavey & Son of Bisley, and the whole of the electrical installation was done by Mr Bert Castle assisted by Mr Ted Hill and Mr Castle's son, Neil.

The work was completed for the 'Grand Opening and Stage Show' on Thursday 26th April 1962. A 'Grand Inaugural Dance' was held the following Saturday evening, a 'Jive & Twist Dance' two days later, and a 'May Fair and Grand Draw' on Saturday 5th May 1962. George Bogle remarked[(6)] 'Raising an average of about £9 a week for six years in a community of only 1,200 people is a remarkable achievement of which the village can be justly proud.' Local businesses that had sponsored the opening events included: Aldershot & District Traction Co (bus services and private hire coaches), A Cavey (building contractor), Cherryman Dairy (milkman), A F Coxon (haulage contractor and builders' merchant), Fox Garage (car sales, service and petrol), Glosters (seedsmen and domestic fuel merchants), Hugh Harris (men's tailor), W H Hone (grocer and confectioner), D W Hughes (electrical appliances), Knaphill Service Garage (car sales and petrol), Alan Lawrence (baker and post office), G E Mayhew (butcher), F G Rice (ironmonger), Stanley Wood (newsagent and grocer), Woods Bros (TV, radio, cycles and prams) and Wootton Construction (building contractor).

Loans had been secured and it took several years to clear the outstanding debt of around £500, even though one last big event – a Christmas Fair on Saturday 7th December 1963 – was held to pay off part of the overdraft from the bank.

Not long after this, the vehicular access from the A322 was closed following a fatal accident when a van emerged from the car park hitting a motorcyclist on the main road.

For just over 10 years, there was a flat behind the kitchen with a bedroom upstairs which was let to a resident caretaker, the first being Lee Bailey and the second, and last, one was Rex Evans. These rooms are now used for storage of equipment.

Some years later dry rot was discovered spreading from the main entrance porch into the hall. This doorway was sealed until 1982 when it was made into an interconnecting passage into the new Jubilee Room, belatedly named to commemorate Her Majesty's Silver Jubilee some five years earlier. In 2009, the hitherto flat-roofed Jubilee Room was fitted with a pitched roof and slates matching the main part of the building. This was a vast improvement on the previous roof design which had never blended with the rest of the hall and had started to leak in places. The work was carried out by Howard Parnell Contractors of Lightwater, who also replaced the windows in the Jubilee Room.

---

(1) William Birkbeck Wakefield 1867-1941.

(2) Land that had recently been cleared of vegetation between the original Bisley Church of England Primary School and Ford Road.

(3) *The Woking Review*. March 1957.

(4) *Woking News & Mail*. 3rd May 1962

(5) Bisley Church Youth Club (leader: Richard Clifton) and Bisley Youth Club (leader: Jim Cheeseman).

(6) May Fair programme Saturday 5th May 1962.

Chapter 15

A PLACE TO LIVE

Helen Allingham was a well-known Surrey artist who portrayed many beautiful pastoral scenes of picturesque cottages and farms, depicting images of serenity and cleanliness that seldom, if ever, really existed. A dilapidated property with holes in the thatch, and dirty children in threadbare clothes running around in the dirt in the lane would be transformed into an idyllic scene of Victorian tranquillity, with doves perched on the quaintly undulating cottage roof, smoke gently rising from the chimney, flowers in full bloom in the well-stocked garden, mother with a shining white apron lingering by the garden gate to watch spotlessly clean children at play outside, and so on. Mrs Allingham's watercolour paintings remain in great demand and are reproduced for greetings cards and other goods mainly for those attracted by romantic images of life in the countryside.

The reality of rural housing in this part of Surrey during the Victorian era was often totally different. Few could afford to keep small country cottages in a good state of repair and the occupants lived very hard lives by today's standards, seldom having the time to relax or to wear their best clothes. For instance, Thatched Cottage on The Green at Bisley, the home of Topper (Henry) Gosden, still had a 'dirt' floor in 1934. Thatched roofs would have to be in serious need of attention before they were repaired or replaced, walls tended to be damp, doors and windows were ill-fitting, lanes were dusty in summer and rutted and muddy in winter, and nobody ever took for granted, in the way we do now, the availability of such essentials as proper sanitation, heating, lighting, and water.

In 1909 the Sanitation Inspector reported[(1)] that 'Bisley had approx 40% Privy Cesspits, 40% pail closets, 20% water closets', adding that 'Chertsey RDC[(2)] has purchased a sewage cart with pump and hose but has not yet undertaken scavenging or sewage disposal of the parishes'. The Inspector's report in 1946 included the following recommendation:-

> Many cases of serious nuisance from sewage effluent and inadequate drainage of houses continued to arise during the year in Chobham, West End and Bisley. These conditions are bound to recur, particularly in low lying districts in wet weather, and can only be temporarily abated. Many areas are now too urbanised to permit of (*sic*) primitive methods of disposal of water waste and contents of pail closets to small back gardens. From the aesthetic as well as the Public Health aspect, provision of main drainage is an essential requirement.

The long-awaited and much-needed main drainage sewerage system was at last approved by Bagshot Rural District Council in May 1956 and laid along the main road a few months later. Part of Queens Road was linked to it in 1960 and this section was extended two years later, by which time most of the village had been connected to the sewer.

In 1952 more than half-a-dozen little cottages had no electricity or gas and in 1968 there was still one house (No 3 Reidon Hill Cottages) with only gas lighting downstairs and candles for upstairs. Some small houses had just a range for both cooking and heating before the days of electricity. This would keep one room warm in winter but the rest of the house remained cold. Paraffin oil-heaters were relatively cheap and widely used. There were several local stockists of paraffin, including Underwoods of Bagshot who continued to provide a convenient weekly doorstep delivery of 'Esso Blue' paraffin into the 1960s.

In 1944 the Sanitation Inspector declared[(3)] 'many properties in the Chobham and Bisley area especially have to rely on shallow well waters and many residents have not yet taken advantage of a piped supply even when this exists in proximity to their dwelling'. In 1954 there were 302 houses, of which 19 still relied on wells for drinking water. Almost every cottage in Bisley either had its own well or shared with just one or two others, simply because there was no concentration of houses in any particular place. The wells tended to be quite shallow as there is a high water-table throughout much of the village; some wells were as little as 15 feet deep (4.5 metres). They were usually constructed close to the house and some were even connected by pipework to a tank in the loft from which water could be drawn for daily use once the tank had been filled using a semi-rotary manual pump.

In 1961 West Surrey Farmers' Association were asked to quote for providing a water supply to Strawberry Farm. The offer stated:-

> To supply 970 feet of ¾″ galvanised wrapped and treated iron piping from the cherry tree beside Stafford Lake Road inclusive of trenching… inclusive of backfilling, stop-cock, etc. and Engineers' time, and a charge of £36 3s. 0d. for easement to the Lord of the Manor for crossing the common, all for the sum of £226 0s. 0d.

It may seem very odd that the provision of what are now regarded as essential services never materialised earlier, but the country had been greatly impoverished by the Second World War and afterwards people had endured considerable austerity for a decade or more.

Notwithstanding these difficult times and shortages of materials, Bisley was given street lighting in 1948 after a lengthy fight between those wanted it and those who didn't. It was nothing like as extensive as the network in place today, nor was the illumination in any way comparable with the output of modern lighting fitments. Six swan-neck lampposts were installed at strategic places along the main road, three more in Queens Road, two in Church Lane and one in Shaftesbury Road.

In reality the installation of twelve small street lights with standard filament-bulbs was never going to make a huge impact in terms of illumination, but it did attract wide attention as a result of vociferous condemnation by a small Luddite fraternity within the community who had perceived it as unacceptable urbanisation and who had fought hard to prevent it. This is how it was reported in the *Woking News and Mail*:-

> After 14 years of campaigning by residents, the village of Bisley now has street lighting. The battle started in 1934 when public meetings were held and 'no lighting' advocates won their case. When the campaign for street lighting started Bisley was the most publicised village in the country with newspapers carrying stories about 'England's Darkest Spot... with inhabitants living like savages... 101 years behind the times'. The early meetings were called by Mr J Fuller, who is the present Chairman of the Parish Council, and after two defeats a poll was demanded and again the verdict was against street lighting. The project was then shelved. In 1947 and engineer from Woking Electric Supply Company was invited to explain the technicalities of the scheme and a proposition to install lighting was carried unanimously. Now Bisley has street lighting and the cost is being borne by the Parish Council, which will mean a 3d. rate.

One could expect certain daily rags to use florid language and make disparaging comparisons with 'savages', but their assessment of the time-warp may have been a touch disconcerting as it accorded all too well with the Revd Joseph Cater's opinion in the first chapter of 'Bisley Bits' of how backward these 'natives' actually were:-

> Commercial enterprise has never located in Bisley, for there is not a single shopkeeper in the parish – not even a 'store' in which the trader may vend his varied wares… in humble retirement in a window at the end of some cottage garden may be seen indications that a few sweetmeats are procurable for sufficient consideration. No tradesman, no dealer, nor huckster, no market-place, no fair… and moreover, such a sober, honest, law-abiding people have the inhabitants of this parish ever been, that they have not, and never have had, either the old-fashioned parish constable nor the more modern village policeman. It is true that periodic visits are paid by an official of the kind, who comes from a neighbouring hamlet; but only in order that he may assure himself that such services as he could render are never required. In short, the natives of Bisley are so intensely conservative a people that… they are at least a hundred years behind the times.

So closely-packed are all the houses and bungalows along the A322 today that there is scarcely room to put another dwelling between them. Yet in 1900, going northwards along Port Lane, as it was then called, the traveller would have passed only six properties before reaching the cross-roads at Miles Green: The Willows, The 'Fox Inn' and Rose Cottage on the right-hand side, and Pound Farm and Bedford Cottages on the left. Then continuing up the road to the 'Hen and Chickens', one would have seen just three more: Wilcot House on the right, and Holly Lodge and The Firs on the left-hand side.

Mr William Sidery, a local school teacher writing in 1949, noted:-

> There have been many improvements in the village in the last quarter of a century. Some agricultural land has been sold for building plots where some modern houses and bungalows have been erected to suit the taste of newcomers who appreciate the quiet of the countryside. Enterprising tradesmen have established flourishing businesses so that bread, meat, provisions, coal, etc. can be obtained close at hand. A flourishing transport company has given frequent means of travel to and from the busier centres of the county. The telephone has been introduced. Post Office business is conducted by the village green. A county police station with resident Police Officer has been provided.

> The high road from Guildford to Bagshot has been widened and well paved, and side lanes as well have been made fit for modern traffic. Many of the old cottages and farmhouses are still picturesque and of considerable antiquity. Some have been rendered more fit for habitation by such improvements as lean-to additions and corrugated roofing.

On the subject of corrugated roofing, number 300 Guildford Road, Bisley, was built for the Ellen family just over 50 years ago. It was called Weavers and it replaced an ancient pair of houses, originally called Bedford Cottages, that were later converted into a single dwelling known as Thatched Cottage. However, the thatch on the roof had deteriorated decades before and had been completely replaced with sheets of corrugated iron. These, in turn, had not weathered well, almost rusting through in places. The cottage stood on what was once the far end of Pound Green and the last occupants were Edwin and Mary Hill. The holly hedge in the front garden overhung the footpath so much that people had to step out into the road every time they passed the property.

Sarah Chandler at Combers.

Unless farms and cottages were associated with some local feature, such as Newbridge Farm, Stafford Lake Farm or Pound Farm, they were usually given the name of the folk who lived there. Goodeners, Cobbett's Farm, Combers and Clew's Farm are good examples; all continued to be known by these names long after the respective families had moved out.

The following old buildings have survived to the present time, though some of their ages have been disputed: Newbridge Cottage and Old Cottage are believed to 14th century, Cowshot Manor and Clews Farm originate from the 15th and 16th centuries respectively, Cherry Trees (c1550), Pound Cottage, Bullhousen Farm, Reidonhurst and Heathcote are all said to be 17th century, and the 'Hen and Chickens' public house and 'The Fox' public house date from the 18th century.

Quite a lot of very ancient dwellings that would have been attractive subjects for Mrs Allingham to paint have been knocked down, including: Snowdrop Farm (1964), Lavender Farm, Frythmead, Strawberry Farm (2000), Scott's Farm, Thatched Cottage on The Green, Pole Oak (1850s?), Steadmans Farm (1895), Lafords Farm, Combers (1979), Cobbetts Farm, Thatched Cottage on Guildford Road (1958) and Charity Cottages (1973). The dates in parenthesis indicate when they were demolished. In some cases the houses that replaced them have retained their old name.

Some old places had curious design features that would be regarded as most odd today. For example, the only means of access to the upper floor at Clews Farm was, until the 1940s, a step ladder poking through a hole in the ceiling and, once ascended, one had to be careful to avoid a low beam only 5 feet (1.5 metres) above the floor, slung across the centre of two of the bedrooms. Access to the guest bedroom was through an aperture only 4 feet (1.2 metres) high. Clews Farm also had a priest-hole which was revealed[(4)] when an old iron range was removed from what had once been the kitchen. Heathcote had a hook for holding cured bacon, and a bread oven inside the Inglenook fireplace. Stafford Lake Farm had a sharply sloping floor in one of the bedrooms. Snowdrop Farm, built in 1643, had a tiny staircase, scarcely more than 2 feet (600mm) wide, which made one complete turn up to the bedroom above – not wide enough to admit a chair, let alone a bed!

Wye family at Stafford Lake Farm.

Though Bisley has never had a manor house or any resident gentry, there were some individuals who enjoyed relative prosperity, owning their own land and giving employment to the needy. We shall learn more about them later, but firstly we should look back through the centuries to see how parishioners acquired property, how landholding has evolved and how modern society has developed locally.

Almost all residential dwellings these days are either rented, leased for a fixed period, or in freehold ownership; the last category covering both wholly-owned and mortgaged property. These forms of tenure developed from the feudal system, that was introduced after the Norman Conquest. William the Conqueror claimed that all the land in England belonged to him and he retained about a fifth for his own use. A small amount was entrusted to the church but the largest proportion was, in effect, leased to those Normans who had helped him defeat Harold. These barons, earls and dukes who were allowed to hold land had to swear an oath of allegiance to the king and had to provide him with knights for military service when he demanded it. The barons had complete control of their land, which was known as a manor. These lords of the manor kept as much as they wanted for their own use and divided the rest among their trusted knights. Each knight also had to swear an oath of loyalty and had to provide soldiers, protect the baron and his family from attack and collect taxes when required. The knights, in turn, kept what land they required and distributed the rest to villeins (serfs, who were scarcely better than slaves) and also to a very limited number of free peasants who could pay rent. This created a robust pyramid of power which lasted for several centuries and gave the king the ability to raise an army without the expense of keeping soldiers at his royal court. Everyone knew their place, although many aspired to climb the hierarchical ladder.

The main local unit of power under the feudal system was the manor, controlling judicial, administrative and social organisation with strict control. So much so, in fact, that those at the bottom of the pyramid could be evicted from their patch of land at the will of the lord. They were usually not allowed to leave the manor, they had to ask their lord's permission before they could marry and they had to render a considerable amount of service without remuneration. A small number of peasants were freemen who were in a position to pay an agreed fee for renting their land, but the vast majority were certainly not free and were often treated harshly by their master and his bailiff. The Black Death killed so many up and down the country that some people found themselves able to demand rights and gain concessions. Then there were tradesmen and merchants who became increasingly wealthy and who did not fit into the feudal structure at all and often challenged the system by paying for privileges and marrying into the nobility. Gradually the feudal system became increasingly blurred and started to crumble. By the 1600s the link with military service and national security had almost disappeared, but the basic manorial structure was so strong that in some places it persisted into the twentieth century. At Bisley, for instance, parts of it lasted until the 1920s.

All tenants under the Lord of the Manor had to attend the manorial court at which the lord or his representative presided. Land transfers were recorded on 'court rolls' and, latterly, tenants were given a copy of the entry in the court roll granting them their parcel of land. This became known as copyhold and gave the holders a substantial amount of security, though this form of tenure gradually diminished as more and more tenants became able to pay a small rent rather than render service. The system of succession of title to copyhold land was thus: Upon the death of a man or woman shown on the court roll as being the copyholder, his or her estate owed a 'heriot', normally the best beast, to the Lord of the Manor unless there was sufficient money to pay for the burial of the deceased. When the manorial court was next convened, the heir to the estate would be 'admitted', that is to say entered on the court roll, as the new copyholder upon payment of a small fee, sometimes waived. Copyhold was finally abolished under the Law of Property Act in 1922 and all land held under this form of tenure was made freehold.

Most Bisley folk were very poor, some owning pitifully few possessions, and consequently they were usually treated leniently when rents, fees and taxes became due. Some interesting details are to be found in the records of The General Courts Baron of the Lord of the Manor of Bisley.[(5)] The Chief Steward's Deputy presided at the court on Monday 5th June 1871 which was convened to record the death of Mary Hill, the copyholder of Radsell's Grove (later to become Strawberry Farm), and to allow the admittance (to the copyhold) of James Hill (her son). The legal transfer, shown here, is fairly typical:-

> <u>Death of Mary Hill</u>
> THE HOMAGE present that Mary Hill late one of the Copyhold or Customary Tenants of this Manor who held to her and her heirs by Copy of Court Roll at the will of the Lord according to the custom of the said Manor subject to a Conditional Surrender thereof made by the said Mary Hill to William made and dated the eleventh day of April one thousand eight hundred and forty The several parts and parcels hereinafter mentioned and described of ALL that Copyhold messuage or tenement called Radsell's Grove

with the Barn buildings Orchards gardens and all the Lands thereto belonging with the appurtenances containing by estimation five acres more or less in the Parish of Bisley late in the occupation of John Hill that is to say the north end of the said messuage a small piece of ground before it half the Barn half the yard South end and garden behind the Barn two plots of ground the West side against the other a road to it from the yard about two and a half acres (more or less) also the Hogsty against the Common Held since the last Court so thereof seized Whereupon a Heriot of the best beast became due to the Lord of this Manor but none was seized because the said Mary Hill had no live beast at the time of her death.

Her Will

THE HOMAGE also present the Will of the said Mary Hill dated the sixth day of March one thousand eight hundred and sixty five the original whereof is now produced and read in open Court whereby she gave and devised unto her son James his heirs and assigns ALL that Copyhold messuage or tenement garden ground and pieces or parcels of Arable Land thereunto adjoining and belonging containing in the whole by estimation two acres and a half more or less situate lying and being in the Parish of Bisley then in the occupation of herself and the said James Hill To hold the same unto and to the use of her said son James Hill his heirs and assigns forever.

Admittance of James Hill

NOW at this Court upon the first Proclamation came here into Court in his proper person the said James Hill and humbly prayed to be admitted tenant to The several parts and parcels hereinafter mentioned and described of ALL that Copyhold messuage or Tenement called Radsell's Grove with the barn buildings Orchards Gardens and all the Lands thereto belonging with the appurtenances containing by estimation five acres more or less in the Parish of Bisley late in the occupation of John Hill that is to say the North end of the said messuage a small piece of ground before it half the Barn half the yard south end and garden behind the Barn two plats of ground the West side against the other a road to it from the yard about two and a half acres (more or less) also the Hogsty against the common which came into the hands of the Lord of this Manor on the death of the said Mary Hill to whom the Lord of the Manor aforesaid by his Deputy Steward aforesaid granted the

> same and delivered seizin thereof by Heriot To hold unto the same James Hill his heirs and assigns for ever (subject to the before mentioned Conditional Surrender) by copy of Court Roll at the will of the Lord according to the custom of the said Manor by the yearly apportioned rent of one penny Heriot when it shall happen suit of Court and other services Rent 1d Heriot and customs therefore formerly due and of right accustomed and so he was admitted Tenant thereof in form aforesaid Gave to the Lord as a fine for such his admittance as appears in the margin and his fealty was respited.
> Fine £12 Examined W Haydon Smallpiece, Steward

The quaint words and expressions, such as ‘messuage’, ‘seizin’ and ‘fealty was respited’,[6] were standard legal terms of the day, and the format for Surrender and Admittance was much the same in almost every case, with only property and tenancy details changing to suit the circumstances of each new agreement. However, the farm called Radsell’s Grove, small as it was, had previously been divided equally between two brothers, hence the ‘half of this’ and ‘half of that’, which must have presented something of a challenge to record with any accuracy on the Court Roll. To add to the confusion, one brother had called his half Raspberry Grove. Luckily, both parts of the property were quickly reunited.

An amusing story passed down through three generations of the Hill family, and of which there is no reason to doubt, concerned the heriot mentioned in the first paragraph of this Admittance document. Lord Onslow's bailiff accepted there was no beast on the farm because, by the time he arrived, kindly neighbours had spirited away the livestock to other parts of the village and cleaned and scrubbed the yard and buildings so well that no trace of recent animal occupation remained. For all we know, this ruse may have been tried on other occasions but nobody would dare record the trick for risk of incriminating those responsible.

There was an almshouse at Wokingham, founded with a bequest of £7,000 from the Reverend Henry Lucas, in which nine elderly Bisley residents[(7)] were given accommodation. The Henry Lucas Hospital was built in 1663 to take in 16 elderly male occupants. To qualify for a place, they had to be 'single men when elected, and should so continue, should be of the age of 50 years at least, of sober life and conversation, poor and impotent persons, decayed in estate by sickness or other misfortune and not by their own wicked courses, not having of their own the clear value of £20, such as should be born, or inhabiting three years at least, in some of the parishes…' in the Forest of Berkshire or the Bailiwick of Surrey in or near the forest. None the certificates of entry of those from Bisley convey any indication of the straitened circumstances of these old gentlemen, but the bureaucratic procedure and the cost to the parish in securing a place for at least one of them was not insignificant:-

		L	s	d
1852	To the expenses of taking JAMES KEATES to OAKINGHAM HOSPITAL	L	s	d
Nov 1	Hire of horse	0	6	0
	Paid on the road at Bracknell for Refreshment	0	0	8½
	Ditto the gates for two carts	0	0	8
	Do. for refreshment at Oakingham for five	0	6	5
	Do. for ostler	0	0	4
	Do. at Bracknell on return	0	0	10
	Do. at Chobham	0	3	6
Dec 2	Do. for refreshments 7 other expenses to London	0	8	2
	Fairs for three to and from London by rail	0	18	0
	Officers costs London 2/6 each	0	5	0
	To taking of JAMES KEATES & his goods to HOSPITAL OAKINGHAM	0	10	0
		2	19	7½

		L	s	d
1852				
Dec 9	To a part of the expenses of taking JAMES KEATES to OAKINGHAM HOSPITAL to present him to the MASTER of the said HOSPITAL	L	s	d
	A hired horse	0	6	0
	For refreshments on the road at Bracknell	0	0	8½
	To the gate for two carts	0	0	8
	For refreshments at Oakingham for five	0	6	5
	To Horseler (ostler)	0	0	4
	Do. at Chobham	0	3	6
	Fare for one Churchwarden to London by rail	0	6	0
	Refreshments for him	0	1	0
		1	4	7½

These expenses were incurred by Stephen Steptoe who may already have been an Overseer at this time. The original claim, written in his own hand, was kindly made available by his great grand-daughter, Miss Eva Elizabeth Steptoe.

There were several Bisley men who were just 'day labourers'; that is to say they sought work today not knowing whether they would be hired again tomorrow. Some of them were probably single men but others may have had a family to support. However, for two centuries prior to 1834, the poorest of the poor had to rely on parish support which was controlled by an Overseer for the Poor. In Bisley, as in other parishes, the Overseer was appointed annually by the vestry, comprising the minister, churchwardens and elected parishioners. He had to ensure the welfare of the poorest sort and was empowered to raise charitable funds. If he was good at his job he might retain the post of Overseer for several years.

People suddenly finding themselves without shelter might occasionally be received by a kindly neighbour with a spare room, but villages sometimes had a 'poor house' for these unfortunates. Some villages also had a 'Pest House' as well, where anyone who had contracted a contagious disease would live in isolation until they recovered, or died. The is no record of a Pest House in Bisley but there was a 'poor' or 'parish house' in 1686 because the Churchwarden's account for that year included 3s.6d 'given for thatching ye parish house'.

When the Revd Dr Andrew Lamont died twenty-five years later, leaving £100 in his Will for the poor, it was agreed to acquire more parish houses, spending £50 10s. 0d on two semi-detached cottages in Queens Road and letting them at a concessionary rent. These Charity Cottages, as they would become known, needed extensive repairs and improvements but fortunately the remainder of the legacy was just about enough to cover the cost. One of these cottages had a sitting tenant in his mid-eighties, William Tunnell, who was allowed to remain there for the rest of his life.

Ann Hill and Daniel Stevens at Charity Cottages.

What became of the original poor house is not known, but a century-and-a-half later the families living in Charity Cottages, George and Ann Hill on one side and Daniel and Maria Stevens on the other, had their names recorded in the Baptism Register in 1862 when Jane Hill and Benjamin George Stevens were christened on 16th February and 6th April respectively. Moving forward another hundred years, the old cottages were sold for redevelopment following the death of the last tenant, Mrs Pocock. The name Charity Cottage, however, lives on as the name of the replacement dwelling.

Annual accounts in the 17th and 18th centuries show payments in kind as well as money being given to individuals 'for relief'. The Overseers were supposed to be fair to the poor without being too lenient. They could not be extravagant with parish money and they had to be very firm with those who came a-begging from outside the parish, moving them on swiftly. Necessitous individuals who received parish relief were generally those who could not work, or who were too old to work and had nobody to look after them, people who had fallen upon hard times, orphans and the mentally ill. Vagabonds received little or no assistance but on one occasion a sickly vagrant was paid 2d. to leave because, had he died in Bisley, the parish would have had to pay for his burial.

Everything changed, or was supposed to change, under the notorious Poor Law Amendment Act of 1834, which provided a simple solution to the seemingly intractable problem of how to deal with able-bodied paupers who chose not to work but to live off the meagre parish rate instead. The Act created a national administrative framework for the relief of poverty by establishing 'workhouses'. If a parish was not large enough to establish its own workhouse, it had to collaborate with neighbouring villages to build and operate a 'Union Workhouse' for all of the villages in the 'Union'. The principle was simply this: outdoor relief for the able-bodied was abolished, conditions in workhouses had to be harsher than that experienced by the lowest-paid workers in order to discourage the idle poor from seeking refuge, and those who were incarcerated were required to work to nationally-approved standards.

Each workhouse had strict segregation of men, women and children, and so destitute families were separated with little or no further contact between them. Only infants were allowed contact with their mothers, while brothers and sisters were kept apart and denied access to their parents. All semblance of family support, love and dignity was stripped away. Workhouse attire consisted of coarse cotton shirts or shapeless shifts and rough trousers. The daily regime started early, the food was meagre and the work was arduous and repetitive. People were free to leave at any time but, if they had other family members there, they had to leave together. It is little wonder that the Victorian poor lived in fear of the workhouse. Many impoverished folk preferred to avoid the ignominy of having to go there, suffering dreadful living conditions while maintaining an independent existence outside.

Guildford had a workhouse adjacent to St Luke's Hospital and the one at Bagshot was located next to the old Fire Station in Guildford Road, but the one to which the paupers of Bisley usually went was the Chertsey Union Workhouse at Ottershaw. Most of those who entered its dreaded portals would never have the wherewithal to leave. Sometimes those who were able to get out of the establishment and regain a dignified life in the village fell upon hard times again and had to return. Twenty-three people from Bisley died inside that institution between 1860 and 1900 at ages ranging from 1 (Edward Gosden who died just a few weeks after entering the workhouse in 1871 with his mother) to 91 (Elizabeth Stevens who departed this world in 1869).

The harshness of the workhouse was the primary reason why the former parish-based regime continued to exist in many places, including Bisley, well into mid-Victorian times. Stephen Steptoe, who was the Overseer at Bisley in 1864, made a list (**Appendix I**) of the recipients of a purchase from Arthur Cutler, a grocer and draper at Knaphill, totalling £7 19s. 6d, which was spent solely for the benefit of the poor. The handwritten order has been preserved and it includes the value of goods each person received, but unfortunately there are no details of the items supplied, though we may suppose that they included clothing as well as food.

Radical changes to the Welfare State occurred in 1946 and 1948 with the introduction of National Insurance and a National Health Service that ensures benefit for unemployment and sickness and free treatment for illness. However, the workhouses did not close immediately, but developed into doss-houses for vagrants who would otherwise have slipped through the net of the Welfare State. These 'men of the road' knew the location of each 'spike', as the workhouse was known, some of which would become regular stopping points on their circuit of the countryside, where they could get a bath, a shave, some food and a bed for the night in exchange for a token amount of work. The regime at the workhouses had become far less strict than in their heyday but most of them would not allow tramps to stay longer than one night. The Common Lodging House at Bagshot was registered(8) to accommodate 32 male lodgers, but rarely had more than a few staying overnight at any one time.

These vagrants were a familiar sight as they passed through Bisley making their way on foot between Bagshot and Guildford carrying all their meagre belongings. Occasionally they would stop to ask for water or unwanted clothing from kind-hearted villagers. They had a clever system of fixing bottle-tops in discreet places to identify houses where other itinerants might receive sympathetic attention. These tramps preferred the road to a settled existence and some of them were surprisingly well-educated yet had lost everything as a result of alcoholism, family problems or being unable to settle down after war service.

As early as the 16th century some people in Bisley had become relatively prosperous and made a Will for the disposal of their possessions after death. The Will of John Cobbat was made on 3rd January 1592 and the inventory of his belongings for probate was valued at £5 15s. 9d:-

It	*he hade in his purse*		*xijd*
It	*his a parrell*	*vs*	
It	*a tabell a forme and arounde tabell &*		
	a chare to stoles		*xviijd*
It	*a cobbard with xi oulde platters & to peuter pottes*		
	thre canstickes	*xs*	
It	*the brass*	*xs*	
It	*all the sylve weare*	*ijs*	*xid*
It	*all the beddinge of to beddes and that long*		
	the to them	*xiijs*	*iiijd*
It	*thre oulde chestes*		*xiid*
It	*all the Lomber*	*iiijs*	*iiijd*
It	*a Cowe and a mare*	*xxvjs*	*viijd*
It	*the corne upon the grounde and the fodder*		
	in the barne	*xxxs*	
It	*foure flytches of bacen and iiij egges*	*xs*	

John Hone made a Will on 23rd February 1594 in the presence of John Kobbat the elder, John Avis, Thomas Goringe and William Hone. This inventory, totalling £9 1s. 0d, has even more unfortunate spelling errors than the one listed above:-

It	*primis he had in his purse*			*xiid*
It	*his wearinge aparrill*		*vis*	*viijd*
It	*a table and a forme, to stoles*			*xijd*
It	*the brasse and pewter*		*iijs*	
It	*a broche and a tryfte & potthockes*			*viijd*
It	*to flocke beddes with the bolsters and coverlyts and a blankat & a peare of shetes*		*viis*	*xd*
It	*a bedsted, to chestes and all other Lomber*		*iijs*	
It	*foure bushells of Rye in the House*		*vis*	
It	*thre akars of winter corne one the grounde*		*xxxs*	
It	*five akars of ottes on the grounde*		*xvs*	
It	*on Cow, to hekefers and foure small bollockes and a lyttell mare*	*vl*		
It	*on tegge*			*xviijd*
It	*a Karte and a donge potte*		*iijs*	*iiijd*
It	*fyve hennes and a Coke*		*ijs*	
	Sum	*ixl*		*xiid*

Possessions such as these were rather more than most villagers owned in the sixteenth century, and therefore it was important to make a Will. Several people left legacies for the benefit of the poor of the parish: John Farnham died and was buried on the same day as his Will was written,[(9)] 23rd April 1585. Among his bequests was 8d. for 'the poor men's box at Bisley'. Likewise, Thomas Underwood left 4d.

for the poor men's box (1585). The widowed Alice Bonsey gave £12 12s. 0d. (1614), Miss Agnes Attfield left £12 0s. 0d. (1623), John Hone provided £2 10s. 0d. (1677) from which accrued interest was to be paid annually to the poor and, as previously noted, the Revd Dr Andrew Lamont bequeathed the grand sum of £100 0s. 0d. (1709) which was wisely invested.

A series of events involving territorial dispossession and repossession nearly seven hundred years ago resulted in a quite extraordinary boundary settlement that has endured to this day. Two consecutive years of unusually bad weather ruined the harvest in 1314 and 1315, which compounded the plight of many people who were already suffering terrible hardship under the punitive regime of Edward II. Many died of starvation because they were suddenly unable to feed themselves and could not afford the highly inflated prices of basic food. These unsettled times had far-reaching repercussions, with fluctuating labour sometimes leading to land disposals. It is not stated exactly why Amicia and Thomas, her son, had to part with their sizeable property in Bisley but it is recorded that this roughly triangular area of nearly 43 acres (17.4 hectares) of arable land in the north-east corner of the village was acquired legitimately by John and Agnes Arderne. The Arderne family was of some standing in Surrey and John's grandson became Sheriff of Surrey in 1409.[(10)]

Now King Edward's close relationship with Piers Gaveston, a much despised courtier in royal circles, was known throughout the kingdom and even reached the ears of the King of France after Edward's marriage to his daughter, Isabella. Gaveston took great advantage of this favouritism and humiliated other noblemen at court. The King himself alienated the lords by placing Gaveston in a powerful position, granting him great titles and giving him vast estates. The King's overt closeness to Gaveston quickly became a great embarrassment to Queen Isabella and she eventually left him and returned to the continent. Meanwhile, Gaveston was captured at Warwick Castle by several knights and killed with an axe. Edward II instructed a steward to take possession of Gaveston's estates on behalf of the Crown and the Arderne's estate was mistakenly seized. The King abdicated in 1327 but within a few months was murdered by members of his former entourage '*with a hotte broche putte thro the secret place posteralle*'.

John Arderne and his wife then petitioned for the restitution of their land, taking the matter to Parliament and Edward III. Their property was soon returned to them but, during the period of misappropriation, the parish boundary of Bisley had receded from the edge of Scotts Grove Road to the other side of Sandpit Lane, leaving their land some 250 metres from the nearest point of the village boundary. This separated area became known as Bisley Detached, and has remained a detached portion of the civil parish of Bisley ever since. It is now bounded by Horsell on two sides and Chobham on the other.

---

(1) *Health & Sanitary Conditions*, Chertsey RDC 1909.

(2) RDC = Rural District Council. Bagshot RDC was established as the new district authority in 1933.

(3) *Health & Sanitary Conditions*, Chertsey RDC 1944.

(4) *Woking Review*, November 1949.

(5) Rt Hon William Hillier Onslow, GCMG, PC, 4th Earl of Onslow, 1853-1911, Lord of the Manor 1870-1911.

(6) Messuage = dwelling-house with outbuildings and land. Seizin = posession of land by freehold. Fealty was respited = suspension of the oath of fidelity and allegiance to the Lord of the Manor.

(7) John Cobbett 26-03-1672, George Massey 01-08-1681, Thomas Taylor 05-08-1700, Henry Daborn 01-08-1720, Humphrey ffield 06-08-1753, John Stiles 02-08-1784, James Fleet 29-02-1816, William Cobbett 03-11-1831 and James Kates 02-12-1852.

(8) *Health & Sanitary Conditions*, Chertsey RDC1921.

(9) *Surrey Probate Inventories*.

(10) *A History of Chobham*.

Chapter 16

FROM FARMING TO FACTORY

We have no clear picture of the extent to which the inhabitants of Bisley were reliant upon help from Chertsey Abbey in the early days, but we know they were basically subsistence farmers who were scarcely able to provide for the needs of themselves and their families by working the infertile land. We presume they received assistance in return for supplying small quantities of produce that they could ill-afford to hand over, and that gradually, as economic and social frameworks began to develop, payment was received for surplus produce and goods and services were purchased from travelling peddlers and tradesmen. Parishioners developed certain skills of their own and by the sixteenth and seventeenth centuries skilled tradesmen were so proficient and well organised that nobody was allowed to practise certain trades until an apprenticeship had been completed.

In 1668 Henry Pritchard, a Bisley labourer, had to appear at the Quarter Sessions for trying to set up as a blacksmith without having firstly served the required seven-year apprenticeship. Likewise, seven years later, Thomas Blundell, who was a tailor, had to face the court for attempting to be a mercer (draper), aromater (grocer) and tallow-chandler, trades to which he had not been apprenticed. In all probability these activities presented competition to established tradesmen in Bisley or neighbouring villages, who duly reported the upstarts to the Lord of the Manor.

Around this time the population of the village was around 200 to 250 souls, possibly not much more than it had been three hundred years earlier when the Black Death severely depleted both urban and rural communities alike. The main difference in the seventeenth century was that, by then, a highly developed social hierarchy of freemen (mostly larger farmers), copyholders (smaller farmers and tradesmen), villeins (tied peasants), day labourers and the poor had evolved and which was structured upon the manorial system that prevailed across most of the country. In Bisley, for instance, one was not allowed to sit in church on Sunday wherever one chose, as seating was allocated according to the family's position in the community; labourers had to stand at the back.

Many free and tied tenant farmers would undoubtedly have had other jobs, practicing some craft or trade to augment their income, and some would be elected by the vestry to hold an essential parochial office, such as parish clerk, churchwarden, way-warden, overseer or constable. Then there were other obligations: mending roads, keeping water-courses flowing, repairing rails around the church and, of course, compulsory archery practice on Sundays. Bisley had a two-acre archery field, called the 'Butts', situated in part of the copyhold belonging to a member of the large Cobbett family and which adjoined Nultrow

Common Field. An earth bank would have formed the butts for catching arrows that missed the targets.

It is difficult to build an accurate picture of the gradual move from cultivation of the land and rearing livestock to taking up other employment, because occupation is so rarely shown in manorial records, parish records or wills. Most of the non-agricultural occupations that are recorded between 1500 and 1851 for Bisley are shown below, but there are not enough of them to give any meaningful indication of this transition:-

linen weaver	William Rickson	1584	(Quarter Sessions)
tailor	Edward Oslam	1598	(Quarter Sessions)
miller	John Swayne	1601	(Quarter Sessions)
victualler	Thomas Chandler	1637	(Will)
cooper	Thomas Rogers	1639	(Burial)
thatcher	Henry Cobbett	1641	(Burial)
weaver	George Wickman	1661	(Lay Subsidies)
weaver	John Cobbett	1661	(Lay Subsidies)
tailor	Thomas Blundell	1675	(Quarter Sessions)
flax dresser	Thomas Taylor	1700	(Burial)
weaver	Henry Wickman	1706	(Burial)
weaver	Henry Whittall	1729	(Burial)
brick burner	George Kidder	1732	(Will)
poulterer	John Whitehall	1754	(Burial)
brickmaker	George Hill	1806	(Father of baptised child)
wheelwright	James Daborn	1806	(Father of baptised child)
innkeeper	Edward Smith	1813	(Father of baptised child)
brewer	James Burchett	1818	(Will)
broom-maker	Samuel Cheeseman	1819	(Father of baptised child)
shopkeeper	Thomas Gosden	1821	(Father of baptised child)
thatcher	Stephen Steptoe	1823	(Will)
chimney-sweeper	John Bath	1834	(Father of baptised child)

sweep	John Bath	1841	(Bisley Census)
nurseryman	James Hone	1841	(Bisley Census)
shoe maker	James Blackman	1841	(Bisley Census)
schoolmaster	Thomas Martin	1841	(Bisley Census)
schoolmistress	Charlotte Spong	1841	(Bisley Census)
sawyer	George Grey	1841	(Bisley Census)
publican	Edward Smith	1841	(Bisley Census)
chandler	Charles Ellis	1841	(Bisley Census)
grocer	George Sawkins	1841	(Bisley Census)
haybinder	Frank Taylor	1851	(Bisley Census)
sawyer	William Oliver	1851	(Bisley Census)
police constable	William Lambert	1851	(Bisley Census)
grocer and baker	John Slyfield	1851	(Bisley Census)
governess	Mary Hepham	1851	(Bisley Census)
victualler	Edward Smith	1851	(Bisley Census)
railway labourer	George Robinson	1851	(Bisley Census)
launderess	Amelia Hill	1851	(Bisley Census)
blacksmith	John Mose	1851	(Bisley Census)
dressmaker	Elizabeth Harding	1851	(Bisley Census)

When the 1812 Parochial Registers Act took effect at the beginning of the following year, parishes had to show the father's occupation of each child recorded in the Baptism Register.

We can now see that 341 babies were baptised in Bisley during the 37 year period from 1813 to 1850 (an average of about nine per year, of which many died in infancy). The more interesting statistics are that 230 fathers were agricultural labourers (67%) and another 58 were farmers (17%). Of the remaining children entered in the book, many were 'baseborn', the offspring of unmarried mothers, in which case the father's name was rarely recorded, even when known.

Lawrence's bakery delivery van.
Photo: Burn & Martin Collection by courtesy of Surrey History Centre

In the year of Queen Victoria's death (1901), 29 babies' names were entered in the register but only four of their fathers (14%) were labourers, the others being: baker, nursery gardener, carpenter (twice), handle maker, ironmonger, painter (twice), butcher (twice), horse keeper (twice), barber, solicitor, core maker, plumber, bandmaster, engineer, bookbinder, cabinet maker, bricklayer (twice), teapot handle maker, traveller and bottle maker. What had hitherto been a slow but progressive movement away from land-based employment rose sharply during the Victorian era in much of the countryside; Bisley being no exception. Valerie Porter asserts[(1)] that 'by 1850, for the first time in Britain's history, as many people were living in towns as in the countryside but their roots remained rural; most town dwellers still had close relatives in the countryside and liked to make day trips there for fresh air and the scenery'.

The incumbent of the parish church sometimes worked the land but his main remuneration came from parishioners who were obliged to give one-tenth (a tithe) of the 'fruits of the land'. Cash payments in lieu of harvest produce increasingly became the accepted form of settlement, but resentment and bitterness over one's liability had festered for generations in those who believed the system was inherently unfair. Tithe apportionment was enacted to ensure a more equitable arrangement by assessing each person's holding and setting a notional value upon it. This entailed making an accurate Tithe Map and Apportionment for each parish to set a fair rent-charge, and introducing the flexibility to apply indexation as commodity prices rose. Even as late as 1911 a re-apportionment of the Rent Charge had to be carried out on Field No 107 (3 acres, 1 rod and 23 perches, approx 1.33 hectares) which was to be sub-divided to form 13 valuable building plots. No action could be taken until individual amounts had been established. The total amount payable to the Rector was only £1 3s. 0d. per year for the whole field, but due process had to be followed, and settlement reached on a fair division of 23 shillings into 13 portions, before the new houses[(2)] could be built and a new track created (the one that now provides pedestrian access from Clews Lane to Bisley Primary School). Tithing was finally abolished throughout the land in 1936.

The valuer who conducted the 1846 Tithe Apportionment for Bisley estimated that there were 948 acres and thirteen perches (approximately 384 hectares)[(3)] of which:-

Acres	Roods	Perches		
503	-	38	53.2%	arable
259	2	19	27.3%	heath and common
100	-	-	10.5%	meadow and pasture
30	-	-	3.2%	houses and gardens
20	1	2	2.1%	glebe
20	-	-	2.1%	copse
14	3	35	1.6%	roads

(The discrepancy of one perch is negligible.) One can calculate that arable land represented over three-quarters of all land available for agricultural use (arable, meadow and pasture, glebe and copse) yet a hundred years later the proportion had dropped dramatically despite the more widespread use of mechanised equipment, and the powers introduced during the war years (1939-1945) under the Cultivation of Lands Order 1939 to require as much land as possible to be cultivated. In 1846 a total of 170.9 bushels[(4)] of wheat were produced, 303.2 bushels of barley and 436.4 bushels of oats, the respective prices being 7s. 0¼d., 3s. 11d. and 2s. 9d. per bushel.

Bert Hill accompanied by a young boy. 1960

Up to the nineteenth century, farming had been the primary source of Britain's wealth and in 1900 there were still 22 farms and smallholdings in Bisley. A century ago one could scratch a living for a family of four by farming just an acre or two, yet one cannot support an average-sized family on less than a hundred acres (approximately 40 hectares) today. At the present time less than 4% of land in the village is being actively tilled for agriculture or horticulture. The last farm with dairy cows in the village ceased milk production a decade ago, when the market price of milk was being artificially suppressed to below the cost of production by aggressive third-party retailing. The only people still farming land in Bisley today are doing so on a part-time basis and have additional occupations to supplement their income from the land.

The Act of Parliament that changed the landscape of Bisley more profoundly than any other was the General Enclosure Act of 1836. This ended the farming system of strip cultivation in open fields, usually called 'common fields', which had been practised in the village and in many other places for centuries. One should note that the term 'field' meant an unenclosed area where open field farming was carried out. Conversely, if the land was enclosed it was called a 'close'.

Common fields were large unenclosed tracts of arable land, owned by the Lord of the Manor, where tenants were allocated a strip, or strips, in all the fields so that they could rotate crop production and include a fallow year. There would be at least three common fields to achieve this rotation, though Bisley had five comparatively small ones, suggesting that two or three of them may have been grouped together. Though there is no information on this point, it may have been necessary to operate a four-year rotation of crops here, instead of the more usual three, because the soil in this district is so deficient in nitrogen. This would enable beans (legumes) to be included in the cycle to improve the uptake of nitrogen in succeeding years. In the four-and-a-half centuries that Bisley operated strip cultivation, the names of the five common fields changed thus:-

1405	1605	1712	1792	1847[5]
Le Eltrowe	Neltrow	Nottrough	Neltro	Nultrow
Wydecroft	Widcroft		Whitecroft	Wilcot
	Southash	Southerge		Southridge
Northull	Northill	North Hills	North Hill	Churchbourne Mead
	Burcroft	Burah		Burkit

Nultrow Common Field extended westwards from the A322 incorporating what is now Arethusa Way and South Road.

Wilcot Common Field adjoined the eastern side of the A322 all the way up from Bisley Primary School to Wilcot Gardens and stretching three-quarters of the way over to Church Lane where it abutted Southridge Common Field.

Southridge Common Field had its southern and eastern boundaries along the roadside in Clews Lane between the Rectory to the T-junction and, from there, up Church Lane to the rear gardens of the houses at the end of Orchid Drive.

Churchbourne Mead started on the other side of the T-junction at the end of Clews Lane running roughly northwards towards Chobham in a narrow belt each side of the little stream as far as the nursery now called North Hills.

Burkit Common Field lay against the parish boundary on the high ground a little to the south of Oldhouse Lane.

Commenting on the allocation of individual plots in the seventeenth century survey, Gray[6] remarks that the 'few small common fields' at Bisley together comprised about 100 acres but there was 'no symmetrical distribution of acres among the field divisions', adding that this mattered little from the agricultural point of view because nearly all the open fields fell within a dozen copyholds and the total area was greatly exceeded by the acreage of enclosed land in the village. Dr Gray added that 'nor had the Bisley fields changed much during the two centuries preceding the (1605) survey, if we may judge from the mention of three of them[7] in an indenture of 6 (the sixth year of the reign of) Henry IV'.

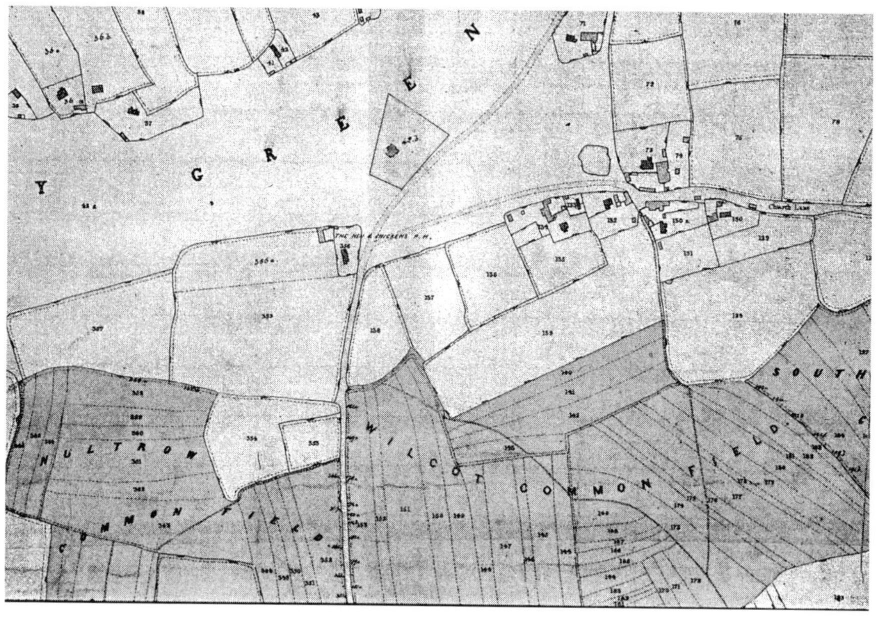

Part of the common fields.

The open field system had generally been in decline for some time but Bisley became one of the last villages in Surrey to abandon it, even though each person was to be allocated a more compact parcel of land roughly equal in area to the strips he tilled in the common fields. Possible reasons for the delay could have been a general reluctance to invest time and effort in putting in stock-proof boundaries, or simply failure to see the benefit of making such a radical change in arable farming.

The abandonment of communal tillage had taken place in much of the country without recourse to legislation, but from the mid-1700s there were literally thousands of acts of Parliament for specific enclosures, including almost 50 in Surrey. The law was simplified by the 1836 Act which allowed commissioners to continue with the process of enclosure without direct reference to Parliament. The Final Award for Bisley was not made until 1858 and it was some decades later before it was reluctantly implemented.

Manorial control of parts of Bisley did not disappear altogether with enclosure, but continued right up to 17th May 1968 when the last vestiges of manorial land – the commons and some remaining pieces of roadside verges[(8)] – were acquired by Surrey County Council.

Generations ago very few individuals who led sober, honest and God-fearing lives had any details about their personal lives recorded for posterity. For instance, we should never have known that John Swaine was a miller, had he not been indicted for grand larceny in 1601. Where did he practise his trade, one wonders? There were no windmills within reasonable daily walking distance of Bisley and the four nearest water-driven corn mills were situated in neighbouring villages. There were two on the Windle Brook at Windlesham (Hook Mill and Windlesham Mill) and two on the Mill Bourne at Chobham (Hurst Mill[(9)] and Emmett's Mill). A third type of mill called a malt quern, of which the one at Frimley Green[(10)] is believed to have been the only example of its kind in the district, was driven by a horse-gin which turned the millstone.

George Kidder, George Hill and others who made bricks, tiles and drains in the eighteenth and nineteenth centuries made a good living from this trade. There were half-a-dozen brick fields in Bisley, Knaphill and Chobham during this time, though the one in Kiln Lane at Bisley was the first to go out of business, either because the clay seam became exhausted or because of the brick tax introduced in 1784. Kiln Lane brickworks produced hand-made clay roofing tiles as well as red bricks,[(11)] baked in a kiln or a clamp, many of which had distinctive dark blue ends thought to result from gorse being introduced during firing to increase the temperature in the kiln. The last remaining cottages built with Bisley bricks have quite recently been demolished, but a few whole bricks have been salvaged and fragments of tiles and brick may still be found halfway along Kiln Lane where the business was located. The brick kiln and the adjacent 4 acre (1.6 hectare) clay field called Kiln Close were mentioned in the 1666 marriage settlement between Thomas Collier and Susan Cocks, and the Will of Stephen Steptoe of 1823 also refers to '… one close of land called or known by the name of Brickkiln Close'.

Frank Taylor's stated trade as a hay-binder hardly seems to have been a full-time occupation, but he may also have been a rope-maker, such was the great demand for rope and twine made from flax.

Thomas Taylor had been a flax-dresser in the seventeenth century, and flax-dressing was one of several stages in the process to turn the fibre from the flax, or linseed, plant into linen. Flax was widely grown in the area mainly for its fibre to make linen and flax hemp rope, but linseed oil, medicines and dye could also be extracted from various parts of the plant. Flexlands at Chobham takes its name from flax, and examples of clothing made from local linen woven in the 1700s and 1800s, and preserved today, are as strong as the day they were made. The number of weavers and tailors in Bisley in early days suggests that linen cloth-and-garment making was a common cottage industry.

The Fox Inn. 1931

Travelling forward to the nineteenth and twentieth centuries, inn-keeping was carried out at more establishments in Bisley than is generally realised. 'The Fox Inn' provided bed and breakfast until the 1960s, and welcomed passing coaches with a large notice proclaiming 'Tea Rooms', which was affixed to a separate corrugated sheet steel building with a wooden frame located at the side of the pub. This 'tin' refreshment room became a regular stopping point for coaches which often parked on the forecourt of the Fox Garage which closed on Sundays, much to the annoyance of Reg Burn, who had no hesitation in making them move off his premises. Although a line of posts was eventually installed between the two frontages to overcome this problem, there was no animosity between the Burns and the Taylors at 'The Fox Inn', as Terry Burn, the garage proprietor's eldest son, became engaged to Barbara Taylor, the licensee's daughter. 'The Fox Café' closed years ago but the building was not demolished until 1988. The inn had been strategically located at the crossroads in the days when Kiln Lane, and the continuation of the track across the common to Pirbright and beyond, had been a well-used thoroughfare. The original part of the building is still visible from the outside, though now surrounded by later extensions. 'The Fox' was once owned by Ashby Brewery in Staines which was taken over by Simonds of Reading in 1930. The sign of 'The Hop Leaf', the trademark of H & G Simonds, was displayed at both 'The Fox' and the 'Hen and Chickens' until Simonds was bought by Courage in 1960. The 'Hen and Chickens' public house is also a thriving business and is well-situated in the heart of the village. It too has been much altered in the course of time and, like 'The Fox', part of the original structure can still be seen from the outside.

The Barley Mow.

Few people these days know that Bisley once had two other public houses, both of which are believed to have provided overnight accommodation for travellers now and again. One was called 'The Yew Tree'. It was situated near the junction of what is now School Close and the A322 and was demolished in early Victorian times. Its last licensee was Henry Eacott, the great-grandfather of Albert Eacott who lived at the end of Ford Road and who will be remembered by some of the older generation. The fourth pub was called 'The Barley Mow' and was to be found at the junction of Chobham Road and Barley Mow Lane. This establishment finally closed its doors to the public in 1921 by which time that part of Bisley had been transferred to Knaphill.

The Post Office in Bisley has moved from shop to shop. It started in the front room of Elm House (later Elmfield) in Church Lane where Mr & Mrs Percival Whitehorn had a village grocery. It was transferred to Lawrence's bakery next to the 'Hen & Chickens', and then back across the road to the stores on the corner, where it has remained ever since.

Queenie and Alan Lawrence at their bakery and post office.
Photo: Burn & Martin Collection by courtesy of Surrey History Centre

People who set up in business in a small way during the reigns of Victoria and Edward VII often worked at home and had a sign by the gate advertising some trade or craft, such as 'Boot maker' or 'Seamstress'; while those needing retail premises for selling to the public and for storing goods either took over existing shops or used one room in their house as a shop. In Bisley and the surrounding villages there were many of these 'front-room shops', some of which were in very strange locations and never seemed to have any customers, although one or two even survived into the second half of the twentieth century.

Among those who started successful enterprises in the early 1900s were: W D Bayliss (tree surgeon), Albert Cavey (general builder), Frederick Coxon (haulage and builder's merchant), W Dealtry (newsagent), M J Fennell (grocer), William Figg (vetinary surgeon), W H Hawkins (refreshment bar), Charles Hilder (coal merchant), William Hoad (carman), Arthur Knighton (butcher), Alan Lawrence (baker), D W Thorogood (grocer), George Titcombe (dairyman) and Percy Wood (general dealer).

Rose Cottage demolished in 1937 for the expansion of The Fox Garage (Ivy Daborn as a child).

Three firms that were associated with factory production for the war effort during the Second World War, and which flourished during peacetime, deserve special attention. The Fox Garage, which had started in wooden stables rented from 'The Fox Inn', was established by Reginald Burn in 1923. He repaired cars and sold Redline petrol and soon began selling second-hand cars as well. The business prospered and Edward (Ted) Hill became his first mechanic, soon to be assisted by Joe North and the young Geoffrey Garland. Mr Burn took the opportunity to expand the enterprise by buying the adjacent Rose Cottage, which he demolished in 1937 to provide space for a purpose-built garage and workshop with a large forecourt on which a range of motor spirit(12) was provided. The former stables then became the stores and were connected to a new service bay. During World War Two, the Government provided machine tools to manufacture small parts desperately needed for armaments, and much of his workshop was turned into a factory. After the war Reg Burn bought the lathes and milling machines and in 1952 moved them out of the workshop and into a purpose-made factory, called Fox Engineering, which was built for him in an orchard next to the garage. This enabled him to convert the front of the garage into a showroom for car sales, and the Fox Garage then became agents for Austin, Morris, MG, Singer, Humber, Sunbeam and Commer. Barrie Burn, the second of three sons, took over the garage in 1968 upon the death of his father and decided to discontinue petrol retailing which had become unprofitable. The Fox Garage later became a main agent for Vauxhall around the time that

Simon became the third generation of the Burn family to run the firm. Another branch was opened at Camberley, and in 2009 the two parts of the business were consolidated into a single operation at Camberley, whereupon both the garage and the engineering factory at Bisley were closed. Planning permission has been granted to replace the garage premises with residential housing.

The Fox Garage. 1920s

During the war a small factory was hurriedly constructed almost next to the Fox Garage.[13] In the early 1950s the building was acquired for the production of heat-sealing equipment for plastics, an innovative development at that time. The firm was called Tavak, a name derived from a combination of the initials of the owners. Fox Engineering took over the firm in the late 1960s, continuing the polythene packaging business, but two decades later it became part of another specialist heat-sealing company and diversified into manufacturing other associated products. The new company folded in 2006 and the building was sold. The name Tavak has been revived under a management buy-out which now operates from premises in West End.

The name 'Bisley' was once just synonymous with shooting, but now it is also immediately recognised as the country's leading manufacturer of steel office equipment. Frederick Brown was already a friend of Reginald Burn before the Second World War, as they both had well-established local firms in different branches of the motor trade and did business together. Freddy Brown moved to Bisley during the war and also became very involved with military contracts. He designed and made containers for dropping by parachute. When war ended in 1945, Freddy turned his attention to the manufacture of steel wastepaper bins. Within a few decades the Queens Road factory, operating under the name of F C Brown (Steel Equipment) Limited, was making a range of steel office products. Tony Brown joined the family firm in 1960 and took over from his father in 1970. Under his management the factory started to grow more rapidly. A large extension and parking area was built in 1982, enveloping the former Snowdrop Farm and Hayward's nursery at the end of Chatton Row. The firm increased production and kept expanding into new product lines, and another factory was opened at Newport in South Wales in 1988. The company became known as Bisley Steel Office Equipment and prospered both in Britain and in export markets. It has twice received the prestigious

Queen's Award for Export Achievement and is now one of the largest producers of office equipment in Europe. Tony Brown, the proprietor, employs a large workforce at Bisley and generously supports several local voluntary and charitable organisations.

---

(1) *Yesterday's Countryside.*
(2) Orchard House (since demolished), 259 to 279 Guildford Road (Napoli Tiles), and in Clews Lane: Fairlight and Fair View (both demolished, now Donnafields).
(3) 1885 Ordnance Survey: Bisley comprised 921.917 acres (including 42.847 in Bisley Detached).
(4) Bushel = 8 gallons (approx. 35.6 litres)
(5) In 1847: Nultrow Common Field comprised 23 acres and was divided into 21 plots, Wilcot was 41 acres and had 35 plots, Southridge was 12 acres and had 8 plots, Churchbourne Mead was 9 acres and had 10 plots, and Burkit was 8 acres and had 15 plots.
(6) *English Field Systems.*
(7) In 1405 tithes were owed by John Willere of Bisley from 5 acres of arable land '*una acra iacet in Campo vocato Northull, et una acra et dimidia pariter iacet in Campo vocato Wydecroft, et una acra iacet in Campo vocato Eltrowe, et una acra et dimidia partier iacet in Campo vocato Westeworth.*' (Where was Westeworth?)
(8) Collectively called 'manorial waste' despite including significant heathland tracts now regarded and ecologically valuable.

(9) The original name of Town Mill (Industrial History of Surrey Heath).

(10) *Life & Work on Surrey Heath.*

(11) Early bricks from Kiln Lane, Bisley, were 2 inches thick, but later ones were 2½ inches thick (probably to comply with the attempted standardisation under an Act of Parliament in 1769).

(12) Redline, Pratts, BP, Shell & National Benzole, (pre-war), and National Benzole, Power, BP, Shell, paraffin and Shell-Mex which later became Super Shell, (post-war).

(13) Located between 315 and 321 Guildford Road, Bisley.

Chapter 17

COMMON GROUND

Bisley and its surrounding villages have a multi-purpose leisure facility that is free, convenient and open day and night, yet it is often undervalued or taken for granted. This precious asset is the expanse of heathland covering large parts of north-west Surrey as well as the border area of Berkshire and parts of Hampshire. Though some of it is used for military training and is either closed altogether or has restricted access, one does not have to go very far to find attractive areas of dry heath which the public may use for informal recreation. Many English counties have no lowland heath at all, and in far too many places in the countryside one has to observe the privacy and restrictions of enclosed land by opening and closing gates, sticking to narrow rights-of-way and often having to retrace one's steps when there is no convenient circular route. By contrast, open heaths provide the choice of going freely on or off the paths for walking, exercising the dog, horse riding, finding a quiet place for a picnic, observing wildlife or simply getting out into the fresh air.

Bisley Common comprises several areas of a once vast stretch of heath that was formed upon the unique geological soil structure called the Bagshot, Bracklesham and

Barton Series of Sands, generally called the Bagshot Beds, that stretches from Ash northwards to the county boundary and beyond. This once unbroken block of heathland included Wyke Common, Pirbright Common, Sheets Heath, Cowshot Common, Colony Bog, West End Common, Lightwater Moor and Bagshot Heath. Many of these large areas contain smaller distinguishable sites which also have names indicating a common or a heath. However, there has been a considerable loss of heathland and fragmentation in the course of time, particularly during the last two centuries because of human interference such as housing development, railways and roads; and also as a result of natural succession as woodland develops.

Looking firstly at the massive tract of dry heath, wet heath and bog that stretches westwards from Bisley and West End over to The Maultway on the Chobham Ridges, and also northwards from Pirbright and Bisley Ranges to Red Road, it is now the largest block of heath this side of the New Forest and is recognised internationally as being one of the most important places for wildlife in Europe. The thousand-acre site carries an impressive range of ecological designations and contains certain species found nowhere else in Britain. The rifle ranges at Pirbright and Bisley in the south, and the mortar ranges in the north, occupy only a very small proportion of the heath but the enormous central danger area for any stray bullets that miss the stop butts ironically protects an enormous wealth of plants, mammals and insects contained within the various heathland habitats. The whole block has a high security fence around the perimeter.

Firing points on Century Range.

Prior to the arrival of the National Rifle Association, there were five tracks traversing the heath from Bisley and West End to the Chobham Ridges, skirting around the dangerously marshy parts of Colony Bog, Strawberry Bottom and Great Bottom. These tracks were recorded on the first large-scale Ordnance Survey map[(1)] of the district. Three of these tracks fell into disuse soon after Bisley Ranges were established in 1890 and were no longer visible on the ground by 1915. Despite regular activity on Bisley and Pirbright ranges, one of the tracks was still being used sufficiently often to be recorded as a Right of Way under the National Parks & Access to the Countryside Act 1949, and was still designated as a Public Footpath on the 1961 Definitive Map and Statement by Surrey County Council. Identified as

Public Footpath No126A, it was almost exactly three miles long (4.8 kilometres), meandering across the common in a roughly south-westerly direction passing Furze Farm and High Hoglees, crossing Stickledown Range between the firing points and the targets, veering slightly more southwards upon reaching a mound indicating the boundary of Pirbright Parish, and proceeding up Mainstone Hill where it then turned sharply north-westwards continuing more or less straight to Colony Gate at the junction of The Maultway and Old Bisley Road. It seems quite bizarre that the right to walk this route was not extinguished when the ranges were put in place, but the fact remained that the use of this path took precedence over shooting and so the Range Officer was forced to halt all firing, not just on Stickledown, but on all the ranges if anyone came into sight. The *Woking News & Mail* reported in September 1950 that Bisley Parish Council wanted to 'preserve' it, but one member who walked it said, 'It seems to me only suitable for the very nimble.' It was not until the early 1980s when the Ministry of Defence erected the security fence around the whole range and overshoot complex that a Diversion Order was made to re-route the footpath around the northern end of the fence, making it possibly the longest diversion of any right-of-way in the country. The ancient route across the heath was not very suitable for wheeled vehicles and may have been used mainly by people on horseback or on foot, whereas the onward extension from Colony Gate to Frimley, which is still called The Old Bisley Road, has become heavily used by all types of traffic.

This military danger zone used to contain just a few

small cottages at Colony and Hagthorn which had to be vacated and pulled down once public access was denied. However some vestiges of human occupation remain: the hedge banks are still there, so too are a few old apple trees and there is a brick-lined well which, surprisingly, does not appear on Ordnance Survey maps. However, in the space of little over a century most of the local names of topographical features within the danger area have been all but forgotten, even though they are shown on maps. Polled Oak Slade, Godley Lane, Straight Oak, Bending Oak, Cow Moor, Strawberry Bottom, Brock Hill and so on have lost their significance, while Stickle Back Down has been contracted to Stickledown. The name Coldingley, which was the ancient form of Colony, has been revived for use as the name of a local prison.

In general, public exclusion from the land behind Bisley Ranges has benefited wildlife and we are informed[(2)] that 'there are diminutive trout in the small peaty streams which rise in Colony and Hagthorn Bogs, but sadly the curlews which at one time arrived regularly to nest behind Siberia come no more, and the coveys of partridges and occasional nightjar which frequented the ranges in former years are no longer in evidence'.

We now turn our attention away from the military and NRA land and towards the parts of Bisley Common which were owned by the Lords of the Manor of Bisley until as recently as 1968 when the Earl of Onslow[(3)] sold them to Surrey County Council. These commons, village greens and odd pockets of unenclosed land usually at the side of a road were regarded as 'the waste of the manor' and in former times the Lord sometimes gave certain tenants 'common rights' in lieu of payment where substantial services had been rendered. This cost him absolutely nothing but conferred privilege upon the recipient who could take advantage of the practical benefits.

To many local people 'common' and 'heathland' are almost synonymous because virtually all the commons in this locality were, and in places still are, covered with heather and other plants and trees that live on acid sandy soils. Common Land refers to the 'common rights'[(4)] normally given to certain properties in perpetuity but it does not mean that the land is in common ownership – it hardly ever is so. These ancient rights were proved in law a little while ago for two Bisley properties after submitting parchment title deeds over 200 years old to the Commons Commissioners, in accordance with new legislation requiring all such rights to be registered. On 6th June 1981 the rights of estovers and turbary were confirmed for Hassells and Strawberry Farm; the latter property also having the right of pasture. A few residents were granted 'personal rights' that will lapse upon their death, but the general public can only enjoy the 'right of air and exercise' on Bisley Common. Village greens were once part of the common but they have been separately classified since the Commons Registration Act of 1965.

The Reidon Hill and Shaftesbury (or Bisley Green) areas of Bisley Common, comprising 67 acres and 52 acres respectively (27 & 21 hectares), were used for military purposes during the Second World War when slit trenches were dug for training, an observation post was set up on a vantage point close to Stafford Lake Road, and alder buckthorn bushes were harvested to make high quality charcoal for military fuses. Further disturbance took place in 1955 when the A322 was lowered by six feet at the junction of Stafford Lake Road in order to remove a blind spot for traffic emerging from Limecroft Road. Hundreds of tons of sand were excavated and redistributed on the common in a thin layer, just north of the informal car park (now closed) that was situated opposite this potentially dangerous T-junction. Despite these and other disturbances (some may say, because of them), these comparatively small parcels of heath still contain significant amounts of distinctive heathland vegetation, typically heather, gorse and broom, that is well adapted to the extremely acidic and nutrient deficient sandy soil. Then there are pioneer species, such as silver birch and rowan, that can tolerate a range of harsh environments; and in places where the soil has been enriched by years of leaf litter, holly and oak are now taking hold. A survey of higher plants[(5)] was undertaken on these two areas in 1974, which was about the time that the variety of plants was at its greatest after the disruption during the Second World War and immediate post-war years. The results are shown in **Appendix J** because a significant number of plants are no longer to be found and in decades to come further losses may be expected.

It is generally accepted that acid heath developed as a result of clearance of oak forest that covered most of Southern England in primaeval times. By removing the trees for cultivation, our forebears little realised that a natural process of impoverishment would occur on the thin layer of soil overlying the sand. Animal dung applied as a fertiliser after shallow ploughing soon leached through the sandy soil along with any essential minerals that were already present, and within a few years the ground became extremely acid and nutrient deficient as these constituents, essential to crop production, sank below the reach of shallow-rooted cereals and vegetables. Further cultivation was futile, but one of the few benefits of this developing heath to local farmers was that they could put livestock out to graze upon the plants and grasses which quickly colonised these areas.

Even today, there are Bisley people who can remember when cattle were grazed on the commons during the inter-war years. The animals would generally be 'minded' by a boy or a girl who would take them out in the morning around a familiar route which had good grazing, returning home in the afternoon. Even after the Second World War, Bob Worsfold regularly tethered a number of goats on the common, each having a chain long enough for at least a day's grazing. The goats would eat almost anything within reach and were thus an important factor in holding back the natural succession of scrub and woodland.

The pond near The Farm School (with Cobbetts Farm and the Williams Memorial Cottages behind).
Photo: Joan Roberts

Myxamotosis, the ghastly disease of rabbits brought to England from France in 1953, quickly spread across the country and within two years had killed around 95% of the rabbit population. It was late arriving in this district but no less deadly for that. The pitiful signs of infection were first observed in Bisley early in 1955 and by the end of the year not one rabbit was to be seen. Since then the disease has become endemic, re-emerging in different parts of the country every so often as populations begin to increase. The immunity passed on to offspring by rabbits that survived gradually decreased in successive generations. Rabbits habitually used to burrow to a noticeably greater extent than they do these days, as if they now know that transmission of the disease by the rabbit flea is more likely to occur underground. Another controlling fact has been the mutation of the virus into less virulent forms, thus increasing survival rates and immunity in rabbit colonies. The purpose for introducing the subject of myxamotosis is because, in pre-myxamotosis days, the rabbits had such a profound effect upon the countryside, so great was their population density. One can well recall seeing cropping margins around every field of young crops and hay meadows, ending at the extreme distance that a rabbit could run safely for cover. Banks were particularly favoured for burrowing and the sides of ditches would often collapse as a result of these excavations. Evidence of rabbits could be seen everywhere on the common, not because they chose heathland vegetation but because their numbers were always so large in preferential feeding areas that a proportion of the population moved on to the less favourable heath. Large patches of grass on dry heath resembled closely-mown lawns, few birch seedlings ever grew more than an inch or two, even gorse was kept so short that it formed small mounds a few inches high where young growth on the outside was kept in check, leaving little mounds of tougher stems resembling pin cushions. All this changed virtually overnight, never to re-appear, at least not in Bisley, simply because the disease always strikes again before the population approaches a high density. Perhaps the nearest resemblance to 'pre-myxi' days is the heavy cropping by ponies and other animals in the New Forest. Collectively, the rabbits were probably more instrumental in preventing the widespread establishment of self-seeding trees on Bisley Common than all other forms of intervention, including domesticated livestock grazing and conservation work.

Aerial photographs of Bisley Common and mapping of the pattern of predominant vegetation by Bisley Common Society in 1975, provided an accurate picture of the extent of bracken, pure stand of ling heather, areas of scrub and woodland encroachment, and the network of paths that criss-crossed the area. Now, in the space of less than four decades, the picture has changed appreciably. Two sizeable blocks of bracken and some invasive scrub have disappeared as a result of sustained conservation management, but it has not been possible to maintain the stands of heather which have considerably diminished, particularly after heath fires, because heather is so slow growing and cannot compete as successfully as faster developing plants, such as purple moor grass and silver birch. Unfortunately, under certain adverse conditions, the proportions of dense heather and sparse grass can all too readily be reversed within just two or three years.

Well-known paths across the common can easily fall into disuse, become re-routed around obstacles such as gorse bushes and fallen trees, or may be replaced by new tracks. Only the most heavily used paths, which are generally those connected to points of access, are likely to remain unchanged. Even the soft sandy circles devoid of vegetation, known as 'pony-circles', that were formed in the 1950s by repeated use of a lunge to train horses, cannot be distinguished from surrounding growth these days. An even larger bare patch, where sand was deposited on the common when the A322 was lowered on Reidon Hill, has now developed a thick cover of natural vegetation.

Both Shaftesbury and Reidon Hill suffer considerable pressure these days from dog walking which has increased appreciably in the last few decades. Ground-nesting and low-nesting birds, such as the skylark, wheatear, willow warbler and chiffchaff, that regularly nested here up to the 1960s and 1970s, never return these days. General human pressure, rather than just inquisitive dogs, may also account for the loss of the stonechat and whinchat, and there is a completely different reason for no longer hearing the nightjar near Bullhousen Farm or seeing goldfinches along Stafford Lake Road. The answer is loss of suitable habitat. The nightjar requires very special conditions for its feeding ground and the colourful flock of goldfinches along Stafford Lake Road used to feed upon the seeds of knapweed, wild carrot and other seed-bearing flowers which grew in abundance on both sides of the road, but which have now been shaded out by the belt of trees. However, the marked decline in population of some plants and animals, some of which have disappeared altogether, is less clear and sometimes are completely inexplicable. For instance, the delicate little flower we call harebell, confusingly known as bluebell in Scotland, has recently vanished from Bisley Common and other dry heaths in NW Surrey, seemingly without reason, yet it flourished and was widespread until just a few decades ago.

Changes such as these are by no means confined to the last half century. In the 1880s, one of the men travelling around the countryside looking for a suitable permanent location for shooting ranges to replace the enormously successful annual NRA meeting at Wimbledon, was Lord Cottesloe. After one of his visits to what is now Bisley Ranges, he remarked that it was 'but an open expanse of typical north-west Surrey heathland, a home of snipe and black game, wild and windswept, with light sandy soil, covered with heather, gorse and bracken, traversed by a few tracks made by drovers and local inhabitants crossing the heath from Fox Hills (Chobham Ridges) to Bisley Village'.[6] He recorded that he had flushed a grey hen (a female black grouse) which he thought must have been 'one of the last of her species to remain on the wild Surrey heaths'. Not only did it disappear from the heaths of Surrey, but in the following half century it vanished from the rest of lowland Britain. The large tortoiseshell and marsh fritillary butterflies that were regularly observed around this district dwindled during the first half of the 1900s, finally disappearing altogether in the 1960s. At the same time the comma and white admiral butterflies became more plentiful, extending their range, and can now be seen on or around the wooded margins of the heath. Population fluctuations occur in the countryside all the time, and have done so for centuries, but a matter of greater concern to the naturalist is the total loss of a species that lacks the mobility to re-colonise a particular area where it formerly existed.

The decline and loss of characteristic heathland flowers as woodland encroaches, usually from the margins towards the centre, are difficult to reverse because silver birch and other trees germinate readily and raise the nutrient level, enriching the surface of the ground to the detriment of plants and insects that thrive upon impoverished acid soils. Narrow belts and isolated pockets of heath, such as the Shaftesbury and Reidon Hill areas of Bisley Common, are particularly vulnerable to this stage of succession in the vegetation.

Somewhat incongruously in a place seemingly devoid of naturally occurring rocks and stones, a pale-grey material, with pieces ranging in size from small lumps to large boulders, occurs on all the local heaths. It is called sarsen stone, or heathstone, deposited during the last ice age and which has peculiar characteristics that made it particularly valuable for construction work in former times. Richard Lucock Wilson, a lifelong resident of the district and local historian, has explained the way in which this material was extracted and used. An article[7] of his, published in 1996, described the process:-

> A walker on the heaths that encircled the villages of West End and Chobham, picking his way between the gorse and broom bushes, may see lying amongst the heather, long blocks of unhewn sandstone. Such a thing is unusual on the sandy heaths of Surrey.
>
> A hundred years ago you would have found at almost any season of the year, except perhaps hay and corn harvest, a group of men busy at one of these rock sites digging as fast as they could. The block of stone would be slowly uncovered and found, as a rule to be of a rusty brown or

> dark ochre colour, the men struggling all the while to free it, working up to their thighs in water, for the heaths are very boggy and crossed by small streams.
>
> As soon as they had hoisted up the block of stone, usually by means of a rope or chain or pulley, the men would begin at once cutting it with special saws into rough squares, measuring anything from about six inches to two feet wide. Saws were used, for while the sandstone was wet and had not been exposed to the air, it was comparatively soft and easy to cut.
>
> That done, the blocks were stacked up on the heath and soon had become as hard and firm as any brick.
>
> Almost in the centre of the scattered village of West End is a tiny church built entirely from block of this stone, in the year 1842. Every farmer in the village – my own great grandfather amongst them – lent a cart and a man to dig that stone off the common. A century of exposure to the air has made it exceedingly hard now and bleached to a very lovely pale grey.

Sarsen stone was a very valuable commodity in this district where no other natural outcrop of stone of useable size exists. One enormous boulder of sarsen stone was perched on the top of High Curley at Lightwater, but it was accidentally split in two in 1945 by the heat of a bonfire built upon it. Very few such examples are to be found on the surface of the heaths nowadays.

Almost three hundred years ago, Daniel Defoe made very derogatory statements of our local heaths on a journey[(8)] from Chertsey to Basingstoke:-

> Crossing the Black Desert, as I call'd it, of Bagshot Heath… here is a vast tract of land, some of it within seventeen or eighteen miles of the capital city; which is not only poor, but even quite steril, given up to barrenness, horrid and frightful to look on, not only good for little, but good for nothing; much of it is a sandy desert… for in passing this heath in a windy day, I was so far in danger of smothering with the clouds of sand, which were raised by the storm, that I cou'd neither keep it out of my mouth, nose or eyes; and when the wind was over, the sand appeared spread over the adjacent fields… so as that it ruins the very soil. This sand indeed is checked by the heath, or heather, which grows in it… but the ground is otherwise so poor and barren, that the product of it feeds no creatures, but some very small sheep, who feed chiefly on the said heather, and but very few of these, nor are there any villages, worth mentioning, and but few

> houses, or people for many miles far and wide; this desart lyes extended so much, that some say, there is not less than a hundred thousand acres of this barren land that lyes all together, reaching out every way in the three counties of Surrey, Hampshire and Berkshire.

Many other travellers had good reason to dislike crossing the bleak and desolate heaths in times past, particularly as daylight faded and during the hours of darkness, because of the risk of being waylaid by lurking highwaymen. There were certainly such men operating around the district during the hundred years or so before the arrival of railways. The openness of the terrain well suited their trade, but the risk of being stopped, let alone being harmed, was more perceived than actual.

Extinguishing a fire on Bisley Common.

The author, when a young boy in 1954, found by chance on Bisley Common the remains of a pistol that was later identified by an antique firearms expert as 'probably having been a highwayman's weapon'. A heath fire had spread closer than most towards the main track in front of Snowdrop Farm, and in those days local boys loved to scratch around after such fires and would sometimes find a coin or two, or similar 'treasures'. On this occasion the barrel and action of a pistol lay underneath the burnt and blackened debris just beside the track, some 220 yards (200 metres) from what was once the cross-roads at 'The Fox Inn'. The wooden stock, of which there was no trace, had obviously been burnt long ago in previous fires, or just rotted away. The metalwork was pitted with rust beneath the blackened surface and there was no visible decoration other than a very thin silver-coloured strip of platinum cross-wise on the hexagonal barrel.

The only other find on the common worth mentioning was an 18th century horseshoe found on the Shaftesbury area of Bisley Common in the 1970s, close to the shallow trench delineating the Ministry of Defence boundary.

---

(1) OS map 1871 Sheet XVI.3 surveyed 1870. Scale 1:2,500 (approx 25 inches to 1 mile).

(2) *Bisley: The National Shooting Centre*. NRA.

(3) Michael William Coplestone Onslow, 7th Earl of Onslow (b1938)

(4) Pasture (the right to graze animals), turbary (dig peat or turf for fuel), pannage (to allow pigs to eat

acorns and beech mast), estovers (take brushwood and bracken), piscary (take fish) and common in the soil (take sand, stone or minerals).

(5) Excludes non-vascular plants, such as fungi, mosses, liverworts and algae.

(6) *The Story of Bisley*. Cole.

(7) *Bisley & West End Parish News*. October 1996.

(8) *A Tour Thro' the Whole Island of Great Britain*. Defoe.

Chapter 18

PLUCKED FROM THE ANNALS

All ancient records, no matter how incomplete or restricted in scope they may be, provide essential historical information, though the local historian always hopes for more than he finds. Registers of baptisms, marriages and burials provide a continuous link from generation to generation but tell us little about the daily lives of parishioners. Census returns are most important in certain respects but, again, they have their limitations because they did not commence until 1841 and there are ten-year intervals between each one of them. Similarly, taxation lists show the relative wealth of taxable individuals but in general they impart no more than a snapshot in time. Then there are parish documents indicating local obligations for equipping soldiers, personal responsibility for maintaining rails around the churchyard, churchwardens' accounts, payments for relief of the poor, and so on.

Of all the different records stretching back several hundred years, court records of the Surrey Assizes and Quarter Sessions are among the most interesting for giving a detailed picture of social and economic life in Bisley and the customs and values of former generations.

Wearily returning home.

Surrey Assizes

Five hundred years ago, anyone accused of a crime in the village could expect to be dealt with at the Court of Quarter Sessions, though the more serious offences would normally be heard at the Surrey Assizes held twice a year, either at Kingston, Guildford or Croydon. Circuit judges presided at the Assizes, going around several counties and dealing with a wide range of criminal activities, not just felonies such as murder, highway robbery and rape, but also other crimes considered to be very serious in their day, including theft of goods worth in excess of 12d (a capital offence in the 16th century), failing to go to church once a week[(1)] and witchcraft.

A Bisley spinster, Bridget Hitchcoke, was indicted on three charges of witchcraft: that she bewitched a mare to death at Horsell on 15th June 1573, and that she did the same to a cow on 25th August that year, and allegedly bewitching another mare on 26th May 1577. All three animals (collectively worth £5 17s. 4d.) had belonged to John Mellist, a member of a Bisley family who appeared to have some connection with Horsell.[(2)] Miss Hitchcoke was tried as a witch but was acquitted of all three charges. She then left the district, presumably in some haste.

The year 1573 seems to have been an inauspicious one for other local folk because John and William Hone, both husbandmen from Bisley, were had up for stealing two sheep, valued at 4s. 4d. each, the property of two Frimley men. It was stated that one of the animals was taken from Colony. John Hone was found guilty and 'allowed clergy' (at his execution) but William was still 'at large' during the trial.

The same year John Beard of Bisley and another man from Camberwell were charged with vagrancy at Bisley, Lambeth and other places. Beard was 'ill' and the other man was 'sentenced according to statute'.

Two Bisley men, Richard Romsey (? Rumsey), a husbandman, and William Rickson, a linen weaver, were charged at the Assizes with grand larceny, namely that they broke into a field at Send on the night of 31st March 1583 and stole a calf worth 6s. 8d. belonging to Robert Boughton. Rickson was also indicted for stealing a brass kettle worth 7s. 0d. from Robert Waterer at Woking a few days earlier. Romsey was found not guilty on 30th June 1584 but Rickson, who was 'at large', was found guilty and later apprehended.

Another individual, of whom we have previously been informed was a miller, John Swayne, who was indicted for grand larceny for stealing a fowling-piece worth £1 0s. 0d., a gold ring (6s. 0d.) and 13s. 3d. in money. He too was at large and was tried in his absence.

Richard Burchett of Bisley was tried, together with another man from Pyrford, for stealing a cow worth £3 0s. 0d. at Beddington on 30th September 1592 but he was found not guilty.

Another Burchett, Thomas (Byrchett) who also lived at Bisley, husbandman, admitted stealing a sheep valued at 11d. from John Attwood Jnr at Woking on 20th December 1591 and was sentenced to be flogged. Had the animal been more valuable, Burchett would have swung for his crime in the usual way.

William Hone of Bisley (one of many Williams, but obviously not the one who was in trouble in 1573) was found guilty and whipped for the theft of three tanned buckskins from someone in Chobham on 30th November 1594. The buckskins were worth a total of 11d. which, coincidentally, was the same price as the previous item and just 1d. below the amount that would result in capital punishment upon conviction, and so one cannot help wondering if these valuations by the aggrieved parties that seemingly went unchallenged were, in effect, a way of granting leniency.

Edward Remnant had his white cow (£2 0s. 0d.) stolen from Bisley on 28th December 1595. Robert Elliott, a tanner from Bagshot, was charged with the offence but found not guilty.

John Porter had his house in Bisley burgled on 6th March 1598 and several men were arrested for the offence, including a Bisley tailor named Edward Oslam. Some of the defendants who also faced other charges were found guilty and hanged, but Oslam was acquitted.

Quarter Sessions

The Quarter Sessions, as the name suggests, were held every three months at which all manner of offences were brought before the bench. Taking a representative period of seventeen years from 1663 to 1680, eleven wrong-doers from Bisley were sentenced and duly fined; one of them was up in court several times, as we shall see.

At the July Sessions at Guildford in 1663, the ditches of John Cobbett 'near the highway from Purbright… were overflowing for want of scouring…' and two years later 'Humphrey Field late of Bisley yeoman ever since the 1st June has allowed his watercourse leading from Trulley Lane to a bridge commonly called Newbridge in the said parish to overflow in rainy weather'. Similarly, Robert Davys was in trouble in 1680 for '… allowing his ditches next to the highway leading from Newbridge to his house to be out of repair'.

A presentment was made at the Quarter Sessions in October 1667 in which a witness attested to the fact that a former Horsell man had rooted up wood and underwood in 20 acres of woodland in Bisley, and converted it to tillage.

In 1664 a regular offender 'up before the Beak' at Guildford was recorded thus: 'Thomas Blundell, late of Bisley, labourer, ever since 3 July has been "*communis et publicus venator et destruor Jocalium domini regis Anglice*" a common potcher and destroyer of the king's Game'.

At Croydon Quarter Sessions on 10th January 1665: 'Thomas Blundell, late of Bisley, yeoman, 1 Nov, made assault and affray there, with "*Tormento Anglice*" a hand gun, and other weapons, upon George Remnant, Bisley, yeoman'.

He soon returned to Bisley and by 1688 he had a trade: 'Thomas Blundell (14th October 1668) tailor of Byssley recognisance for £20 if he do never hereafter destroy any more game contra unto the law, that is to say, Deere, Pheasants, Partridges, Heathpoults, Ducks, etc.' He also had to pledge a further £10 to 'keep the peace'" towards Edward Goreing, one of the Bisley Constables, who he had attacked while being served with a writ. On 14th December he was in trouble again for keeping '… a sitting dog and a gun with the intention of killing pheasants, etc… not having lands in his or his wife's right to the value of £100 per annum, shot at partridges with a hand gun charged with gunpowder and nail-shot'.

Goreing ceased to be the Constable the following year and moved away but Blundell, it seems, took revenge and reported him to the authorities, for it is recorded thus: 'Edward Goreing late of Bisley, husbandman, being 16 years of age or over 20th June for three Sundays following did not repair to… (the) parish church nor to any place of common prayer.'

There are similar cases of non-attendance at church: Thomas Longe, late of Bisley, yeoman, being 16 years and more 24 June last, (with 3 others) was indicted at Guildford on 12th July 1664 for having not 'repaired to their parish churches nor to any place of public worship'.

In 1672 recognisance of £10 was required of Thomas Bird, yeoman, Bisley, '…to answer for speaking bawdy and filthy, obscene words to ye wife of Richard Massey of Bysely and to keep the peace towards her'.

At the April Quarter Sessions held at Reigate in 1674, James Hone, Bisley, (and a Chobham man) '…neither being a son and heir of an esquire, etc nor owners, etc of forests, parks, etc for keeping guns' were found guilty and duly prosecuted.

The same year there was a 'riotous assembly' at Brookwood when Matthew Hone, George Harding, Richard Collier were among about a hundred other labourers living in the area who had embarked upon a token poaching expedition to demonstrate against the destruction of their crops resulting from 'the King causing Deere to be put into Brookwood'.

Three years later Richard Towers was punished for forcible entry into a close 'called le Hogleaze (Hoglees at Cowshot) and digging up and carrying off four young oaken tellows[(3)] worth five shillings'. In those days acorns were regularly planted on enclosed parcels of land to replace mature oak trees felled for timber.

Also within this particular seventeen year period, John

Towers, Richard's father, was convicted of 'erecting a wooden Turfe-House on the highway between Bisley and Guildford thereby obstructing it'. The offending structure was a fuel store for peat situated next to The Willows at Reidon Hill; but why John Towers should chose to build it where it partly blocked the road, is a mystery.

Parish Registers

Bisley has a complete record of 'Christeninges', 'Weddinges' and 'Burialls' stretching back almost 450 years, which is an unusually long time. It is also extremely fortunate that every record from 1561 was entered into a bound book at a later date, as there is now no trace of the original loose parchment leaves from which the entries were transcribed into the new register. This volume, the first of several compiled by the church, is headed:-

> *The Register booke of the parish Churche of Bisley in ye countie of Surrey, newly written in the yeare of our Lord God 1598 and in the fortieth yeare of the raigne of o^r^ most gracious Sovraigne Ladie Elizabeth by the grace of God Queen of England France and Ireland, Defender of the ancient Christian Catholic Faith &c. wherein is contayned all christenings, weddings, & burialls commanded by her Matie to be made for Diverse good causes & considerations.*

The very first entry is a christening, one of seven that year, which reads:-

Dorithy Braye was baptised at chobham one[4] *maunday Thursday ——— 1561*
There was just one marriage during that year:-
John Cobbet and Margaret Remnante were marryed the xxth *daye of June ——— 1561*
There were six burials, the first being:-
Rose Goringe y^{e} *daughter of Robt was buried y*^{e} *xij*th *of march ——— 1561*

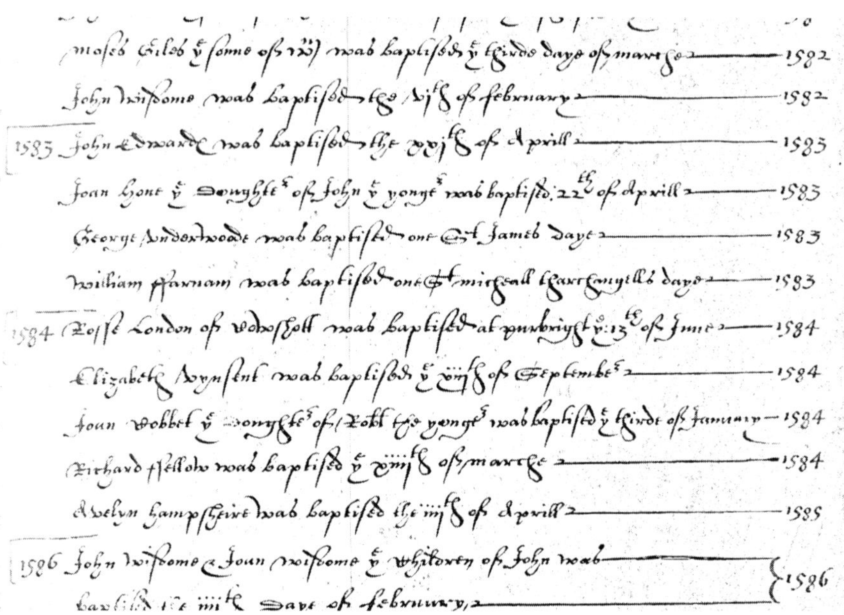

moses Giles ye sonne of [illegible] was baptised ye thirde daye of marche — 1582
John Wisdome was baptised the vjth of februarye — 1582
1583 John Edwarde was baptised the xvjth of Aprill — 1583
Joan hont ye doughter of John ye yonger was baptised 22th of Aprill — 1583
George Underwoode was baptised one St James daye — 1583
William ffarnam was baptised one St michaell tharchangells daye — 1583
1584 Rose London of [illegible] was baptised at [illegible] ye 13th of June — 1584
Elizabeth [illegible] was baptised ye xiiijth of September — 1584
Joan Cobbet ye doughter of Robt the yonger was baptised ye thirde of January — 1584
Richard ffellow was baptised ye xiiijth of marche — 1584
Avelyn hampshire was baptised the iiijth of Aprill — 1585
1586 John Wisdome & Joan Wisdome ye children of John was baptised the iiijth daye of februarye — 1586

16th century entries in the baptism register.

Whoever made sure that the retrospective records were included, did so in a very neat hand, filling six pages with christenings, two for marriages and four for burials. In marked contrast, the handwriting that follows is very poor and almost indecipherable. The information in the registers is not always confined to the purpose for which they were intended as we see on the last page of this one, where thankfully there is yet another change of handwriting, which this time is considerably more legible:-

> *October 19th 1679.*
> *The day and yeare above said John Edglar a Quaker and an Excommunicated person came into the parish church of Bisley in the time of Divine Service while the minister was reading the Bendictus and disturbed the Congregation there assembled.*
>
> *He did the same again on the next Sunday following which was the 26th day of October 1679 in the forenoon when the people were singing one of the psalmes.*
>
> *He did the same again on Sunday the 9th of November 1679 in the time of Divine Service, in the Communion service when the minister was reading the Collect after the Lord's prayer.*
>
> *Memorand : that the said John Edglar was received into the church again on the twenty fourth day of October, being Sunday 1686 at Bisley by me Andrew Lamont, Rector, ibid.*

Later baptisms, marriages and burials were recorded in separate books. The first entry in the 1678 Burials Register confirms that the interment complied with the Burial in Wool Act of that year which demanded that all bodies, except plague victims, were to be buried in a woollen shirt, shift or shroud, and in no other material whatsoever, thereby increasing the wool trade:-

> *Hannah Cobbett, the daughter of John Cobbett and Hannah his wife, was buried at Bisley in wool only, Octob10th. The affidavit was made before Sr Thomas ffoster by Mary Whittwell widdow and Anne Edgelor Oct 15th 1678.*

Palmer**(5)** states that the provisions of the Act had to be complied with, even in the case of Damaris Gunner who was interred without church rites. This Act was an early example of state protectionist policy as the wool industry was a major part of the national wealth. Initially an affidavit had to be sworn for each corpse, but later it became sufficient for a witness to testify to a Justice of the Peace. Despite the threat of heavy fines, the law was soon largely ignored as contraventions were difficult to prove without exhumation but, as unpopular as it was, the law was not repealed until 1814 – long after it had ceased to be enforced. Other interesting details among the shorter entries include:-

9th Nov 1692	Damaris Gunner committed suicide and was allowed burial in the churchyard but without 'divine service'.
19th Mar 1869	Two Daborn boys (aged 1½ and 4) died of whooping cough within a few hours of each other.
14th Jul 1877	John Cheeseman (35) was run over by a wagon and died instantly.

26th May 1883	Amy Stevens (15) was buried after being 'overworked in service'.
16th Aug 1894	Revd Joseph Cater (who wrote *Bisley Bits*) buried Violet, his 17 month old daughter who died of diphtheria.
14th Aug 1899	James Hill of Strawberry Farm (85) was the last man in Bisley to wear a smock frock.

This last entry is interesting in that one would expect comments in a book of burials to be confined to causes of death, burial details or, as we have already seen, other matters of some importance. Whoever made the entry must have regarded the wearing of this type of protective garment at almost the turn of the century as being so outmoded that it warranted mentioning for posterity.

The Cobbett and Hone families were very large, even in the Elizabethan era, and, between them, 44 members were buried in the churchyard during the hundred years from 1565 to 1665. However, the ages of the departed are rarely recorded prior to 1800 but we may presume that a significant proportion died in early childhood, particularly as sixty infants from Bisley families died without reaching their fourth birthday in the fifty years from 1810 to 1860. This was an extremely high death rate, possibly in the region of thirty to forty per cent of all babies, bearing in mind the population of the village was no more than 600 to 700.

An infant born out of wedlock was often recorded in Bisley as being a 'base child' or 'base-born' and all too often the mother was a young domestic servant. There is an interesting legal avouchment against one such entry in 1602. The mother had been delivered of her baby at a house at 'Bisley Bridge' (Newbridge Cottage?) the home of one of two named men bound in the recognisance of £20 to pay for the upbringing of the child. One presumes that William Hone was the baby's maternal grandfather and that Thomas Caule was the baby's father, but then why was Elizabeth's surname Griffin?

> *1602. Anne Griffin base born and christened in the parish of Bisley, Elizabeth Griffin her mother being delivered of her at Wm Hone's house at Bisley bridge, being baptised the xij^th day of November. For discharge of the parish of the said child, one Thomas Caule of Aldershot and William Hone of Bisley became bound to the churchwardens Richard Millist and John Castell, being for the same year, and to their support from tyme to tyme in a bond of xx^£ to save and keep the said parish of Bisley from all manner charges of the said child, which bond remaineth in the parish of Bisley.*
> *Executed September 1602.*

These Churchwardens were pragmatic men, and what better place than the Baptism Register could there have been in which to document this bastardy bond. The Overseers were largely responsible for tracking down fathers of healthy infants born to unmarried mothers, and making them pay towards the children's upkeep, so that the cost of raising these youngsters would not be borne by the parish. An absentee father traced to another parish would receive little sympathy for his behaviour from that community once it became public knowledge.

From the mid-1300s when the infamous and devastating Black Death swept through the country, the plague re-emerged intermittently here and there for another four centuries; the most severe being the Great Plague (1665–6), though some claim that these two diseases were not the same pestilence. Nevertheless, three members of one Bisley family died of the plague within a fortnight of each other in August 1635. They were Richard Edmead, Catherine 'a widow' (probably his mother), and Henry his son.

A number of unidentified corpses were found from time to time in the village which had to be 'buried on the parish'. Any vagrant who appeared to be close to death would be given a few pence to move on to the next parish, in order to avoid the considerable cost of burial being paid out of the public purse. Perhaps some of these unfortunates who died at Bisley had already been moved on in this way from elsewhere.

The Registers show that gypsies often encamped at Bisley for short periods. Those who died here were accorded a decent burial, and parents of young children were encouraged to have them christened in church. In almost 250 years[(6)] the Baptism Registers do not once mention the word gypsy, merely stating, in what is now called in politically correct terms, that the person was 'encamped at Bisley' or 'from a travelling van passing through Bisley'.

This is a little surprising since the epithet 'gypsy' had been widely used elsewhere to describe these nomadic people as far back as the 16th century. Perhaps the word was disliked as much then as it is now by those to whom it refers. In fact the term gypsy does not appear in the registers before 1876, where it is written twice. However, the Revd Walter Eaton chose to revert to the use of the description 'traveller' in an entry the following year.

Of the several dozen poverty-stricken individuals from Bisley who were forced to enter the Chertsey Union Workhouse, 23 died there. Some of them fell victim to contagious diseases such as smallpox, diphtheria, consumption, typhoid and scarlet fever, which often spread rapidly through such confined communities.

Even though Bisley was largely a poor village until quite recently, it still seems to have had more than its fair share of 'day labourers', the poorest of all earners. They would be hired just for the one day and would have to seek work again the next morning. If they were lucky the work would last for several consecutive days, even weeks, though the likelihood diminished as competition increased. Some day labourers died with little more in the way of possessions than the clothes they were wearing.

At the opposite end of the social scale, there have been only two people accorded the great honour of having their bodies interred in the chancel of the parish church, as befitting those of great standing. They were both relatively prosperous, at least by the standards of this village. The first was Thomas Kombes, who died in 1611, although we simply do not know if he was permitted burial in the chancel because he was the son of a courtier, or whether he achieved sufficient distinction in his own right. The second person was the great benefactor and Rector for over fifty years, the Revd Dr Andrew Lamont, who expressed the wish in his Will of 1709 that his body 'be decently buried in the Chancel of the Church of Bisley by the discretion of my Executors'. There is no indication that this wish was not fulfilled.

Briefs

These were letters patent issued by the sovereign authorising voluntary collections for a wide range of charitable purposes. The briefs were acted upon by lay officials within the community and also by the church. These are some of the causes to which Bisley inhabitants contributed:-

1678 For rebuilding St. Paul's Cathedral (10s. 0d.)
1683 Wapping White Chapel[7] (5s. 7d.)
1688 For French Protestants (8s. 7d.)
1689 For Irish Protestants
1692 Fire at Norwich
1692 Redemption of captives out of Turkish slavery (6s. 6d.)
1699 For French Protestants (9s. 1d.)
1700 Relief of Christians under the Emperor of Fez and Morocco
1702 For Chester Cathedral
1703 Widows and orphans of seamen lost in the 'dreadful storm and tempest'
1706 Darlington Church repairs

The simmering animosity and distrust between Protestants and Catholics frequently resulted in persecution of whichever denomination was in the minority, not just Catholics in England, but also Protestants living in France, Ireland, Spain and other strongly Catholic countries.

Bisley had able-bodied men who would have been drafted into military service to defend the country had the Spanish Armada actually reached these shores to overthrow Queen Elizabeth I and reinstate Roman Catholicism. There were supposed to have been 40,000 militia men,[(8)] ready armed and trained, to defend the Queen against a Spanish invasion, yet the collective skills of those from Bisley listed on the 1583 Surrey Muster Rolls[(9)] are sadly unimpressive:-

Pikemen selected	Robert Cobbett Junior
	Thomas Underwood
Bill men selected	Rychard Fellowe
	Thomas Cowper
	William Hone
Bill men of the best sorte	Henry Byrchatt
	John Symondes
	Ambrose Hampsheire
	Robert Gyles
Bill men of the second sorte	Robert Cobbett
	John Farnam
	John Hone
	John Cobbatt
	William Gyles
	John Shorter
	Thomas Edwardes

Lawrence Heather
William Russell
John Goringe
Edward Attfeild
Thomas Feild
Archers selected Rychard Roumsnye(10)

Although England would not have an effective standing army for another hundred years, she was not defenceless. The provision of arms for knights by the more wealthy people in society was well organised and so too were the regular musters, listing men according to their ability and, in some districts, noting the weapons they possessed.

Rails around the Churchyard

Records were also kept of individuals responsible for maintaining a section of the 'railes' (fencing) around the churchyard to keep out livestock. The extent of liability varied from one person to another according to the size of his, or her, property and so the length in feet had to be noted in every case. Everyone knew which bit of fence was theirs and presumably who was responsible for the adjoining section on each side. The total length of rails listed in 1698 was 453 feet, divided between 42 properties. It seems that the owners of five properties incurred the greatest liability which was limited to a maximum of 24 feet. They were Thos Collyer, Mary Davy, Mr Hornby, Mr fford, and James Hone, although Mary Davy's obligation was reduced when George Remnant Junr kindly undertook to look after eight feet of her allocation in addition to his own.

Taxation

A major source of taxation for the Crown from the Middle Ages was called the Lay Subsidies, which generally applied to the value of the estates owned by the laity; the clergy and the poor being exempted. Lay Subsidies were assessed according to one's personal income from land and certain possessions, and more than half-a-dozen people in Bisley were taxable.

National taxes have been raised in numerous, sometimes ingenious, ways throughout history, but taxation regarded by the population as being unfairly applied generally does not last long. The first Poll Tax was imposed to cover the high cost of military campaigns and similarly Hearth Tax, Land Tax and Window Tax were equally unpopular and short-lived. The 1664 Hearth Tax for Bisley was assessed by George Rempnant who was the Constable and who found that there were 18 properties with 47 hearths that qualified; a further 21 properties were not chargeable. Rempnant himself had six hearths, more than anyone else in the village. Land Tax followed a few decades later and Window Tax came very soon after that. There was a flat rate for a stipulated number of windows but larger properties sometimes avoided paying a surcharge for exceeding the quota by blocking up some windows. The tax was abolished in 1851 but some local buildings have never re-opened these bricked up windows.

Parochial Accounts

The earliest extant records of Churchwardens' and Overseers' accounts are over 300 years old. Part of the first one has been torn and is missing, leaving just six entries:-

Ye Accounpts of Henry Collier one of the wardens of Bisley for the year of our Lord	*1673.*	*s d*
It(em) spt at Bishopps when we came into our office	*)*	*02 06*
It pd at the Visitaton Court for taking My Ooath and for the dinner for the old churchwardens and my selfe	*)*	*05 08*
It given to the Ringers on the kings Birthday	*)*	*01 06*
It paid for helping upp with the Bell	*)*	*02 06*
It pd to Henry Whittwell for mending the Bell wheele	*)*	*01 02*
It pd to Edward Tanner for mending the Bell	*)*	*02 03*
It pd to Mrs West		

The following was submitted by the Overseer in 1682 and is also incomplete:-

The Account of George Wickman for the poorest of the poors of the parish of Bisley for the year of our Lord 1682.		*L s d*
It pd to Widd Marston for releefe severall times. May the 7th	*)*	*0 5 6*
Item pd to Widd Whittwell for releefe Monthe May the 7th	*)*	*0 4 0*
It pd to Thomas Young for releefe Month May the 7th	*)*	*0 3 4*
It pd to Widd Hone for releefe Month May the 7th	*)*	*0 2 0*
It pd to Willm Rogers for keeping a Bastard child. Month May the 7th	*)*	*...*

Several interesting recurrent items appear in the Churchwardens' accounts which are complete for the following years – 1737, 1740, 1743, 1744, 1751, 1758 and 1773:-

	L	s	d
paid for washing the surplis	0	1	0
spent on Gunpowder treson	0	2	6
paid for Riting my a counte	0	1	0

Some of these years have interesting single entries:-

paid for ye bel Ropes	0	6	6
Paid for ware from the Kill (kiln)	0	7	4
For fetching the ware	0	2	6
Paid for 2 days cutting of bushes	0	3	0
for going to the Ospitall	0	1	0

Several observations may be made from these few extracts, firstly one might question whether the surplice was actually washed as frequently as stated, sometimes several times a year. Two shillings and six pence would have been a very large expenditure for commemorating the Gunpowder Plot of 1605. The Clerk's indifferent spelling mattered not if neither Churchwarden could write. Bell ropes were very expensive in those days. The bricks, tiles and drains would have been made in Kiln Lane. Presumably several people were involved in the two-day task of cutting bushes for the amount stated. Which hospital? Maybe it was the alms house[11] at Wokingham.

---

(1) Every man had to attend church once a week (Act of Uniformity 1558 [1559]) or be fined 12d.
(2) *Bisley People in the 16th & 17th Centuries.*
(3) Oak saplings.
(4) The letter 'e' is frequently added to the end of some words in this document, though its use here does not change the preposition 'on' into the cardinal number 'one', since Maundy Thursday occurs just once in the year.
(5) *Bisley People in the 16th & 17th Centuries.*
(6) Between1628 and 1884 there were 10 baptisms of children from travelling vans.
(7) The name 'Wapping White Chapel' was used to distinguish this hamlet from the one known as Wapping-Stepney.
(8) *English Social History.*
(9) *Surrey Record Society. Surrey Musters*: Bisley 27th Jan 1583.
(10) In 1584 his name was spelt 'Romsye'.
(11) The Henry Lucas Hospital built in 1663, to which several Bisley men were taken.

Chapter 19

COLOURFUL CHARACTERS OF FOND MEMORY

At this juncture one has to tread most carefully to avoid offence. For very good reasons there are stories, often verified, about Bisley people and events that would be of great embarrassment or annoyance to some folk, and which therefore must be omitted. It would also be improper to write about anyone still living, no matter how meritorious their actions or estimable their lives. The field is narrowing. In this subjective area no two persons are likely to agree upon whom to include or exclude, no matter how lengthy the list, so we shall keep it short, be aware that there are significant omissions, and be mindful that this is merely a sample of individuals who stood out from the crowd. No inference should be drawn from the order in which names appear nor the lengthiness or brevity of any passage, merely noting the fact that they, and others like them, have enriched our lives in one way or another, and that their respective deeds or personalities have left a lasting impression.

Reg Burn

Reg was extremely well-known as the founder of The Fox Garage, the very successful motor car business that he established in 1923 and continued to run until his death in 1965. Reg was an exceptionally clever and prosperous businessman, but he also had a very generous nature as well as a great sense of humour. Employees thought the world of him and their loyalty was reciprocated. When asked, he would give sound advice on important matters and he helped many people in the village in various ways, even lending somebody a car for the duration of a holiday. Reg had been a tall man, but lying on damp ground under cars in the early days of the garage business, he developed arthritis in his back and he became doubled over as a result. This did not stop him rushing over from his house to confront thieves on each occasion they broke into the garage in the middle of the night, setting off the alarm.

The Fox Garage. 1960s

Ted Hill

Ted was born in Bisley but lived in Kings Road West End for many years. He was the first person to be employed as a mechanic by Reg Burn soon after The Fox Garage was established. He literally worked there all his life because years after he drew his final wages, he would turn up every day on his 'sit-up-and-beg' bicycle to feed the cat and find useful little jobs to do. Ted was a quiet-spoken man with a very likeable personality and he was very clever. He installed electrical wiring systems throughout Fox Engineering and Cavey's joinery workshop, and he could make almost anything in metal without the need for a construction plan. Ted made a plough and a harrow for Reg Burn's grey Ferguson tractor and used them for cultivating the field at the end of Chatton Row where he grew vegetables for the garage canteen.

Bisley Fire Brigade. 1960
Left to right (rear): Benny Hearn, Sid Mitchell, Bert Castle, Len Mansfield, Alex Hutchinson, John Beavis, Charlie Hilder.
(front): Joe North, Ted Hill, Ron Small.
Photo Burn & Martin Collection by courtesy of Surrey History Centre.

Ted Hill was one of the retained (part-time) firemen with Bisley Fire Brigade and, as the Senior Officer, was proud to wear his white helmet. The firemen(1) were fully trained professionals who had full-time employment outside the fire service, but all of them worked within a short distance of Bisley Primary School where the fire engine was kept. The fire alarm was mounted on a post behind the school and when it sounded it could be heard for miles. The fire engine would be driven around the village, quickly picking up firemen before rushing off to some incident. Despite being extremely short-sighted, Ted insisted upon being the relief driver and, on the rare occasions he had to drive, his nose would appear to be pressed against the windscreen as the appliance left the garage forecourt. Ted built the first Bisley fire engine by converting an old Hillman 14 lorry.

The first Bisley fire engine.
Photo Burn & Martin Collection by courtesy of Surrey History Centre.

Mrs Hawkins

Florence Edith Hawkins, known to one and all simply as 'Mrs Hawkins', was born in 1880 into the wealthy Sainsbury family, of which she was very proud. However, all her relatives shunned her on account of her eccentricity. She had lived in Bisley since 1917 but it was not until some thirty years later that she started a strange hobby that grew into an obsession.

For anyone travelling down Queens Road in the 1950s and 1960s, the most remarkable sight came into view as one approached the bend by the firing points of Century Range. Mrs Hawkins' garden – using the term loosely – was quite unique. The whole area was filled with an adornment of broken pieces of crockery, coloured glass and bits of mirror, cemented together into odd shapes and sizes, displaying a dazzling array of coloured mosaic taking the form of jagged shards of sculpture standing up to 5 feet (1.5 metres) high, all interspersed with busts, antlers, bric-à-brac, statuettes, plates, shells, curved horns, gnomes, and the 'penny'. The penny, as it was generally known, was a plate, approximately 4 feet (1.2 metres) in diameter, fixed upright, having a leaf pattern around the perimeter and a huge embossed silhouette of the head of a lady, similar to the way in which the Queen's head is shown on British coins – hence the 'penny'.

Some of these recycled pieces of china and plaster work were raised on plinths to give them added prominence, though they were all packed so tightly together one could scarcely see between them. Each year more pieces would be added to the collection. Even the quaint green and white traditional gypsy caravan standing in the centre of the garden was adorned with strange bits and pieces to make it an integral part of the whole assemblage. In other circumstances, the gaudily-painted caravan would have been immediately apparent to the eye, particularly as it was raised on blocks, necessitating a flight of 9 steps up to floor level, but lost in this awesome spectacle of colour and form it almost blended into the background. The whole bizarre scene would not have been out of place in Alice in Wonderland.

The unique art gallery stretched right down to the narrow grass verge at the edge of the road where the small white entrance gate hung with warning bells to announce the arrival of intruders. There were wires and string set along the short path to the caravan all connected to bells, making it difficult to gain entry without setting off the early warning system, rather like a loose spider's web to catch its prey. An old parrot swung in a cage at the door of the caravan, and young boys would be sent packing if Mrs Hawkins was in earshot of their efforts to teach the parrot a few choice words.

Needless to say, Mrs Hawkins had a poor opinion of boys:-[(2)] 'Many of them are young lunatics,' she would say. 'They are too educated and have too much easy money. It is difficult to get people to work. I couldn't get a boy to cut my brambles last year for any money. People are just not available for any sort of repair work either. I suppose I shall have to mend the greenhouse myself,' she conceded, when a pane of glass needed replacing.

People from all over the world come to shoot at Bisley and some of those who stood in Queens Road marvelling at the display would send home photos of the weird spectacle. Sometimes in the summer there were queues of cars parked outside. Pictures of this strange garden display appeared in publications in far away places, including Canada, Kenya, Malaysia and New Zealand.

Mrs Hawkins was a tall lady, who used to be a staunch member of the W.I., the Knaphill Legionnaires and other local clubs. She was noted for her generosity in providing produce from her greenhouse for the raffles. She went to Guildford Market every Tuesday to find suitable articles to add to her collection. When she went shopping in Guildford or Woking, she would dress in a flamboyant style with a brightly-coloured frock, and often paint her bicycle the same colour. The following week it might be red, or yellow or green.

Mrs Hawkins was certainly a colourful character – in more than one sense – and she lived into her late 80s. She once told a local press reporter,(3) 'I just won't know what to do with all these things when I die. None of my relations want them.'

Mrs Hawkins' caravan. 1959

Heaven knows what became of her caravan after she died, but some months later the penny was spotted in the window of an antique shop in Woodbridge Road, Guildford, appropriately facing the old cattle market that she regularly used to visit.

John Cooper

John was a very self-effacing gentleman with a mischievous sense of humour. He moved to Clews Farm with his family in 1964 and became very involved with Bisley Church, becoming a Churchwarden in 1968 and later qualifying as a Reader. He claimed that emptying the chemical toilet regularly was his main duty to the church.

John was born in 1917 and served in the Fleet Air Arm during the Second World War. He never talked about his wartime service other than to say that it had been difficult flying in the Norwegian fjords. It was only after his death in 1998 that *The Daily Telegraph* published[(4)] a full page obituary, stating that John had been an outstanding fighter pilot and had won the Distinguished Service Cross and Bar. The article mentioned that on one occasion he had flown so close to a fjord-side cliff that a radio aerial on the belly of his plane had been broken off. He had flown 29 types of aircraft and made more than 100 deck landings and, as a Lieutenant Commander, had been the Commanding Officer of an aircraft carrier squadron. John Cooper was a keen sportsman throughout his life, even having a go at windsurfing in his 70s, but he was also a talented artist and had exhibited watercolour paintings at the Royal Academy. He made some wonderful paintings of local scenes, including many of St John the Baptist Church, Bisley.

Albert Henbest

Bert, as he was always called, lived at Compton in Church Lane, not far from Bisley Church where he was the Verger from 1928 until 1972. Bert led the responses at church service in a loud voice from the back of the church, rang the bells, laid out vestments, lit the candles, acted as sidesman at weddings and funerals, turned the boiler on and off, carried water up to the central heating tank in the bell tower, apprehended a thief in the vestry[(5)] on one occasion, and did almost everything to keep the place ticking over smoothly. Moreover, he single-handedly kept the whole churchyard in immaculate condition – a feat which whole bands of volunteers have never since been able to achieve, no matter how great their number. This he accomplished by going there very regularly, often several times a day even if for only half an hour or so, to mow the grass, edge the drive, cut the hedges, remove dead flowers from graves, and so on. Bert did this so well, and for so long, that few realised just how much time he devoted to this duty, or how difficult the task became for others once he had gone. Bert did much for Bisley but it is this churchyard work for which he is best remembered.

Bert Henbest.
Photo: Jim Henbest

The Reverend John Gwyon

John Gwyon was born in 1863 and became Rector of Bisley from 1895 to 1928. He was a scholar but he became increasingly eccentric in later life and his congregation at church dwindled to a mere handful.

An Inquest was held at the Coroner's Court next to Woking Police Station on 28th December 1928, following his tragic death on Boxing Day. The *Surrey Advertiser and County Times* report[6] of the Inquest stated that the Rector had lodged with William Fennell of Bisley Post Office for six years. Gwyon did not live at the Rectory, despite being urged to do so by the ecclesiastical authorities. Evidence from some witnesses indicated that he had felt he was being forced to choose between resigning or living in the Rectory which he hated, and that the slightest thing would worry him, even the arrival of letters.

Gwyon's doctor, who knew him well, said that he had always been eccentric. He would go about the roads with a hangdog look, and with his hands behind his back. He always wore very filthy collars and his shirt was dreadful. A month before his death, the doctor had examined him for an insurance pension scheme. His heart was in a very bad state. He said he was always terribly afraid that 'something would happen mentally'. 'Really he was in a very bad way,' he concluded.

The Bishop of Guildford was represented at the Inquest by his secretary, who denied that any pressure had been put on Gwyon to retire though he had been offered a handsome pension of £175 if he were to do so (the net value of his stipend was £233 a year).

It was stated that in the course of conversation with his landlord at the Post Office on Christmas evening, Gwyon had mentioned that there was 'nothing in the Bible indicating where a suicide goes'. Fennell had not been at all perturbed by this remark, as the Rector was the last man he would have expected to commit suicide, though he conceded that the Rector had been very nervous during the past month.

Gwyon had been reported missing during the evening on Boxing Day, and at about 8.30am the following morning the rectory was forcibly entered by two people – one a policeman – and Gwyon's body was found hanging from the skylight, the cords of which were tied around his neck. The post-mortem established that death was 'due to asphyxia by suffocation by hanging'. The jury returned a verdict that 'Mr Gwyon committed suicide while insane, having become a mental and physical wreck'. After this dreadful event the Rectory was declared unsuitable for further use as a parsonage and was sold under the name of Bisley House. In 1947 it was again renamed, this time Coombe Manor, and in 1995 it was demolished, by which time the redevelopment value of the site had exceeded the resale value of the house.

The Reverend John Gwyon. 1922
boys, left to right: Percy Morton, Edward Lines, Claude Elmer, Tom Morton, Joseph Lines.

There are several extant copies of what seems to be the only photograph of him taken at close quarters. It shows him standing behind five boys in the church porch. One copy carries a message on the back in his own hand:- 'Mr & Mrs R B. Roberts from Rev J Gwyon. Rector of Bisley Surrey – Since 1895. With compliments. August 1922.'

The Reverend John Gwyon's Will was even more extraordinary than his behaviour during his lifetime. At his death, he left an estate of £9,976, which was a very substantial sum in those days. It has never been explained how he managed to amass such a large fortune. The fact that he had so much money came as a surprise to his former parishioners at Bisley who always thought he never had 'two pennies to rub together'.

He bequeathed that the estate (£7,974 net) was to be devoted entirely to a charitable foundation called 'Gwyon's Foundation for Clothing Boys', of which the trustees would be the Farnham Urban District Council. This charity was to provide the boys of Farnham with knickers (knicker-bockers) and 'for no other purpose whatsoever whether educational or otherwise'. One of the strangest aspects is that nobody in Farnham or Bisley could ever recall Gwyon having any interest in, or connection with, the town of Farnham.

The details of the bequest become more and more bizarre :-

> A tailor was to be appointed in Easter week each year.
>
> Boys aged no younger than 10 nor older than 18, living in Farnham or with 3 miles of the town were to receive one garment each year.
>
> The words 'GWYON'S PRESENT' must be written in capital letters on the lining of the waist on the right-hand side. Provided the words have not been defaced or removed from the garment, the boys were to be eligible for another pair the following year.

> 'No sporting or fancy knickers of any kind will be permitted, such as football knickers, cricket knickers, military knickers, Boy Scout knickers or riding knickers, and in no case shall the knickers be of the pattern known as shorts.'
>
> If at any time the annual interest exceeded the expenditure on these garments, then the surplus was to be used in the same way for knickers for boys in Windlesham, Chobham, Egham, Woking and Reigate (though Bisley was not mentioned).

Gwyon had appointed the Public Trustee to be his executor, but the Will was successfully contested in the High Court and ruled null and void. The judge had to decide whether the trusts declared in the 1912 Will and five codicils were valid in creating this charity. The judgement was that, because of the restrictive conditions to be applied to boys benefiting from the bequest, it could not be regarded as a charitable trust and so he ruled that it was wholly void and that the estate was to be dissolved under intestacy law (the proceeds reverting to the Crown). Meanwhile, the national press had taken up the story with glee and made sure that Gwyon's name became known throughout the land.

Henry Lawson

Henry Peter Lawson had been a widely known and respected stockbroker who, in retirement, lived at Lynbrook, formerly

Clinton Farm and which at one time had been in the Parish of Bisley. He became involved in many local organisations and was a staunch member of the congregation of Bisley Church. He commissioned two of the stained glass windows in St John the Baptist Church and quietly helped in many practical ways. Mr Lawson twice restored the cover on the Holy Well, and when the old churchyard lawnmower broke down, a new professional machine designed to withstand heavy use mysteriously appeared. He died in 1956 aged 89.

Major Robin Fulton

Robin was an immensely self-motivated man, one could say single-minded almost to the point of obsession, and he was determined to emulate the success of his father and grandfather by winning the most prestigious prize in the world of rifle shooting – the Queen's Prize. He modestly claimed that his father and grandfather were naturally brilliant shots and that he was just a determined plodder.[(7)] Whether this was true or not, he matched their achievement by winning it in 1958 and nearly repeated it the following year when he was narrowly beaten into second place. Robin was a Queen's finalist twenty-one times, and represented Britain as a member or coach of the shooting team on twelve occasions abroad and seventeen times at home. Robin put his heart and soul into everything he embarked upon, including hunting. He founded the Fulton Harriers in 1951 which became the Bisley and Sandhurst Foxhounds in 1958, and the sound of a pack of excited hounds at feeding time at his home at Chaseley could be heard throughout the village.

Richard Clifton

Richard embarked on a promising career as a city accountant but gave it up when an opportunity arose to work in his uncle's[8] hardware shop in Knaphill. He soon took charge of mower repairs and servicing which, in those days, included annual re-grinding of cylinders blades. Richard soon branched out on his own and built up a very successful garden machinery business which is still thriving.

From early boyhood, Richard had a deep love of the countryside, particularly insects, and kept bees all his life. He had a powerful tenor voice and sang in Bisley Church Choir for many years. Richard took over as Clerk to the Bisley Parish Council and was instrumental in setting up Bisley Church Youth Club, which he ran single-handedly for many years, taking the table tennis table on the roof of his Morris 1000 saloon car from home to the former Fire Brigade rest room where the club met every Tuesday evening. Richard had a magnanimous personality and a wonderful sense of humour.

---

(1) John Beavis, Bert Castle, Benny Hearn, Charlie Hilder, Ted Hill, Alex Hutchinson, Len Mansfield, Sid Mitchell, Joe North & Ron Small.
(2) *Woking Review*, May 1965.
(3) *Woking News & Mail*, 23rd February 1962.
(4) *Daily Telegraph*, 24th February 1998.
(5) *Surrey Advertiser*, 21st October 1939.
(6) *Surrey Advertiser*, 5th January 1929.
(7) *NRA Official Millennium Souvenir 1910-2000.*
(8) F G Rice.

Chapter 20

MISCELLANY

'King's Evil', which we now call scrofula – a disease that disappeared in this country as milk became tuberculosis-free – was most common in children and resulted in unsightly swellings of the neck. There was a widely-held belief, which had originated from the time of Edward the Confessor, that successive monarchs inherited a God-given power to heal the afflicted merely by touching them or giving them a coin or medallion which had been touched by the king. The coin would be pierced and hung on a ribbon around the neck, and in time the patient would supposedly be healed. Three young people from Bisley received certificates from the Rector and Churchwardens as credentials allowing them to be brought before King James II. The first two, Elizabeth Collier and her cousin, Thomas Collier, who were aged 15 and 4 respectively, were taken to a mass ceremony in 1686 for sufferers of the disease. Two years later Sarah Massey, the Rector's daughter, was afflicted and she too was given a certificate. There is no record of whether any of them were cured but this procedure was given added credence by the introduction of a prayer(1) into the Book of Common Prayer to be used during the ceremony.

Scrofula was one of many diseases for which exaggerated claims were made in 1657 in the first newspaper advertisement[2] for coffee:-

> *... the drink called Coffee (which is a very wholesome and Physical drink, having many excellent vertues), closes the Orifice of the Stomack, fortifies the heat within, helpeth Digestion, quickneth the Spirits, maketh the heart lightsome, is good against Eye-sores, Coughs, or Colds, Rhumes, Consumptions, Head-ach, Dropsie, Gout, Scurvy, Kings Evil, and many others...*

The village Pound, where stray animals were 'impounded', was situated on the edge of the common across the road from the beer garden of 'The Fox Inn'. It was shown on the 1871 Ordnance Survey map but it had gone by the time the 1915 edition was published. Pound Cottage (now 320 Guildford Road) was formerly Pound Farm.

Bombs dropped on Bisley recorded by Bagshot Rural District Council:-

22nd October 1940	–	5 (high explosive) at Stickledown
8th November 1940	–	5 (high explosive) at the Refuge Farm School
22nd November 1940	–	1 at The Copse, Bisley
3rd February 1944	–	2 at Queens Road

After the retirement of the Revd Charles Montagu Horley as Rector of Bisley, a Diocesan proposal to amalgamate the benefices of Bisley and West End was passionately resisted. At the Annual Parochial Meeting in February 1955, the Reverend D P Davis, who was Vicar of West End and had been made Priest in Charge at Bisley during the interregnum, said he understood why many people disliked 'turning out on a cold night and going down the dark lanes to church with no lighting, and instead of paths, deep ditches on either side, but' he added 'fill your church and by doing this you will gain a Rector'. The concerted efforts of the Churchwardens and Parochial Church Council(3) were successful in rejecting the scheme. Bisley was to have two new Rectors before eventually being united with West End by Order of the Privy Council in 1976.

Biplane in the kitchen garden at The Farm School.

A biplane made an emergency landing in the vegetable garden of the Farm School during the First World War, and a light aircraft from Chobham Airfield, flying low in very turbulent weather, crashed into trees beside Coombe Manor in 1962.

The short front garden of 287 Guildford Road became so crammed with trees and shrubs that it eventually became completely obscured by them, leaving just a small arched gap beneath the screen of foliage leading to the front door.

Cutting from a local newspaper in 1899:-

> An octogenarian native of Bisley died last week in the person of Mr James Hill (1814-1899), farmer, who for a great number of years made regular journeys to Richmond to dispose of his produce. He was well known along the road, where some 30 years ago an experience befell him which nearly cost him his life. He was set upon and left insensible by some roughs he had prosecuted for theft, and who on leaving prison resolved to have their revenge. As the result of this outrage, his life for a time was despaired of, but getting the better of his injuries he lived to a ripe and active age. In parochial affairs, the deceased was for many years an active participant, among the offices he held being that of Churchwarden.

A newspaper cutting without a date or name:-

> A meeting of the Bisley Parish Council was held on Tuesday, Mr WJ Fuller presiding. Other members present were Messrs Cheeseman, Steptoe, Mitchell, Graham, Cherryman and the Clerk (Mr W Miles). The Clerk reported the receipt of a letter from the District Council stating that owing

> to the economy being exercised nationally, the suggested widening of Port Lane (A322) had been held up.
>
> The question of the danger arising to pedestrians on the main road was raised, and it was resolved to suggest to the District Council that even if a permanent footpath could not be provided at the present time, the services of the Council could be utilised in taking preliminary steps in levelling the roadside waste[(4)] between the Post Office and Reidon Hill with a view to the other work being placed in hand at the earliest possible date.

The A322 was straightened and considerably widened in places through the southern end of the village in the late 1950s. The re-alignment started outside the Fox Garage and finished opposite Port Way. It left a redundant section of road, 12 feet (3.7 metres) wide at its widest point, in front of 309 to 315 Guildford Road. An even wider section, outside the shop on the corner of Clews Lane (279 Guildford Road), was turned into a filter lane when traffic lights were installed. The green at the end of Queens Road was reduced even more in size by further road widening and forming a kink at the end of Queens Road to stagger the crossroads on the A322. The green had once been large enough for children to play cricket in comparative safety, but at that time there was only light passing traffic and no trees to interrupt the game.

There were two very well patronised youth clubs in the 1960s – one was run by Jim Cheeseman and the other by Richard Clifton.

'Coldingly More' is named on the John Senex map of 1729. On the same map, the East-West route passing the Fox Inn is shown to be straighter and more obvious than the North-South route that we now call the A322, thus giving weight to the assertion that Kiln Lane was once the more heavily used road.

In 1948 the Olympic Torch was carried along the A322 through Bisley. It was handed over at Crossways Cottage by K W Botting (Surrey Constabulary Athletics Club) to R J Turner (Walton Athletics Club) who then handed on to the next runner who was awaiting its arrival at the Gordon Boys' School in West End.

Peace celebrations 1945: 'Best float'.
left to right (adults): R. Underwood, Mrs V. M. Halls, Ted Wye, Reg Barrett, Mrs Connie Barrett, Mrs Underwood, Miss Jessie Matthews, Miss Hazel Underwood, Mrs Irene Elliot, Arthur Clifton, John Elliot.
(children): June Halls, Richard Clifton, Lorna Elliot, Marilyn Elliot.

Woking News & Mail, 28th September 1945:-

> Outstanding success attended the Bisley Victory Celebrations held on September 22nd, the main programme being held out of doors. The proceedings included sports, entertainment and a tea for the children, with sideshows for the grown-ups in the afternoon, followed in the evening by a torchlight procession, bonfire and dancing. The celebrations commenced with a procession of children in fancy dress led by two

pipers from the Scots Guards. There was a large number of competitors and much ingenuity had been used in evolving the dresses under ration conditions. The fancy dress prizes were distributed by the judges, Mr and Mrs Eatherley and Mrs MacArthur. After a comprehensive sports programme and free swing and pony rides, about 400 children were entertained to tea. After tea victory medals[(5)] were presented to each child by Mr RW Burn before they filed out to the sports field, where a Punch and Judy show was given followed by a conjuring entertainment.

In the evening a procession with flaming torchlights took place, starting at the Garibaldi and proceeding to the Hen and Chickens for judging. It was headed by the Drum and Pipe Band of the Scots Guards. A 30ft. tall bonfire, lighted by the Victory Queen, Miss Sheila Linger, and aided by fireworks made a fitting finale to the gay pageantry of the procession.

The evening festivities continued with a dance on the school playground under floodlighting, and an exhibition parade by the Drum and Pipe Band of the Scots Guards.

The members of the planning committee for the celebrations were Messrs Urban, Beavis, Fuller, Smallridge, Winton, Miss

> Lyming and Mrs Harris, and about 60 other Bisley residents gave of their time and energy in preparing and running the festivities.

A long-running dispute over a footpath in Bisley was settled in the Royal Courts of Justice in 1914. The tenant farmer, Frederick Street, had challenged the right to use the path through Bullhousen Farm to Lucas Green Common. He had tried to stop walkers from using the path (Public Footpath No23), and so too had his father, also called Frederick, and John and Isaac Gosden, who had occupied the farm as tenants from 1822. In the opinion of the judge, Mr Justice Astbury, the case hinged upon whether the public had used it as of right prior to the first tenancy. A witness, James Collier, whose personal recollection went back to 1844, stated that his father had spoken of the existence of the path at least as far back as 1822. Another witness, Mary Ann Elson stated that her father told her, in around 1850, that the right-of-way existed before the first tenancy. Many other witnesses were called, some of whom also attested to having been told that people had regularly used the path without let or hindrance before the critical date. One key witness, Stephen Holmes, stated that he had been present when one of the Gosdens had confronted two gypsies on the path and had turned to him saying: 'It is a nuisance these people coming here, but it is a footpath and I cannot stop them; but I do not want to let the likes of them through if I can help it.' The judge stated that there was

a large body of evidence supporting the assertion that a right-of-way existed and ruled that the dedication to the public has existed from some time prior to 1822.
(Now, almost 100 years later, the controversy has been long forgotten, and the path is rarely used).

The delightfully named Snowdrop Farm was a pretty little cottage that nestled on the edge of Bisley Common at the point at which Public Footpath No148A branches off to Reidon Hill from Public Bridleway No147. Snowdrop Farm had almost certainly been built around the middle of the 17th century and the date 1643 was clearly marked on one of the bricks. It was originally called 'Goodeners' and appears to have been given the name Snowdrop Farm about two hundred years later. The front garden hedge was set back from a small barn on the edge of the common, forming an unusual kink in the boundary, still there today. The wooden barn was the last building in the area to be thatched with heather which was so tightly packed that it kept the rain out as well as any other thatching material.

The Steptoe family had lived and farmed there for generations and, confusingly, the first-born son in nearly every generation was named Stephen. The last of the male line, Stephen Charles Steptoe, born in 1886, lived there with his sister, Eva, who was three years younger. In later life they kept only pigs and hens and had a few bee hives in the orchard.

The field at the end of Chatton Row, in which Mr Ernest Hayward had nursery stock and which was later used to grow vegetables for the canteen of the Fox Garage, was originally part of Snowdrop Farm, and so too were the meadows behind the farm which Bert Hill rented for hay and grazing his heavy horses. Brown's steel office equipment factory and car park now covers all three fields.

The Second Lord Teignmouth, recalled[(6)] an incident in Bisley Church on one occasion when his friend, the Reverend James Jerram, Vicar of Chobham from 1810 until 1834, was conducting a service: 'The situation in the church at Bisley was most retired, a favourite resort of owls, who might be heard hooting by day. On one occasion when we were present, Mr Jerram's sermon was disturbed by snoring. He more than once appealed to the suppose sleeper, and at length, peremptorily intimated that unless the good man or woman to whom he attributed the interruption were awakened, he must discontinue his sermon. "Sir," exclaimed a man from a remote part of the church, "it's a howl".'

The farm buildings belonging to the Farm School were in Church Lane opposite The Old Cottage. They comprised brick cart-sheds and stables, an open-sided Dutch barn and a 'model' concreted cow-yard with a cow-shed, calf pens and a dairy that had a steam steriliser. The morning's milk was cooled and delivered to the Farm School, the Shaftesbury School and local houses by seven o'clock each morning. An asphalt playground separated the farm buildings from the Assembly Hall, the Farm Manager's house (now Shallowford) and the Farm School.

From the *Woking News & Mail,* 26th June 1948:-
A number of old school pupils joined the boys of Bisley (Shaftesbury) School on Saturday on the occasion of the unveiling and dedication of a memorial tablet to the 25 old boys who lost their lives in the 1939-45 war. The tablet, which is on the east side of the chapel, is supplemental to the 1914-18 war memorial and has been provided by old boys. **(Appendix E)** Afterwards the company went into the School Hall where the old boys made a presentation of a carpet and a lawn mower to Mr B Read, headmaster, and to Mrs Read, on the occasion of their coming retirement on August 31st after 23 years at the school.

From The *Bisley Parish Magazine,* December 1901:-

> The year now drawing to a close will always be a memorable one in this country, owing to the death of our late beloved Sovereign Queen Victoria. At our Parish Church a Memorial Service was held on Sunday afternoon, February 3rd, the Chancel being draped with black. The school-children marched to the Church to the strains of the Dead March, played by the Farm School Brass Band. The crowded congregation,

including representatives of the Parish Council, was almost entirely dressed in black. The organist, Mr Broderick, played Chopin's Funeral March at the commencement of the Service, and the Funeral Marches of Beethoven and Mendelssohn at the close. The service was fully Choral, and included two solos by Mrs Lansdown and Mr Clayton. The Rector, the Rev J Gwyon, preached the Memorial Sermon.

The Bishop of Winchester has again visited our Parish during the present year, namely, on May 3rd, when he confirmed a number of Farm and Shaftesbury boys at their School Chapel.

Captain George Payne, the People's Warden, is away in South Africa with the Metropolitan Mounted Rifles, Ethelred Payne, one of our choir boys, and two others of Captain Payne's sons being with him. We hope we may, in the coming year, be able to welcome them all home again, safe and sound. The death of Sergeant Major H Glazier, of Bisley Green, which took place at Winberg Hospital while serving with the Imperial Yeomanry in South Africa, is much to be regretted. Others from the village, besides many old boys of the Farm and Shaftesbury Schools, have served, and are serving, at the Front, Bisley having thus

> many ties with the conflict at the present time. May the new year bring peace and prove a bright and prosperous one to all our readers.

George Payne did return at the end of the Second Boer War in 1902 and lived to the ripe old age of 83. His brother, Charles, the Shaftesbury School Bandmaster, had been killed in action in 1899 aged 46.

The village became smaller in the 1930s when the parish boundary was moved away from The Garibaldi public house. Most of the houses in Limecroft Road, Stanley Farm in Chobham Road and a large piece of common were transferred to Horsell Parish, though they are now regarded as being part of Knaphill. At the northern end of the village, the parish boundary still crosses Newbridge and incorporates all the houses on the left-hand side from Newbridge Cottage to the former Elm Tree Nursery which closed after Bill Glazier died. A little chalet bungalow, called Boundary Cottage, opposite the nursery entrance marked the point at which the parish boundary crosses the A322. This dwelling has recently been demolished.

---

(1) The prayer was omitted from 1719.

(2) *Publick Advisor* 26 May 1657 (from The Times 27-03-1969).

(3) Churchwardens:- Horace Cherryman and Charles

Ouin. PCC:- Mrs Cheeseman, Mr J Cherryman, Mrs J Cherryman, Miss Clayton, Mr W Ellen, Mr H Elliot, Mr Graham, Mr Grigg, Mrs Hone, Miss Liming, Mrs Linger, Mrs G Ramage, Mrs Richens, Miss Schmid and Mrs K White.

(4) Grass verge beside the A322.

(5) Aluminium medals specially minted for the occasion, with 'V Celebrations. Bisley. 1945' (obverse side) and St. George slaying the dragon (reverse side) depicted in relief.

(6) Teignmouth. *Reminiscences*.

Chapter 21

REMINISCENCES

This book would not be complete without a selection of interesting, informative and humorous reminiscences of some Bisley residents. Regrettably, so many potential contributors have died and their stories have gone with them. They include two well-known characters who had made arrangements to speak about some memorable events for this book, but who died very recently before passing on their personal recollections.

One should hastily acknowledge that these stories are a mere sample of the wealth of material available, had one the time to seek out everyone with something to contribute. The reader should not doubt the sincerity of the following contributions, but it is possible that a few details may be slightly incorrect as some of the events occurred more than half a century ago and the human mind is not infallible. These snatches from the past are deliberately unattributable, require no explanation and are chronicled completely at random.

Off to the seaside in the charabanc.

'Mr Andy Hayward had a small field for nursery stock on the far side of Reidon Hill where Meadowsong and Reidon Cottage are now situated. At the foot of the hill on the Knaphill side there are now three modern houses[(1)] which were built on the site of a very strange property owned by Miss North. In the 1950s the whole garden was an almost impenetrable jungle of scrub and trees, some were leaning and propped up with posts to stop them falling further. You couldn't see the house from the front for the thicket that surrounded it. It was all very dark and sinister in there. We boys used to call her a witch. Apparently her father built the house but didn't finish the roof to avoid paying rates. Miss North just lived downstairs. She was very eccentric, sat indoors and rarely ventured out. She always seemed to have a chicken in her arms. After she died they pulled the house down for safety but they couldn't do anything with the land for seven years in case there was a relative who could claim it.'

'A bomb fell in Mr & Mrs Pocock's garden, which is now the allotments, and damaged the side of Barnfield Cottages, and as I was going to school an incendiary bomb had dropped further up Queens Road in the night and bits of it were still burning the following morning.'

'My brother Frank joined the church choir in 1912 when it consisted of 20 or more men and boys. He became the principal soloist and, when the regular organists and choirmaster, Alec Graham, was called up, my brother took over these duties at the age of 16. He became a Churchwarden and he served for many years as a Magistrate on the Woking Bench.'

'Topper (*Henry*) Gosden lived in a tiny old bungalow next to Greyfriars. He always seemed to be cooking jacket potatoes on a wood fire. Many a time I sat in there and ate one. It had a dirt floor and no windows. My mum said, "I wish you wouldn't go to Topper Gosden's place".'

'When I was a little boy, my grandfather had to see Topper Gosden about something, and he took me with him. Topper had a beard and whiskers and wore a long sort of gown or smock with an old sack around his shoulders. He asked us in. The place only had an earth floor, and it was all up and down like this. Directly in front of us was an old iron grate fire, and hanging from a hook was a chain and a big pot with something simmering in it.

He had a bit of a shed where he kept two goats which he would tether on the common during the day. He always had a few ducks, and when he let them out in the morning they would scuttle under the gate and across to road to the pond. I remember that well.'

'Miss Watts lived in Ford Road in an old railway carriage. That was a dreadful place too – it had no proper floor. She kept pigs and sold a few gooseberries.'

'The Steptoes at Snowdrop Farm had a small wire-haired terrier that would dash out from the gate and bite passers-by on the ankle, particularly children on bicycles. The dog's name was Nipper.

Mr Steptoe cut turf on the common to use in a clamp to store root vegetable. Similar patches of bare ground from where rectangular pieces of turf had been removed could also be seen on the Shaftesbury area, quite possibly the work of Fred Elson.

After Stephen Steptoe died in 1959, his sister Cis moved to another part of the country and was married at the age of 72. The property was bought by Fred Brown who demolished the farm cottage and built a bungalow a short distance away in the orchard.'

'Miss Sophie Wing married one of the Chandlers. It wasn't either Bert or Bill (*Herbert and William were identical twins. It was Edwin Chandler, a dairy farmer from Horsell*). She wore a brown velvet suit and black lace-up boots and carried a bouquet of wild flowers. She left the house the same evening, never to return. Henceforth she much preferred to be known as Miss Wing, and rarely or never Mrs Chandler.'

'The house on the corner (*of School Close*) where Harry Partridge lived was originally the carter's cottage. He would take Mr Lewry's shire horses with the wagon up to the field, which is now Arethusa Way, where they work all day. When they returned, the carter would turn off Church Lane into the pond, wagon and all, where the horses would stand and drink – it was a lovely scene.'

'Mr Morris was the Farm Bailiff and lived in the black and white farmhouse at Cobbetts Farm which was owned by Brookwood Hospital. The stable and cowshed were at the side of the rickyard. There was a large black tarred barn in which the swing-boats for the annual August Bank Holiday Fête at Brookwood Hospital were stored.'

'My mother, Frances Cowle, lived at Clews Farm for some years and her father was the last person to run it as a farm. She died on her 101st birthday.'

'George Titcombe had a little dairy at the Brambles[2] and Alfred Mitchell, who farmed at Hill Place Farm, started delivering milk around the village and parts of Knaphill. When his son-in-law Jack (*Walter John*) Fuller took over, the milk round got bigger when he bought Fern Dairy at Knaphill next to Grimditch & Webb, opposite The Crown pub. He got the rounds that went with it and also the staff. He had seven people working at Fern Dairy and on the rounds, which then included a lot of Knaphill, a little bit of West End, Connaught Road Brookwood and some of St John's. Jack Fuller got a Trojan van with solid tyres, and later he bought a brand new Austin van from The Fox Garage. A man at the top of Warbury Hill came and did the sign writing.'

'A bull escaped from the cattle market in Guildford and rampaged around the town before being cornered and recaptured. My car was the only one in the whole town that it kicked!'

Jack Herbert, Bill Jaques and Robin Fulton (mounted and with his hounds) outside The Hen and Chickens.
Photo: Burn & Martin Collection by courtesy of Surrey History Centre.

'Although The Barley Mow was no longer a pub in the 1950s, the Bisley and Sandhurst Foxhounds occasionally met there. Riders were handed hot punch by the Debenham lad and his friends. The hunt also met at the Hen & Chickens where they would be welcomed with a drink by Bill Jacques, the Licensee.'

'The church organ filled half the vestry and was separated from the robing area by a wooden partition which had a slot with a wooden level protruding through it for operating the bellows. "Frazzle" Fry, as he was known, who lived in Belper Cottage,(3) was the one who pumped the organ by hand but on more than one occasion the organ unexpectedly ran out of wind after the first few bars of the final hymn because Mr Fry had fallen asleep in the vestry during the sermon. Frazzle was a Dickensian character with long "drainpipe" trousers, pointed black boots, "bottle-lens" glasses and a funny old black hat. He was always dressed in black.'

'When sweets came off ration in 1952, I used to go down to Hill's shop on the corner of Clews Lane and buy a bar of Peter's Chocolate with my pocket money because it was bigger and cheaper than Cadburys. One day when I was nine or ten I had just come out of the shop when I spotted a large pig running hell-for-leather down Mr Rix's drive on the opposite side of the road, where Queens Close houses are now. It must have jumped over the pigsty wall. An old black car, about the size of a Morris Eight, was passing just as the pig emerged. The pig hit the side of the car with great force, bounced off like a rubber ball, and immediately ran back up the drive. The car moved noticeably sideways as the pig hit it but I don't think the driver ever saw the pig. He stopped up the road and looked around scratching his head. I hid in case he spotted me killing myself with laughter.'

'Another pig incident that I well remember happened in 1954. Brown's factory was quite small in those days and vegetables were grown in the field at the rear for the canteen. Major Emerson from Knaphill kept pigs in a line of pigsties at the end of the field. One day, two large pigs occupying one sty were separated when one of them was taken away in a trailer to market. The Land Rover and trailer had hardly travelled a hundred yards before the second pig jumped over the sty and chased after the vehicle. Not realising what had happened, the driver drove out of the factory entrance, down to the main road, turned right again and had reached the Fox Garage before being stopped by Major Emerson who had taken a short cut via the back garden of Old Meadows[(4)] where I lived as a boy. He was standing beside the second pig and was explaining what had transpired when the infuriated pig standing alongside glanced round and saw where the major was standing and jerked his hind quarters round, sending the man flying to the ground. It was the one and only deliberate act of aggression by a pig that I ever encountered, and I spent a lot of time with them helping Major Emerson.'

'Like all the cows around here in those days, ours were brown. We had mostly Shorthorns, a Red Poll, Ayreshires and a Guernsey for the rich milk. We drove the cows up and down Clews Lane each day to the fields at the end, and when they had finished there we took them across the main road and along Queens Road to Sid Baker's fields, shutting gates along the way to stop the cattle going into people's gardens.'

'Houses were festooned with decorations for the Queen's Coronation. Both Browns and the Fox Garage were very colourful. There was a big bonfire and fireworks for the whole village on the common at Reidon Hill opposite Limecroft Road.'

'There was an old soldier who liked to frequent The Crown at Knaphill every Friday evening. He rarely set off for home in a straight line nor without a half bottle of whisky in his pocket, which would be finished somewhere along the route. Before reaching the Princess Christian Homes, these empty bottles would be flung to left or right along Stafford Lake Road, disappearing in the vegetation, only to reappear again in large numbers after common fires.'

'A disabled resident from the Princess Christian Homes, who had a four-wheeled electric invalid car, pulled up at the Fox Garage occasionally if the batteries needed topping up with distilled water. There was no charge for this service but the part-time petrol pump attendant, who was a young lad of about 13, had to top up hundreds of cells in dozens of batteries and, if he was lucky, would receive a thrupenny(5) bit as a tip.'

'When they built a hump-back bridge at the ford between Cowshot Manor and the entrance to Bisley Camp, they installed a gas street lamp which was not electrified until the 1960s.'

'There was a long procession of magnificent floats, decorated cars and cycles on 6th June to mark Her Majesty's Silver Jubilee in 1977. It wound its way through the village, starting on Cowshot Common and finishing on Bisley Green. The judges for the best float were: Tony Brown, Barrie Burn, Gill Burn, Mr & Mrs Green, Douglas Pope, Mrs Rosam and Mrs Wareham. It was lovely sight and most colourful too.'

'There was a tiny cottage a little way down the track off Chatton Row, where old John Loveland and his wife lived. I don't remember much about them except that they kept a house cow, as many cottagers with a little piece of land did in those days, and they were taken to court by the RSPCA for letting a horn grow into its eye. The cottage was demolished when a bungalow was built closer to the road in the 1950s for Miss Kates. She was a kindly lady but she had a deformed neck and always had her head on one shoulder.'

'Jim Hill took over the farm from his father, also named James, and sometimes took produce to Southall market where prices were higher than Guildford, Staines and Richmond. He always had to walk there because the wagon was fully loaded. On one occasion, having quenched his thirst after a good day at the market, he was returning home in a thick fog and dozed off. He awoke in alarm to find the horse walking beside the Thames with the wheels of the wagon on the very edge of the embankment.

Bert Hill said that he and Uncle Jim decided one Sunday to walk from Bisley to St. Paul's Cathedral for a service. They walked there and back!'

'We milked them with a bucket in the early days, and the milk was cooled with a surface cooler with water running through it. The milk was put into a drum above the cooler and the rate at which it ran down the corrugations was controlled by a tap. As the bottles were filled we capped them with a cardboard insert. Later on, the new bottles were sealed with a foil cap.'

'The main road was used by whole platoons of soldiers for route marches and for travelling from place to place, but now they are taken in coaches and lorries. It is said that the large number of apple trees all along Stafford Lake Road have grown from the cores they discarded.'

'Fifty years ago, we took cattle all over the common. It was much bigger in those days but that was before they built Grindstone Crescent right up to the district boundary on the edge of Bisley. We never got compensated for losing our Common Rights to graze that area.'

'The grass verges on either side of Stafford Lake Road were very narrow and one day a chap from the Homes, who had been unable to walk since the war, accidentally veered of the road in his three-wheeler, hitting the ditch with a jolt. He found he could move his legs again and within a short time he was walking again.'

'As a boy during the Second World War, I remember seeing pensioners from the Royal Hospital Chelsea visiting the Princess Christian Homes, possibly staying for a short holiday.'

'It is customary to stand in silence just before the start of a parish council meeting as a mark of respect upon the death of a councillor. I shall never forget an extraordinary coincidence that occurred on one such occasion following the death of Bert Henbest, an old soldier and former councillor who had died on 5th September 1972. In those days the parish council meeting was held in the kitchen of the village hall, and that evening talking on a radio could clearly be heard on the other side of the door into the caretaker's flat. At the very moment we all stood up in remembrance of Bert, and to our great astonishment, the sound of a bugle on the radio played the Last Post. How appropriate!'

'Dad was driving cows along the road to Guildford Market one day and got as far as Brookwood, when one of them turned round and came home. He had to come back with the others to fetch her and start all over again.'

'When I started working at the Fox Garage in 1949, the stores – which had originally been the pub stables – had hay racks on the wall. They were still there in the 1960s because the pub still owned the building. The front half was where the coaches went in and the other end was the stables for the horses.'

'In those days many groceries were delivered to the village shops in bulk, either in sacks, boxes or tins and were weighed at the point of sale. It was said that Mrs Whitehorn would cut a currant in half rather than give the customer over-weight.'

'After the war, Mum used to put eggs in waterglass. I think it was sodium silicate. They were kept in a bucket under the stairs for months as it was so difficult to get eggs during the wintertime.'

'Mr and Mrs Hearn lived in Kings Road, West End, and were a familiar sight along the main road on their horse-drawn wagon. Bert Hill also had a horse up until the 1960s for taking his manure cart and hay wagon around the villages. We had all sorts of home deliveries in those days – the weekly groceries from Salter's, meat from Acock's, coal and firewood from Rice's, fish on Fridays from Davis', bread from Lawrence's, and daily papers and milk, of course.

Knighton's shop and delivery van.
Photo: Burn & Martin Collection by courtesy of Surrey History Centre.

The milk was delivered by Cherrymans, Fullers, Elliots or Renshaw and Trigg, depending on whereabouts in the village you lived. There was a lot of rivalry between local tradesmen over delivery rounds in days gone by.

From time to time a knife grinder would turn up, with sharpening apparatus fixed on the front of his bike, and the French onion seller came knocking on the door once a year.'

'Surrey County Council had a lengthsman who went up and down the main road, clearing a ditch here, sweeping a bit there, and so on. He used an Allen scycthe to cut the grass verges, but it was difficult to control and more than once it ended up in the ditch or on its side.'

'I had to take the accumulator up to the cycle shop at Knaphill when it needed recharging. It was made of thick glass but I had to be careful because it had acid inside. I think the shop was on the corner of the lane where the Co-op is now.'

'They came and put tarmac on the main road when I was a little girl (early 1920s). It had no proper surface before and it was muddy in winter. I used to play with the other children at the ford in Ford Road and we skated on the pond outside The Poplars in the winter.'

'The Chandler brothers lived up the road (*Ford Road*) in Combers; one did the gardening and the other looked after the house. They never interfered with each other's work. They had some valuables which were found under the floor when the house was pulled down after the last one died. They never had any electricity connected to the house.

Bert and Bill's mother looked just like Queen Victoria. She was a little old fat lady with a bonnet and she dressed in black.'

'My rent had been half a crown (*2s. 6d*) a week after the war (*WW2*) but as I was going through some distressing times, my landlord reduced it to 1s.6d and made arrangements to have the electricity connected to the house.'

'When the Archer family moved from Newbridge Farm, it became Newbridge Cottage and Mrs Adeline Morris had tea rooms where the teas were served by Miss Stevens. She had jet black hair and she was the daughter of the cook at the Shaftesbury School.'

'I would take the cattle up and down Warbury Lane for Miss Helen Lawson but you would hardly ever encounter a car in those days.'

'I was sitting at the bottom of the Recreation Ground, which was just part of the common then, when I heard a loud noise as this great thing went overhead. I rushed home and my dad said it was a Zeppelin.'

Cherryman's Dairy. 1985.
Left to right: Nicholas Berry, Caroline Cherryman, Peter Cherryman with Rachel, Nick Hunt with Michael, Joan Cheeseman, Ralph Cheeseman, John Cherryman with Robert, Mrs Elliott, David Levings.
Photo: Nick Hunt

'There were several people delivering milk in the village but there was a gentleman's agreement that you did not poach customers from each other's rounds. A few posh houses had milk delivered twice a day.'

'When pasteurisation came in, I was telling a customer who lived in Brookwood about the benefit of raw milk going through the process to kill harmful bacteria. She replied sternly, "I don't want dead germs floating on my milk, thank you".'

We had all sizes of milk bottles: Quarts, pint-and-a-half, pints, half-pints and also a third-of-a-pint for school children. The pint-and-a-half size was the first to go. Elliot's had a lot of customers who liked pint-and-a-half bottles.'

'Gypsies often camped at each end of Kiln Lane and spread their washing out on bramble bushes to dry. They taught me how to set purse nets and catch rabbits with a ferret.'

---

(1) Boundary House and Sheldrake facing the A322, and Boundary Cottage (56 Grindstone Crescent).
(2) Now replaced by 213 and 215 Guildford Road.
(3) Now renamed Rose Cottage.
(4) Now 318 Guildford Road.
(5) Thrupenny bit = 3d.

APPENDIX A

Variations in the spelling of Bisley in Surrey

Bisleigh		
Bisley	1587	(the first record of the current spelling)
Bisscheleye	1279	
Bisscheleyne	1471	
Bissele	1259	
Bisselegah	1103	& 1259
Bisselegh	1270	
Bisteleye	1277	
Bursele	1346	& 1391
Busele	1279	
Buselegh	1270	
Busheley	1283	
Busselagh		
Bussele	c1270	
Busselegh	1255	
Busseleghe	933	& 967
Busseleye	c1270	
Busshelegh	1402	
Bussley	1283	
Byshley	1535	& 1537
Bysley		

Byssa's Leigh	(doubtful, not validated)
Byssele	1391
Byssheley	1578
Byssley	1471
Bystelye	
Bysterley	

APPENDIX B

RECTORS OF BISLEY	DATE OF INSTITUTION	INCUMBENCY ENDED
Thomas		**- 1316** (Instituted prior to 1283)
William de Lascore	**19th Jan 1317**	**- 1317** (Register lost 1346 - 1366)
Stephen Hayne	**28th Jan 1390**	**- 1391**
John Lotewyke	**15th May 1391**	**- 1396**
John Sherman de Nortwych	**8th Aug 1396**	**- 1397**
Philip Palmer	**9th Nov 1397**	**- 1402** (stated to be Richard in 'Bisley Bits')
John Pynford	**12th Aug 1402**	(Register lost 1414 – 1446, omitted in 'Bisley Bits')
John Browning	**22nd Jan 1451**	**- 1451**
Thomas Smyth	**3rd Dec 1455**	**- 1456**
Thomas Russell	**28th Jan 1456**	**- 1460**
John Everley	**6th Jun 1460**	**- 1465**
Thomas Smyth	**1465**	**- 1465**
Richard Strother	**18th Jul 1465**	**- 1465**
William Horne	**31st Jan 1466**	**- 1466**
John Carethorpe	**13th Aug 1467**	**- 1475**
Richard Cadey	**16th Feb 1475**	**- 1476**
Roger Mortymer	**18th July 1477**	**- 1489**
John Williamson	**9th Nov 1484**	**- 1489** (omitted in 'Bisley Bits') (Register lost 1492 - 1500)
Thomas Preston	**22nd Sep 1509**	**- 1530**
Robert Grous	**25th Nov 1530**	**- 1560**

Richard Ode	**18th May 1560**	**- 1561** (omitted in 'Bisley Bits', also Vicar of Chobham in plurality)
John Hill MA	**26th Mar 1561**	**- 1588** (a Canon of Canterbury and of Westminster, also Rector of Windlesham in plurality)
Anthony Harrison	**25th Oct 1588**	**- 1610**
Richard Massey MA	**15th Nov 1610**	**- 1659** ('Bisley Bits' wrongly states register lost 1628-1644)
Dr Andrew Lamont DD	**8th Aug 1660**	**- 1711**
David Kineir	**18th Jul 1712**	**- 1713**
John Campion	**28th Nov 1713**	**- 1739**
Thomas Ganton	**3rd Sep 1739**	**- 1748** (also Vicar of Chobham in plurality)
Alleyne Walter	**21st Jun 1748**	**-** (still Rector in 1770, also Vicar of Chobham in plurality)
George Clarke-Gayton MA	**12th Oct 1779**	**- 1785** (also Vicar of Chobham in plurality)
Richard Cecil MA	**25th Apr 1786**	**- 1810** (also Vicar of Chobham 1800-1810 in plurality)
John King MA	**18th Oct 1810**	**- 1845**
Robert George Lewis	**30th Apr 1845**	(omitted in 'Bisley Bits')
George Robinson	**14th Oct 1845**	**- 1856**
Francis Bonaventure Gourrier	**18th Nov 1856**	**- 1861**
Thomas Joseph Farr	**27th Jan 1862**	**- 1865** (Torr in 'Bisley Bits')
George J Wild	**1865**	**- 1872**
Walter Eaton MA	**7th May 1872**	**- 1881**
Walter Landon Smith MA	**1881**	**- 1886**
Joseph Cater	**31st Mar 1886**	**- 1895**
John Gwyon LD	**11th Mar 1895**	**- 1928**

Charles Montagu Horley	13th Dec 1929	- 1954
Windsor Roberts	29th Jun 1957	- 1962
William Mervyn Bowen Francis	29th Nov 1962	- 1975
Peter Douglas Gotelee	1st Nov 1976	- 1985
Clive Edmonds	27th Apr 1985	- 1992
Ian Terry	1st Sep 1992	- 2002
Andrew Armitt	26th Aug 2003	-

APPENDIX C

Beating the Bounds: Saturday 7th May 1983

The following notes of the event were taken by Clifford Jepson, one of the Churchwardens:-

(9.30am) 37 adults and 14 children assembled at Church porch. Photographs taken.

(9.40am) Prayer and Blessing in Church by Rector. Brief introduction to 'Beating the Bounds' by Tim Price who was to lead the walk.

(10.00am) Set off across Church Lane and style, flag bearer in front. Along Footpath No9 in glebe field.

(10.07am) Revd. Peter Gotelee (Rector) bumped against second style which was marked with a cross.

(10.20am) Mrs Rosemary Cooper (Churchwarden) bumped at fence beside SE corner of North Hill Nursery. Turf cut to mark spot. Continuation of boundary and Bisley Detached checked against map. Proceeded generally westwards via small meadow with bridge over stream to rejoin boundary where it meets Footpath No134.

(10.37am) Mr Vic Hone (born in Bisley) bumped where corner of unused field projects into Beldam Bridge Nursery. Hazel tree marked with a cross. Followed footpath south-westwards.

(10.45am) Mr Clifford Jepson (Churchwarden) bumped beside top corner of nursery belonging to Mr J Elliott of Fenns Lane. Fence post marked with a cross. Continued clock-wise inside nursery.

(10.55am) Mr Tim Price (Parish Councillor) bumped at next corner. Post marked with a cross.

(11.00am) Louisa Bright (aged 7. Flag Bearer) bumped at gate by Old House Lane. Alder tree marked with a cross. Along Old

House Lane to Guildford Road. Over Newbridge.

(11.12am) Mrs Molly Wareham (Head teacher, Bisley C of E First School) bumped at entrance to Brook Nursery. Cross filed in lamp post. Over the road and proceeded northwards.

(11.18am) Alexandra Bright (aged 11) bumped at front entrance of Elm Tree Nursery. Turf cut. Past Mr R Glazier's house and through his nursery.

(11.22am) Mr John Cooper (Parish Reader) bumped at rear entrance in Lucas Green Road. Gate post marked. Over bridge and clock-wise around nursery field on left.

(11.28am) Matthew Price (aged 3½) bumped where Trulley Brook crosses boundary. Oak tree marked.

(11.34am) Mrs Marilyn Meller (née Elliot. Born in Bisley) bumped at next corner of this field. Turf cut. Back to Lucas Green Road and up to Ford Road. Stopped on bridge to see where boundary continues behind Pine Grove Farm. Back to Ford Cottage.

(11.52am) Mr Colin Honey bumped against oak tree on boundary. Three marked. Back to West End Common and along Footpath No126A towards Furze Farm. Left across style into hay field, along Footpath No23 to Bullhousen Farm.

(12.15pm) Lunch under Dutch barn. Some people went home, others joined here.

(1.05pm) 31 people set off after lunch.

(1.15pm) Mrs Jill Gotelee bumped on bridge on Footpath No23. Side of bridge marked with cross. Through two fields southwards to Bisley Common.

(1.30pm) Sophie Oliver (aged 9) bumped on MoD stone 982. Turf cut beside stone. Along security fence towards Long Siberia Range.

(1.35pm) Mr John Friend (map bearer) bumped on Stoney Road by gate in fence. Turf turned. Up Stoney Road leaving boundary (as Short Siberia range was in use). Along Bridleway No141 to road beside Polledoak Slade. Right to target sheds.

(1.50pm) Mr Arthur Martin bumped against pollarded oak beside range. Tree marked with cross. Back a few yards to the derelict Bolling House.

(1.55pm) Luke Putman Aged 10. Dressed in Scout uniform) bumped against an oak. Cross marked on tree. Back to Bridleway No141, then right. Along Queens Road past Wisdom Corner to junction of Water Lane. Position of boundary on Century Range and Hog Lees noted.

(2.10pm) Claire Sutton (aged 10. 1st Bisley Guides) bumped at end of Water Lane. Turf cut. Along Lane, past Medcote Cottage – the only one in a row of houses to stand within the Parish. Right into Watery Lane.

(2.25pm) Mrs Liz Oliver bumped where boundary crosses lane between field corners on either side. Turf cut. Back a few paces to Water Lane and right.

(2.30pm) Mrs Sue Maclean (née Hone, Born in Bisley) bumped by gate into field belonging to Mr Kirby of Stanley Farm. Cross marked on oak tree. Proceeded to Stafford Lake.

(2.40pm) Amanda Price (aged 10) bumped against crack willow. Cross marked. Into hay field and along headland to first gate.

(2.50pm) Mrs Gillian Honey bumped at this gate by Stafford Lake Road. Post marked with cross. Up to second gate. Over and on to common.

(3.00pm) Jason Oliver (aged 12) bumped at Grindstone Handle Corner. Cross cut in sallow tree near house called Lane End.

(3.05pm) Mrs Brenda Winter bumped by track off first bend in Grindstone Crescent. Cross cut in tree. Straight on to where Mr North's tumbled down house once stood.

(3.10pm) Mrs Jen Martin (née Castle. Born in Bisley) bumped against willow. Cross marked on tree. Over main road.

(3.15pm) Sally Barden (aged 10) bumped on verge. Turf was turned over. Up Reidon Hill beside road and through cut to Limecroft Road.

(3.20pm) Mrs Jo Price (née Coxon. Born in Bisley) bumped opposite driveway to Reidon Grange. Silver birch marked with cross. Up the driveway to car garage by The Copse.

(3.25pm) Mrs Judy Thoroughgood bumped against tree stump. Stump marked with a cross. At far end of drive, through Hangmoor Copse.

(3.35pm) Katie Barden (aged 9) bumped on northern side of wood. Beech tree marked. Northwards along boundary.

(3.45pm) Mrs Anne Jackson bumped in permanent pasture beside corner of Bluebell Wood. A square of turf was dug. Continued to Footpath No11A.

(3.55pm) Mr Brian Oliver bumped against stile on footpath. Cross on gate post. Over into Kiln Lane. Right passing stile on left on Footpath No137B and stopping just before spinney on right.

(4.05pm) Lindsay Jackson (aged 10) bumped here by a large oak. Tree marked with cross. Across green and over Church Lane.

(4.10pm) Mrs Ray Shearer bumped on verge. Turf cut. Finally along Church Lane towards Church entrance.

(4.15pm) Mr Neil Maclean bumped on edge of culvert under road a little before Woodcote. Cut marked in brickwork.

APPENDIX D

The 53 ex-Service personnel and staff from the Princess Christian Homes, who have died since 1991 and whose names are shown on memorial plaques in Bisley Churchyard:-

Top Left	CHARLES MANT	1901-1991	RFC & RAF
	THOMAS JOHN SAMUELS	1914-1991	RE
	WILLIAM CHESSHER	1914-1991	LIGHT INFANTRY
	JOSEPH PARROTT	1919-1991	STAFF PCH
	VICTOR BUSH	1942-1991	RADC
	KEITH HUNT	1926-1991	RN
	WILLIAM TAYLOR	1913-1991	RCASC
	CHARLES FOWLER	1907-1992	RA
	EDDIE FLEMING	1918-1992	ROYAL INNISKILLING
Middle Left	FREDERICK MOORE, MBE	1905-1994	17/21 LANCERS & RASC
	BILL JONES	1914-1994	RWF(ARMY COMMANDO) REME
	VICTOR WILKINSON	1919-1994	RAMC
	PATRICK DENVIR	1915-1995	RASC
	JOHN MASSON	1909-1995	RAF
	WILLIAM BURNETT	1906-1995	QUEENS REGT & WG
	GEORGE HAROLD WARREN	1920-1995	R SIGNALS (ARMY COMMANDO)
	JACK TIMMINS	1924-1995	ROYAL NAVY
	WILLIAM GEORGE NORMAN	1906-1995	CAMERONIANS - RASC

Bottom Left	LESLIE CRITTENDEN	1913-1997	MIDDLESEX REGIMENT
	FREDERICK WOOD	1913-1999	ROYAL ENGINEERS
	PATRICK MCCANN	1913-1998	HAMPSHIRE REGIMENT
	BILL REYNOLDS	1914-1998	ROYAL ARTILLERY
	JOAN NORMAN	1922-1998	ATS
	BILL HODGE	1926-1999	SCOTS GUARDS
	MINNIE HOWELL	1905-1999	ARMY WIDOW
	JANET ROCK	1915-1999	WRAF
	-		
Top Right	JAMES MCNAB	1908-1993	WG, BLUES AND ROYALS, APTC
	SYDNEY ABBOTT	1916-1993	RA
	ALBERT GRITT	1909-1993	RAOC
	ALBERT DANIELS	1921-1993	RA
	ALBERT WOOLLS	1907-1993	RA
	DESMOND LLOYD	1917-1994	ROYAL ULSTER RIFLES
	NOBBY DEVONSHIRE	1920-1994	RAMC
	WILLIAM BARFIELD	1907-1994	RAF
	HARRY INGLEDEW	1915-1994	NORTHUMBERLAND FUSILIERS
Middle Right	REGINALD HARRIS	1910-1995	ROYAL ARTILLERY
	FREDERICK MERRITT	1912-1996	ROYAL ENGINEERS
	GEOFF CAMP	1915-1996	ROYAL AIR FORCE
	HUGH MCLAY	1919-1996	RAF
	ELIZABETH BARFIELD	1907-1996	RAF WIDOW
	LESLIE VICTOR WHITE	1921-1996	PARACHUTE REGIMENT
	JOSEPH HOWET LIVINGSTONE	1911-1996	SEAFORTH HIGHLANDERS
	GWEN CULL	1913-1996	RAF WIDOW
	ELSIE HARVEY	1913-1997	ARMY WIDOW

Bottom Right	WO2 BRIAN HAZZARD	1938-2007	1ST GLOUCESTERSHIRE REGIMENT
	WALTER DRURY	1910-1999	RASC
	JENNY STAIRS	1908-2000	NAVY WIDOW
	SIDNEY CLARKE	1910-2000	ROYAL ARTILLERY
	GEORGE FRY	1915-2000	RAOC/REME
	CLARENCE ARTHUR FOSTER	1905-2000	ARP
	JIM BOLAM	1908-2000	RIFLE BRIGADE
	GERTRUDE WHITE	1904-2000	ATS / ARMY WIDOW
	LAURIE SMITH	1908-2000	HOME GUARD

APPENDIX E

This specification of the church organ was provided by B C Shepherd & Son of Edgware, upon completion of renovation and improvements in 1978:-

'It was rebuilt and tonally remodelled to make it a more lively and effective instrument, despite its rather unfortunate location in a low roofed chancel chamber. The action to the main manual and pedal chests has been converted to electro-pneumatic. New additional chests have direct electric action. The drawstop action remains mechanical for the manual stops, whilst the pedal and coupler stop actions are electric. Solid state switching has been used for the Couplers and Pedal Bourdon unit, also for the extra manual chests.

The manual keys have been recovered with "Ivothene". New ivory drawstop bezels have been fitted to all knobs. A good secondhand radiating and concave pedalboard has been fitted. A new balanced Swell pedal has been fitted in the correct position and controls the mechanical connection to the shutters. The Swell shutters have been made to open at an angle of 90^0 (formerly only opening to an angle of 45^0). A reconditioned "Discus" blower replaces the former BOB blower. The wind pressure has been lowered from 4" to $3^3/_8$" WGP.
A Tremulant has been fitted.

Tonal additions and modification are as follows:

Swell. Violin Diapson replaced by metal Gedackt, wooden bottom octave outside Swellbox. Gamba retained but loudened. Harmonic Flute replaced by Gemshorn. Vox Celeste replaced by 2 rank Mixture, lowest octave on new chest in Swellbox.

Great. Open Diapson retained but softened (especially bass). Stopped Diapson retained but softened. Dulciana replaced by Principal. Fifteenth added on new chest, (Discarded Violin Diapson pipes from Swell used in with new treble pipes, Violin Diapson pipes had originally been part of a fifteenth stop).

Pedal. Bourdon stop retained but loudened slightly. Two extra octaves added on new chest to carry Bourdon up to 8′ and 4′ pitches.

All manual stops are complete and of full compass.

To improve tonal egress the panel to the right of the console has had a metal grille fitted to the frame in place of the oak panels.

Specification **before** rebuild.			Specification **after** rebuild.	
Great			Great	
Open Diapson		8	Open Diapson	8
Stopped Diapson	) Common Base	8	Stopped Diapson	8
Dulciana	)	8	Principal	4
			Fifteenth	2
Swell			Swell	
Violin Diapson	)	8	Leiblich Gedackt	8
Gamba	) Common Bass	8	Gamba (full length bass)	8
Vox Celeste	)	8	Gemshorn	4
Harmonic Flute		4	Mixture (19,22)	2.Rks
			Tremulant	
Pedal			Pedal	
Bourdon		16	Bourdon)	16
			Flute) 54 note rank	8
			Octave Flute)	4
Couplers			Couplers	
			Swell to Octave	
			Swell Octave to Great	
Swell to Great			Swell to Great	
Swell to Pedal			Swell to Pedal	
Great to Pedal			Great to Pedal	
421 speaking pipes.			603 speaking pipes.	

APPENDIX F

Organists From 1865 To 1990

Miss Wild	1865 – 1872	
?	1872 – 1899	
Mr A R J Broderick	1899 – 1901	
Mr A F Moulding	1901 – 1902	
Mr S G Russ	1902 – 1910	
Mr F Beal		
Mr H Spooner		
Mr R Jones		
Mrs F Fertig		
Mr R Tyler		
Mr W J Sidery	1943 – 1950	
Mrs F Fertig	1950 – 1952	(2nd time)
Miss J Halls	1952 – 1956	
Mr D Whale	1956 – 1958	
Mrs F Fertig	1958 – 1990	(3rd time)

APPENDIX G

Memorial Tablets: Farm School and Shaftesbury School

Roll of Honour
1914-1918
In Memory of Our old Boys Who Laid Down
Their Lives in the War. This Sanctuary was
Erected by the Boys Past and Present
and Their Friends

Arnold J W
Attwood W C
Blandford S H
Catley G
Cliff H
Clover W J
Collins F H
Crane S C
Everest A S
Foley A J
Fortens B
Francis G
Goodman W
Harrod A C
Hayes E A
Hayes G F
Hayes V
Hennen F O

Hewitt R A
Jackson J R
Johnson A H
Julius A E
Knight H
Littlewood H
Lockey W F
Montague W
Neale H H
Oldfield J D
Page A
Parker W
Pennyfather A L
Pike T
Pile A
Player A A
Pointing C O
Sewell
Shanks C W

Shorter E G
Springham A
Squire L S
Stagnell J W
Tocher C G Mc L
Tocher N C Mc L
Trigg A C
Webster R T S
White F H
Williams R R
Temple A
Bolton W H
Moxey C B
Thom F S

Ashman J S
Barnes F C
Berry W
Berryman R
Brooks F
Brown F H
Burt H
arey G H C
Church W
Copperthwaite W
Daniels H
Everett R H
Grainger C
Hales E J
Hall A F
Hill F E
Hill H A
James C
Keys C

Knell A
Larkins W C
Last H C
Mansfield F W
Mason J
Mason W E
Plummer H
Porter F J
Shaw A E W
Simons C H
Taylor H W
Vassar G
Wade A
Wallace E R E W
Watson F W
Wetton S A D
White E
Witchlow
Woodbridge H C

Roll of Honour. Second World War
1939-1945

Baughen CHW	Cooper B	Lynas N L	Pollard R	Sowden E
Blackman P D	Gray G	Mainprize J L	Pooley F R	Spooner H
Blaney W	Johnson J G	O'Grady C M	Reynolds P E	Wallace G T
Buck D	Locker D H	Parkyn H W P	Rowlands J R	Wine J F
Collier F S	Lovett S M	Tomes P B	Roberts J M	Seymour A

APPENDIX H

Bisley National School: Text Of Trust Deed Dated 19th January 1847

I Arthur George Earl of Onslow Lord of the Manor of Bisley in the Parish of Bisley in the County of Surrey under the Authority of an Act passed in the 4th and 5th years in the reign of Her Majesty Queen Victoria instituted 'An Act to afford further facilities for the conveyance and endowment of Sites for Schools' Do hereby freely and voluntarily and without any valuable consideration grant and convey to the Reverend George Robinson Rector of the Church and Parish of Bisley aforesaid and Tomas Harrington and John Gosden Churchwardens of the said Parish of Bisley and the Reverend Albert Mangles perpetual Curate and Incumbent of the Church and Parish of Horsell in the said County of Surrey the Reverend James Jerram Vicar of the Church and Parish of Chobham in the said County of Surrey the Reverend Charles Bradshaw Bowles Vicar of the Parish of Woking in the said County of Surrey of All that piece or parcel of land being part of the Waste Land or Common belonging to the Manor of Bisley aforesaid containing by measurement one acre bounded by the Queen's Highway leading to and from Guildford and Bagshot on the East by other part of the said Waste Land or Common called Bisley Green on the North and by a Roadway and by other parts of the said Common on the West and South and as the same is delineated in the Plan thereof drawn in the margin of these Presents And all my Estate Right title and interest to and in the same and every part thereon To hold unto and to the use of the said George Robinson Tomas Harrington John Gosden Albert Mangles James Jerram and Charles Bradshaw Bowles and their successors in their said several and respective Offices for the purposes of the said Act and to be applied as a Site for a School for poor persons of and in the Parish of Bisley aforesaid and for the residence of the Schoolmaster and Schoolmistress of the said School or for either of them and for no other purpose whatsoever. Such school to be open at all reasonable times to the Inspector or Inspectors appointed or to be appointed in conformity with Her Majesty's Order in Council bearing date the 10th day of August 1840 and to be always in unison with the Incorporated National Society for promoting the education of the Poor in the principles of the established Church and conducted according to its Principles and for the furtherance of its ends and designs and subject to and in conformity with the Declaration aforesaid the management direction control and government of the said School and premises and of the Funds and Endowments thereof and the selection appointment and dismissal of the Schoolmaster and Schoolmistress and their Assistants shall be vested in and exercised by the said George Robinson Rector of Bisley aforesaid and his successors for the time being or the Curate to be appointed from time to time by the Rector of the said Parish and Parish Church of Bisley And in case such Rector or his Curate aforesaid shall at any time become incapable or unwilling to act in the management and government of the said School and of the Funds and Endowments thereof or in the appointments of the Schoolmaster and Schoolmistress thereof Then such management of the said School and Premises and of the Funds and Endowments thereof and the appointments and dismissal of the Schoolmaster and Schoolmistress thereof shall be vested in and exercised by a Committee for the time being of not more than five persons one of such persons being the Vicar Officiating Minister of the Parish of Chobham aforesaid for the time being on other of such persons his Curate and the Churchwardens of the said Parish of Bisley for the time being if in Communion with the established Church and the other of such persons to be nominated and appointed by the Vicar of Chobham aforesaid and his Curate and the Churchwardens of Bisley aforesaid as often as such nominated person shall cease to act of the Committee Provided always that any person so nominated as aforesaid shall be in Communion with the established Church and a Contributor to the Funds of the said School by annual Subscription And in case any difference of opinion shall arise in the said Committee regarding the Instruction of the Scholars of the said School or any Regulations connected therewith it shall be lawful for any member of the said Committee to cause a Statement in writing of such matter in difference to be laid before the Bishop of Winchester a copy of such Statement having been previously laid before the said Committee and the said Bishop may thereupon at his discretion enquire concerning and determine such matter and the decision of the said Bishop in writing when laid before the said Committee shall be final and conclusive upon the matter.

In witness whereof I the said George Arthur Earl of Onslow and the other parties have hereunto set their hands and seals this 19th day of January in the year of our Lord 1847.

APPENDIX I

A copy of a hand-written order placed by Stephen Steptoe for distribution to the poor, whose names appear below:

Bt of Arthur Cutler, Draper and Grocer, Post Office, Knaphill.

Goods as to order	Mrs Daborn	3 - 6
" "	Ja^s Sawyer	6 - 0
" "	H^y Hockley	7 - 0
" "	Wm Howard	5 - 0
" "	Widow Stevens	6 - 0
" "	Geo Hill	4 - 6
" "	Solomon Stevens	6 - 0
" "	Thos Eacott	6 - 0
" "	Ja^s Martin	3 - 0
" "	David Collier	4 - 0
" "	John Hill (Pound)	5 - 0
" "	Ja^s Hill (Port Lane)	5 - 0
" "	Matthew Harding	5 - 0
" "	Widow Hill	5 - 0
" "	Leah Martin	5 - 0
" "	Widow Collier	3 - 6
" "	Wm Hill	5 - 0
" "	Wm Spong	7 - 0

"	"	Anne Giles	3 - 0
"	"	Widow Martin	4 - 0
"	"	R Atefield	6 - 0
"	"	Dan Cheeseman	5 - 0
"	"	Geo Jackman	4 - 0
"	"	Wm Glazier	6 - 0
"	"	Ja^{s} Martin	5 - 0
"	"	Henry Chowney	6 - 0
"	"	Abraham Boylett	5 - 0
"	"	Mary Giles	4 - 0
"	"	Geo Daborn	6 - 0
"	"	Wm Hill (Riding Hill)	6 - 0
"	"	Amelia Hill	5 - 0
"	"	Widow Tickner	3 - 0
		£ 7 - 19 - 6	

Settled 9 March 1864

APPENDIX J

Vascular plants recorded on the Shaftesbury and Reidon Hill areas of Bisley Common in 1974:-

Common name	Scientific name
Millfoil or Yarrow	*Achillea millefolium*
Ground Elder	*Aegopodium podagraria*
Horse Chestnut	*Aesculus hippocastanum*
Agrimony	*Agrimonia eupatoria*
Velvet Bent	*Agrostis canina*
Bristle Bent	*Agrostis curtisii*
Common Bent	*Agrostis capillaris*
Silvery Hair Grass	*Aira caryophyllea*
Early Hair Grass	*Aira praecox*
Water Plantain	*Alisma plantago-aquatica*
Garlic Mustard	*Alliaria petiolata*
Meadow Foxtail	*Alopecurus pratensis*
Juneberry	*Amelanchia lamarckii*
Wild Angelica	*Angelica sylvestris*
Barren Brome	*Anisantha tectorum*
Scented Vernal Grass	*Anthoxanthum odoratum*
Cow Parsley	*Anthriscus sylvestris*
Fool's Water Cress	*Apium nodiflorum*
Thale Cress	*Arabidopsis thaliana*
Horse Radish	*Armoracia rusticana*
False Oat Grass	*Arrhenatherum elatius*

Mugwort	*Artemisia vulgaris*
Soft-leaved Orache	*Atriplex prostrata*
Common Orache	*Atriplex patula*
Daisy	*Bellis perennis*
Silver Birch	*Betula pendula*
Hairy Birch or Downy Birch	*Betula pubescens*
Nodding Bur-marigold	*Bidens cernua*
Hard Fern	*Blechnum spicant*
False Brome	*Brachypodium sylvaticum*
Soft Brome	*Bromus hordeaceus*
White Bryony	*Bryonia dioica*
Water Starwort	*Callitriche stagnalis*
Ling Heather	*Calluna vulgaris*
Hedge Bindweed	*Calystegia sepium*
Great Bindweed	*Calystegia sylvatica*
Harebell	*Campanula rotundifola*
Shepherd's Purse	*Capsella bursa-pastoris*
Hairy Bitter Cress	*Cardamine hirsuta*
Lady's Smock or Cuckoo Flower	*Cardamine pratensis*
Spring Sedge	*Carex caryophyllea*
Common Sedge	*Carex nigra*
Oval Sedge	*Carex ovalis*
Carnation Sedge	*Carex panicea*
Greater Tussock Sedge	*Carex paniculata*
Pill Sedge	*Carex pilulifera*
Remote Sedge	*Carex remota*
Knapweed or Hardhead	*Centaurea nigra*
Centaury	*Centaurium erythraea*

Field Mouse-ear	*Cerastium arvense*
Common Mouse-ear	*Cerastium fontanum*
Sticky Mouse-ear	*Cerastium glomeratum*
Rough Chervil	*Chaerophyllum temulum*
Rosebay Willowherb	*Chamerion angustifolium*
Fat Hen	*Chenopodium album*
Creeping Thistle	*Cirsium arvense*
Marsh Thistle	*Cirsium palustre*
Spear Thistle	*Cirsium vulgare*
Pignut	*Conopodium majus*
Canadian Fleabane	*Conyza canadensis*
Hazel	*Corylus avellana*
Hawthorn	*Crataegus monogyna*
Smooth Hawk's-beard	*Crepis capillaris*
Beaked Hawk's-beard	*Crepis vesicaria*
Dodder	*Cuscuta epithymum*
Crested Dog's-tail	*Cynosurus cristatus*
Broom	*Cytisus scoparius*
Cocks-foot	*Dactylis glomerata*
Heath Spotted Orchid	*Dactylorhiza maculata*
Wild Carrot	*Daucus carota*
Tufted Hair Grass	*Deschampsia cespitosa*
Waivy Hair Grass	*Deschampsia flexuosa*
Foxglove	*Digitalis purpurea*
Intermediate Sundew	*Drosera intermedia*
Round-leaved Sundew	*Drosera rotundifolia*
Broad Buckler Fern	*Dryopteris austriaca*
Male Fern	*Dryopteris felix-mas*
Couch Grass	*Elytrigia repens*
Great Willowherb	*Epilobium hirsutum*

Field Horsetail	*Equisetum arvense*
Bell Heather	*Erica cinerea*
Cross-leaved Heath	*Erica tetralix*
Cotton Grass or Bog Cotton	*Eriophorum angustifolium*
English Sticky Eyebright	*Euphrasia anglica*
Spindle	*Euonymus europaeus*
Tall Fescue	*Festuca arundinacea*
Sheep's Fescue	*Festuca ovina*
Meadow Fescue	*Festuca pratensis*
Red Fescue	*Festuca rubra*
Alder Buckthorn	*Frangula alnus*
Ash	*Fraxinus excelsior*
Common Hemp-nettle	*Galeopsis tetrahit*
Cleavers or Goose Grass	*Galium aparine*
Marsh Bedstraw	*Galium palustre*
Heath Bedstraw	*Galium saxatile*
Lady's Bedstraw	*Galium verum*
Petty Whin	*Genista anglica*
Cut-leaved Cranesbill	*Geranium dissectum*
Wood Avens	*Geum urbanum*
Ground Ivy	*Glechoma hederacea*
Floating Sweet Grass	*Glyceria fluitans*
Marsh Cudweed	*Gnaphalium uliginosum*
Ivy	*Hedera helix*
Hogweed	*Heracleum sphondylium*
Yorkshire Fog	*Holcus lanatus*
Creeping Soft Grass	*Holcus mollis*
Wall Barley	*Hordeum murinum*

Hop	*Humulus lupulus*
Bluebell	*Hyacinthoides non-scriptus*
Perforate St John's Wort	*Hypericum perforatum*
Slender St John's Wort	*Hypericum pulchrum*
Common Cat's-ear	*Hypochaeris radicata*
Holly	*Ilex aquifolium*
Sharp-flowered Rush	*Juncus acutiflorus*
Jointed Rush	*Juncus articulatus*
Toad Rush	*Juncus bufonius*
Bulbous Rush	*Juncus bulbosus*
Compact Rush	*Juncus conglomeratus*
Soft Rush	*Juncus effusus*
Heath Rush	*Juncus squarrosus*
Slender Rush	*Juncus tenuis*
Field Scabious	*Knautia arvensis*
White Dead-nettle	*Lamium album*
Red Dead-nettle	*Lamium purpureum*
Yellow Meadow Vetchling	*Lathyrus pratensis*
Ox-eye Daisy or Dog Daisy	*Leucanthemum vulgare*
Privet	*Ligustrum vulgare*
Toadflax	*Linaria vulgaris*
Fairy Flax	*Linum catharticum*
Perennial Rye Grass	*Lolium perenne*
Honeysuckle	*Lonicera periclymenum*
Bird's-foot Trefoil	*Lotus corniculatus*
Field Wood-rush	*Luzula campestris*
Heath Wood-rush	*Luzula multiflora*
Gipsy-wort	*Lycopus eurpoaeus*
Creeping Jenny	*Lysimachia nummularia*
Pineapple Weed	*Matricaria discoidea*

Black Medick	*Medicago lupulina*
Cow-wheat	*Melampyrum pratense*
Water Mint	*Mentha aquatica*
Purple Moor Grass	*Molinia caerulea*
Mat Grass	*Nardus stricta*
Hemlock Water Dropwort	*Oenanthe crocata*
Adder's Tongue	*Ophioglossum vulgatum*
Star of Bethlehem	*Ornithogalum angustifolium*
Lousewort	*Pedicularis sylvatica*
Lesser Cat's-tail	*Phleum nodosum*
Mouse-eared Hawkweed	*Pilosella officinarum*
Scots Pine	*Pinus sylvestris*
Ribwort Plantain	*Plantago lanceolata*
Plantain	*Plantago major*
Annual Meadow Grass	*Poa annua*
Wood Meadow Grass	*Poa nemoralis*
Meadow Grass	*Poa pratensis*
Rough Meadow Grass	*Poa trivialis*
Common Knotweed	*Polygonum aviculare*
Water Pepper	*Persicaria hydropiper*
Pale Persicaria	*Persicaria lapathifolia*
Common Persicaria or Redshank	*Persicaria maculosa*
Aspen	*Populus tremula*
Silverweed	*Potentilla anserina*
Tormentil	*Potentilla erecta*
Blackthorn	*Prunus spinosa*
Bracken	*Pteridium aquilinum*
Fleabane	*Pulicaria dysenterica*
Turkey Oak	*Quercus cerris*

Pedunculate Oak	*Quercus robur*
Meadow Buttercup	*Ranunculus acris*
Bulbous Buttercup	*Ranunculus bulbosus*
Lesser Celandine	*Ranunculus ficaria*
Creeping Buttercup	*Ranunculus repens*
Wild Radish	*Raphanus raphanistrum*
Hayrattle or Yellow Rattle	*Rhinanthus minor*
Field Rose	*Rosa arvensis*
Bramble	*Rubus fruticosus agg.*
Raspberry	*Rubus idaeus*
American Blackberry	*Rubus laciniatus*
Sorrel	*Rumex acetosa*
Sheep's Sorrel	*Rumex acetosella*
Curled Dock	*Rumex crispus*
Ciliate Pearlwort	*Sagina apetala*
Goat Willow	*Salix caprea*
Sallow or Pussy Willow	*Salix cinerea*
Crack Willow	*Salix fragilis*
Creeping Willow	*Salix repens*
Elder	*Sambucus nigra*
Figwort	*Scrophularia nodosa*
Common Ragwort	*Senecio jacobaea*
Oxford Ragwort	*Senecio squalidus*
Wood Groundsel	*Senecio sylvaticus*
Groundsel	*Senecio vulgaris*
Sawwort	*Serratula tinctoria*
Golden Rod	*Solidago virgaurea*
Rowan	*Sorbus aucuparia*
Red Clover	*Trifolium pratense*
White Clover	*Trifolium repens*

Scentless Mayweed	*Tripleurospermum inodorum*
Colts-foot	*Tussilago farfara*
Gorse or Furze	*Ulex europaeus*
Dwarf Gorse	*Ulex minor*
English Elm	*Ulmus procera*
Stinging Nettle	*Urtica dioica*
Bilberry or Whortleberry	*Vaccinium myrtillus*
Germander Speedwell	*Veronica chamaedrys*
Ivy-leaved Speedwell	*Veronica hederifolia*
Guelder Rose	*Viburnum opulus*
Tufted Vetch	*Vicia cracca*
Hairy Tare	*Vicia hirsute*
Common Vetch	*Vicia sativa*
Narrow-leaved Vetch	*Vicia sat. nigra*
Common Dog Violet	*Viola riviniana*

APPENDIX K

Conversion of money expressed as pounds, shillings and pence into decimal amounts, rounded to the nearest whole new pence:-

L.	s.	d.	£	p.
		1		0
		2		1
		3		1
		4		2
		5½		2
		8		3
		8½		4
		10		4
		11		5
	1	0		5
	1	2		6
	1	6		8
	2	0		10
	2	3		11
	2	6		13
	2	9		14
	3	0		15
	3	4		17

	3	6		18
	3	11		20
	4	0		20
	4	7½		23
	5	0		25
	5	6		28
	5	7		28
	5	8		28
	6	0		30
	6	5		32
	6	6		33
	6	8		33
	7	0		35
	7	0¼		35
	7	3		36
	7	4		37
	8	2		41
	8	7		43
	9	1		45
	10	0		50
	12	0		60
	13	3		66
	14	3		71
	14	5		72
	15	9		79
	17	4		87
	18	0		90
	19	6		98
	19	7½		98
1	0	0	1	0

	xij		5
	xviij		8
ij			10
ij	xi		15
iij			15
iij	iiij		17
v			25
vi			30
vi	viij		33
vii	x		39
x			50
xiij	iiij		67
xxvj	viij	1	33
xxx		1	50

BIBLIOGRAPHY

Alderman, HM *The Charm of Old Surrey.* London: Drane. 1927

Anglo-Saxon Charters. http://hwaet.heroku.com/charters/69?q=&page=

Aubrey, J ed Rawlinson. *The Natural History and Antiquities of the County of Surrey*. Vol3. (facsimile of 1718-19 ed) Dorking: Nevinson. Kohler & Coombes. 1975.

Bailey, Marion. *The Chance of a Lifetime – The Story of The Shaftesbury Homes and Arethusa*. Dianthus Publishing. 1996.

Bennett, Mary Ann. *Life and Work on Surrey Heath.* Chichester. Phillimore. 2007.

Birch, W de G (ed). *Cartularium Saxonicum: A Collection of Charters Relating to Anglo-Saxon History.* 4 vols with index. London: 1885-99.

Blair, J *Early Medieval Surrey: Landholding, Church and Settlement before 1300.* Stroud: Sutton/ Surrey Arch Soc. 1991

Brind, H Hanslow. *Health & Sanitary Conditions of the Chertsey RDC, Annual Report 1909*. Weybridge: FE North

Brind, H Hanslow. *Health & Sanitary Conditions of the Chertsey RDC, Annual Report 1939-1944*. Chertsey: Rawlings & Walsh.

British Library. Extra-illustrated copy of Manning & Bray: *The History & Antiquities of the County of Surrey*. Collated by Richard Percival in 1847

British Plant Galls. Swanton. 1912.

Bunch, Christopher C. *The Range Tramways of the National Rifle Association*. NRA Journals: Summer 2006 Winter 2006 & Spring 2007. Vols. LXXXV No.2 to Vol. LXXXVI No.1.

Bunch, Christopher C. *The National Rifle Association, Its Tramways and the London and South Western Railway*. NRA Journals: Spring & Summer 2008 Vol. LXXXVII Nos.1&2

Cater, Rev J *Bisley Bits; or, Records of a Surrey Corner*. London: Simkin et al. 1892.

Cecil, Revd Richard. Intr Pratt. *Remains of the Rev Richard Cecil*. London: Seeley. 1811

Chertsey Abbey. Leaflet No2 Runnymede Borough Council. Undated

Christian Guardian. 1831.

Cole, Lt Col Howard, OBE *The Story of Bisley*. Aldershot: Gale & Polden. 1960.

Cooper, Rosemary F. *St John the Baptist Church, Bisley: A Guide and Short History*. Aldershot: Gale & Polden. 1981.

Cornfield, Susie. *The Queen's Prize: The Story of the National Rifle Association*. London: Pelham Books. 1987.

Curtis, Henry, BS, MD, FRCS. *A List of the Curates and Vicars of Pirbright, Surrey*. London: author. 1924.

Daily Telegraph. 7 May 2002.

Daily Telegraph and Morning Post. 15th September 1961

Defoe, Daniel. *A Tour thro' the whole Island of Great Britain, etc.* Vol 1. Letter 2 Part 3. London: Strahan. 1724-1727.

Domesday Book: Vol 3: Surrey. (ed) Morris, John. Chichester 1975.

Electronic Sawyer. [S.420] 2003. http://www.esawyer.org.uk/content/charter/420.html (14 Jan 2010)

Electronic Sawyer. [S.69] 2003. http://www.esawyer.org.uk/content/charter/69.html (14 Jan 2010)

Field, John. *English Field Names: A Dictionary*. Newton Abbot. 1972

Foster, Joseph. *Alumni Oxonienses: The Members of the University of Oxford 1500-1714*. Oxford:1891

Fulton, Robin. *The Story of Bisley (revised), Part Two*. Guildford. Biddles. 1990.

Gover,JEB, Mawer, A, & Stenton, FM. *The Place Names of Surrey*. Cambridge: University Press. 1934.

Gray, Dr Howard Levi. *English Field Systems*.London: Merlin. 1969

Harding Peter A & Clarke John M. *The Bisley Camp Branch Line*. Woking: Harding. 1986.

Harding, Peter A. *Branch Lines from Brookwood*. Woking: Harding. 2008.

Humphry MVO, A P & Freemantle VD, Lt Col The Hon. *History of the National Rifle Association During its First Fifty Years 1859 to 1909*. Cambridge: Bowes & Bowes. 1914.

Lewis, JM Brownsword, R & Pitt, EEH. *'Medieval "Bronze" Tripod Ewers from Wales'*. Medieval Archaeol. 31 (1987)

Malden, HE. *The Victoria History of the Counties of England: Surrey*. Vol 3. London: Constable.1911.

Manning, O & Bray, W. *The History & Antiquities of the County of Surrey*. Vol 1. 150 & Addenda 1. 1804.

Manson, James A. *Sir Edwin Landseer RA*. London: Walter Scott Publishing. 1902.

Meldrum, Rosemary. *The Three Elcho Shields*. NRA Journal: Summer 2004 Vol. LXXXIII No.2.

Melville, Sir Ronald, KCB. *Bisley Past and Present*. Ashford: Geerings. Undated.

Mills, John. *A Guide to the Industrial History of Surrey Heath*. Guildford. Surrey Ind. Hist. Group. 1995

National Rifle Association. *Bisley: The National Shooting Centre*. 1994.

National Rifle Association. *Official Millennium Souvenir 1910-2000*.

Needham, A. *How to Study an Old Church*. London: Batsford. 1944.

Palmer, R J. *Bisley People in the 16th & 17th Centuries*. Privately published by the author. 1979.

Parish News (Bisley and West End). February 1985, July 1992 & October 1996.

Picture Post. Vol. 32 No. 4 July 27 1946. London. Hulton Press.

Porter, Valerie. *Yesterday's Countryside*. Newton Abbot: David & Charles. 2006.

Regista Honorii III & Les Registres de Martin IV. Archivo Segreto Vaticano.

Sawyer, PH. *Anglo-Saxon Charters: An Annotated List and Bibliography*. 1968.

Schueller, Robert. *A History of Chobham*. Chichester: Phillimore. 1989.

Stevens, P. *Surrey Heath in the Dark Ages*. Stevens & Surrey Heath Local History Club. 1994.

Stahlschmidt, JCL. *Surrey Bells and London Bell-Founders*. London: Stock. 1884.

Surrey Advertiser & County Times. 5th January 1929, 21st October 1939, 10th September 1960 & 16th September 1961.

Surrey Archaeological Society *Surrey Archaeological Collections*. Vol.IV-32

Surrey Archaeological Society. *Surrey Archaeological Collections* Vol 75: 1984. Batley. J C and Moss, G P. A Catalogue of Pictures of Surrey and Elsewhere by John Hassell (1767–1825) and his son Edward (1811–1852).

Surrey County Council. *Log Book of Bisley Church of England School 1934–1974.*

Surrey Record Society. *Surrey Probate Inventories 1558-1603.* London. SRO. 2005.

Surrey Record Society. *Surrey Musters, Part 1.* London. Roworth for SRO. 1914.

Teignmouth, Baron (Charles John Shore). *Reminiscences of Many Years.* Edinburgh: Douglas.1878.

The Builder. Vol.XXVII. 1869.

Trevelyan, G M. *English Social History.* Bath: Pitman Press.1944.

Vatican Secret Archives. *Regesta Honorii III & Les Registres de Martin IV.* Vatican City. Vatican School of Palaeography,

Diplomatics & Archive Administation. *Volunteer Service Gazette and Military Dispatch.* London. 13 July 1877.

Wheeler, Lucy. *Chertsey Abbey: An Existence of the Past.* London. Wells Gardner, Darton.1905.

Wilson, Richard Lucock. Article in Bisley & West End Parish News. October 1996.

Woking News & Mail. 6th October 1922,18th July 1952, 25th July 1952, 23rd February 1962, 3rd May 1962, 23rd May 1969, 12th May 1988 & 25th September 1970.

Woking Opinion. 28 August 1954.

Woking Review. November 1949, March 1957 & May 1965.

INDEX

L

M

Q

R